FROM SURVIVING TO SURVIVOR

By

Sheila Rae Manes

iii

To my husband Allen,

You are the most amazing man, and I am so grateful for all your support and love. From the day we met, you brought sunshine into my darkness and changed my life. Words cannot express how much I love you.

To my daughter,

Thank you for understanding that, for my own well-being, I needed to finish this book. Your recognition of my emotional health gave me the motivation I needed to do so. You never fail to tell me what's on your mind. You are an amazing woman who lights up those around you. I am so glad you are part of my life. I love you with all my heart. Thank you for always having my back.

~ Mom

Acknowledgment

To any individual who is dealing with or has dealt with the darkness that is 'Domestic Violence,' I want you to know you are not alone; I'm listening.

Table of Contents

Prologue: A Failed Extraction

For my team, failure has always been the ultimate heartbreak. Its possibility plagues our every move; it's a dark sentry sitting upon our shoulders with each Domestic Violence case we take on. We carry that possibility as we tramp through a victim's galaxy of hell, we trudge forward through its realm, into the violence that dominates the resident trapped there.

Losses have happened to us before, causing the sentry to make room for the extra weight as it lands and grows heavier each time we come face to face with disaster. The sadness grows sharper and pushes deeper each time; it latches onto our shoulders, where it settles in to do its job adding to our failures. The painful reality festers within our souls, trying to eat away pieces of our resolve and determination to save a life.

Even with that pain we continue to fight and pray that each time we're needed, we can carry the weight of past losses and manage to step out from under the darkness that shrouds our missions so we can prevail. So, we struggle; we push our conflicts to the limit with every breath we take, always packing the constant possibility of failure. But that night, our determination was hampered by unforeseen events, our unwavering resolve took a huge hit, causing not only the extraction plan to fail but our promise of protection to be laughable. As a result, we were left with a leaden sadness settling in to infect us all. But we still pushed through the darkness, knowing with an all-consuming truth that the evil of man had beat us once again. We thought the plan was solid but soon realized the broken life we were entrusted with to protect didn't have a chance. The evidence was unmistakable when we found ourselves standing in the

1

middle of a dark road, looking down in horror at the woman who placed her trust in us to get her away from her abuser.

We stood trembling with regret and self-hate for what we were seeing, wondering how we could have done things differently to change this horrific outcome. The evidence of our failure folded us into its nightmare, while the darkness opened with its liquid judgment, making sure our penance for the disastrous results of our actions would begin immediately. We were all accepting of the pelting rain, as each of us felt we deserved its cold beating. We knew we would always carry this emotional burden, and we knew how. We'd lock it down and place it among the others that arrived before it, because the scene would never be wiped out of our minds. It would be another excerpt to add to our catalog of heavily burdened dreams, another chapter added to our personal stories, because no matter how it's filed away, there's always room for more pain.

Our self-loathing continued in slow motion, fed by minutes of remorse ticked off by neon hands from the gigantic clock of horrors dancing among the rain. And the realization was made worse as the headlights from our vehicles harshly shrouded the small body lying dead and physically broken in front of us. Our shadows stood tall and angry behind us, whispering their sobering ruling of our actions, using our car headlights to illuminate the reflectors affixed to the middle of the asphalt like glowing runway beacons to our failure.

Her name was Jennifer, she was about as broken as a victim could get but was also ready to survive. She listened to the plan for her escape and believed in its success because she wanted it so badly. She believed us, and 'we' believed us, when we assured her we would keep her safe and help her begin a new life. But somehow we failed her, we didn't live up to our promise, and the rain continued to chastise us by adding to our misery. It *began pooling up around our boots and mixing with the bloody puddles she lay in. The vision in front of us was surreal in a nightmare setting and I felt gut-punched with disbelief as my mind tried to catch up with the horrible reality in front of me. It reeked from every pore I have, as my heart pounded and screamed for forgiveness. It beat a deafening rhythm of remorse for letting her down, just adding to my personal shame for being alive, for being able to take my next breath and another and another.*

Her name was Jennifer... and we failed her!!!

Chapter 1

It's been months since that night, and the whole team is still reeling with the raw and blistered feelings of losing Jennifer. Even though the cases we've had since then have given us favorable outcomes, the memory of that night still haunts us deeply with a sadness that seems will never fade. That loss is one we can't put behind us; we need to know what we did or didn't do that caused this horrible outcome. Ever since that night, every one of us has taken a turn dissecting every audio recording and surveillance video we had done. We replayed all the decisions we had made and how we came to our game plan.

We looked at each piece together and separately, hoping we would find something that would lessen the hurt of our failure, hoping we could endure the hardship and eke out the flaw. But unfortunately, we still haven't discovered our answers and are beginning to realize we may never find them. But we aren't ready to walk away and close the chapter on Jennifer, not yet. There must be something we can learn from this unconscionable outcome.

So, we continue to beat ourselves up daily; whether it is a rational beating, or an un-rational one doesn't matter. We are the ones that dropped the ball and lost the battered soul we had promised would have a new life. We still cling to the hope that if we can figure this out, pinpoint our mistake, we'll be able to learn from this senseless loss, shedding the quilt of guilt a bit more allowing us to sleep at night.

It shouldn't be so hard for us because we've dealt with the unpredictability of evil so often we should admit the fact we haven't seen or encountered it all. But as hard as we try, we are continually being slapped in the face with the frightening reality of what it takes for us to do our job. We willingly wallow in the muck with one of the most gruesome of humanity's flaws, leaving us with the devastating realization that we can't outthink evil. Maybe we need to accept what is, accept the fact evil will prevail over our efforts at times, and allow it to make us stronger by lending us the tools needed to ramp up our resolve a notch. I wish I had the answer, but all the team members deal with each mission differently. We each have a story, a personal reason for why we chose to join the team, and because of that, each case touches us individually in some way. My reason for building and leading this team is etched deeply into my face, but my teammates' stories are not so clear or even known. The unwritten rule within the group is; if an individual wants to talk about why they joined the team, they can, but no one is ever to ask another team member outright.

So, what do we do, what can we do, how do we heal after letting someone down by breaking a promise of a new life, one that exists without pain and fear? Over time, we have developed individual routines and have learned to respect the need to follow them to stay sane. We have learned it's just as important to stay mentally and physically strong after a win as after a loss. Our routines hold our souls intact and help us maneuver through our mental processes, no matter what outcome we've achieved. Our souls get bruised and battered, win or lose, but not to the extent that we second-guess ourselves and our motives. We will always move on to the next horror show and the individual who needs our help.

We accept the strength our routines supply, we don't shirk our duties, and we use each other for support in so many ways. We dance the Devils dance across his smoldering stage, becoming willing participants in the game of seduction he instructs his crew of abusers to follow. We commit ourselves selflessly to the interaction to extract, protect, and help mend, as best we can, the victims who have been nothing but unwilling participants in the production playing out on his stage.

The Devil's production portrays the pre-abuser, the one who manipulates and snares his chosen victim. At this point in the seductive show, the stage lighting is soft and alluring; the melody of music flows through speakers affixed above and below the fiery stage to enhance the first act. The groomed abuser has free rein to perform his seduction, so he plays like a cat with a mouse as he executes his presentation flawlessly, manipulating his chosen prey effortlessly. Then, right before the performance comes to an end, the Devil snaps his fingers, and the abuser's smooth, choreographed seduction changes from slow and alluring movements to dark and demented in intensity, yielding to the last intermission. The music, no longer soft begins screeching through the speakers riding on flickers of fire. The abuser stands tall and menacing over his prey, waiting for the curtain to fall, trapping his victim behind the cloth barrier, which is his world. The prey reels from the metamorphosis taking place in front of her; she screams to escape from the production because the realization hits that she's seen hell for the first time. The lost parts of herself, the ones she had given up for him, may still be in reach, and she prays that somehow they will return. The unwilling co-star has yet to learn that the only hope for a curtain call is if we find her before it's too late and have time to choreograph a different encore.

Chapter 2

My name is Regina "Reggie" Reynolds, and the team I keep referring to is my family, at least in every way that counts. We are a privately funded entity and exist under the guise of an elite security firm, where we take on the direst cases of abuse stemming from Domestic Violence.

I decided to help put this team together because *I* was a victim of DV (Domestic Violence). I endured a type of abuse words can't describe, stemming from my husband's continual rage and demented acts. As a result of his last act of brutality, I wear deep facial disfigurements attesting to the horrors and depths of cruelty that *is* Domestic Violence, leaving my body to be made up of replacement parts. A knee made of polyethylene, connected to a titanium femur, helps me to stand upright because an aluminum bat swung with hate and rage destroyed both originals, leaving me with a right leg now held together with pins and screws.

Because of my scars I consider myself the poster child for the team, but the physical scars that destroyed my face and the mental ones that held me hostage didn't stop me from eventually becoming a survivor. And as sick as this sounds, I use my damaged face to prove to victims who are so frightened and broken that there is hope. I want them to realize that if I made it, so can they. I am always honest when the question of how I got out of my violent prison comes up; they want to know if it was the team that helped me. The answer to that question is yes, and no.

Yes, they helped me become the Survivor I am now, but no, they didn't help me escape my abusive husband. My answer to them is hard to put into words, even after all this time, because I honestly believe it was fate or karma that helped me that night. Either way, it doesn't matter; the reason for my darkness had ended, because he ended, and it was the act of forming the team, and the team itself, that put me back together. I'll never be who I should have been, all I can do is embrace the me I have become.

It took me years to stop believing the scars I carried inside and out were my destiny. After I was set free, I accepted that destiny because I thought I deserved it; I felt I had been weak and too scared to stand up for myself. But because of this family and what we do, I now know I wasn't weak at all. I couldn't see it then, but every time he came at me with fists of rage or weapon of choice to beat and bruise my body and mind, I subconsciously fought; I physically healed and continued to breathe. I wasn't weak; being afraid and heeding his threats kept me alive, and that's what I help the victims we rescue to see. Fear is not a weakness; fear is a strength used to protect loved ones and a unique survival mechanism. It's the number one common thread all victims of abuse share, and it's the hardest to overcome. It's instilled in each of us not only by harsh, continual threats but by actions that cause physical and emotional pain. For all victims of Domestic Violence, they receive the pain over time, in hours, days, weeks, and years. My husband, like all abusers, used the methods outlined in the Devil's handbook of Gruesome Pleasures. He followed the instructions in the handbook step by step; he eventually dominated every aspect of my life, and over time destroyed any flicker of hope I had silently held.

But the night I was set free, I hadn't yet learned that I had unknowingly used the fear to my advantage; at that point, I still didn't know any better, and I naïvely believed I didn't care anymore.

I had begun to accept defeat and let the darkness seep into my soul, crushing any thoughts of survival because I believed they were a waste of time. I even told myself to carry the constant and continual pain, to acknowledge I had lost the fight and just let him win, then maybe the end would come, and I'd be set free.

I longed for the light that would supposedly cradle me in its warmth and hold me safe as I exited this existence. I was ready to stop fighting and drift amongst its glow, to stop feeling, to stop being, to be at peace, finally.

The night the cause of my pain ended, I endured, and lived through another drunken atrocity inflicted swiftly by his muscled arms as they delivered an unbelievable hatred. The heavy aluminum bat, ironically my own, came down one more time to connect with my right knee, shattering it, and destroying my femur in the process. All I remember seeing is a streak of silver illuminated by a flash of lightning before it hit, but there was no time to roll out of the way. An explosion of thunder rumbled with its unhindered force to surround our little house, shaking the shingles lose to fly into the street. Its boom of destruction followed the lightning dancing an electric explosion across the sky, amplifying the sound of destruction as it assaulted my body. The crunch of bone was like that of gravel being displaced under hard heeled boots and was followed by waves of agonizing pain rolling up my leg. I screamed out of habit but knew it wouldn't help, because the only one to hear it was the one causing the pain.

He stood over me, eyes full of hatred and rage, still holding the bat in his right hand while reaching for his beer with the left. I tried to gain balance on my hands and un-injured knee, but in doing so I tasted a thick, bloody mucous running from my nose into my mouth. I tried to spit before it ran down my throat to feed the sour nausea that was already churning in my stomach. I remember reaching for the corner of the dining room table to pull myself up, but the pain was worse than the fear at that point and I started to pass out. The next blow was delivered with such force it sent me flying from the floor into a set of glass shelves mounted on the wall, next to the door of the kitchen. The thick glass broke into dozens of large, jagged pieces pummeling downward, hitting barriers of face and skull that slowed their descent, but not the carnage they inflicted along the way. The thick pieces of glass bounced with satisfaction as they hit the floor, leaving it discolored with crimson streaks of blood and pieces of my face.

The blood that surrounded me, soaking into the carpet, was coming from would be my disfigured face. I could do nothing but choke on the seasoned copper thickness running into my mouth. Before I passed out, I hoped the light would come this time as I felt it was my only escape, and I prayed this would be my last dance with the devil's darkness!

A Deputy Sheriff found me when he ironically had come to our house to deliver the news that my husband had died in a drunk driving accident. He'd had wrapped his truck, with his drunk ass behind the wheel, around a pole and died on the scene. But after one look at me, the Deputy figured I wouldn't be grieving for the Bastard for long, if at all. He was right about that, who doesn't love themselves some KARMA!!!

I had spent months in and out of the hospital enduring the pain of reconstruction to my leg, the rehab was a *"bitch"* to say the least. That was bad enough, but I had undergone three plastic surgery attempts to put my face back together during the recovery, but the nerve damage was too extensive. As a result, I have a scar running down the right side of my face starting at my forehead, cutting through my eyebrow and eyelid, then down my cheek to end at my chin. The nerves in my right cheek are severed to the extreme, causing the right side of my mouth to present a permanent frown. So, after the last surgery and at the end of my rehab for my leg and knee, I told Michael, my doctor, no more. His was the first face I saw in the emergency room that night. He was holding my hand as I crawled out of the pain long enough to be pissed off because I didn't get to follow the light. But he was gentle and visibly saddened as he held my broken body in his hands, showing the compassion, he felt on his face and in his eyes. Eventually, he became a trusted friend, and at the time, trust was something so foreign to me I didn't recognize it right away.

It was Michael, his wife Abby, and their son John that changed my life. Abby's sister Michelle was a victim of the violence we fight against. She was brutally murdered by her husband, sending the three of them into a darkened spiral they bravely fought against and won. Eventually, they were able to accept the loss and use it in their conviction to help others. Once they had time to grieve, they decided to do something for Michelle. They wanted to make something good come from the senseless tragedy. They knew in their hearts that doing this would eventually ease the pain of their loss. In addition, the three individuals hoped it would diminish the level of guilt they carried for not saving her. So, with sadness, they decided they would accept their penance and work hard to keep her alive in their hearts. Building a legacy for Michelle was as much for them as it was for all the women it would help, and they thought she would approve. They wanted to help other victims and their families before it was too late, even if it was one victim and one family at a time. So that's what we do, even if it means having our dedication fall short at times. We refer to the team as Mickey, Michelle's nickname as a child, and our base of operations is the Club House.

Chapter 3

Looking at my phone, I'm surprised we'd been driving for about an hour, leaving me to suddenly feel tired of reflecting on all the sadness and memories of how I got here, of what brought me to this day, traveling this road. Through the warming rays of the sun hanging low, streaming through the branches of the trees, I begin to realize that I'm no longer pissed-off about the whole,,, not being able to follow the light thing. It's an additional item I can purge from my past, and the revelation feels so good as I mentally tick it off my list of painful emotions.

I turned my head to look at the passenger seat and smile at my co-pilot,,, Suzie. She's in doggy heaven with her head out the window and nose in the air catching all the wilderness smells as they assault her senses. My hand reaches out to scratch her back lightly, but before she pulls her head in to give me a smile with all her pearly white canines, she shakes her head violently. She barks with pleasure as drool flies from her mouth to land on the back window like small transparent slugs. They slide along the glass, screaming an animated mayday, trying to gain some sticky stability that will help them hold on tightly to the glass. She pulls her head inside and gives me her best doggie wink, not all dogs can do that, but Suzie is special. She's a King German Shepard that wears physical scars and hides emotional ones just like I do. She has been my soul mate from the minute we locked eyes through the cage fencing of the King County Humane Society. The minute we met, we shared stories and displayed our scars stemming from the horror humans can inflict. The scenes of our abuse swirled with sorrowful intensity within our eyes, depicting highlighted passages from our horror novels to make sure we understood the other. Sitting in the cage with her that day, I whispered into a damaged ear promising her two things. First, no one would ever hurt her again, and I've kept that promise so far. And second, I would never stop trying to track down her abuser and inflict the same pain, and to this day, I continue to search with the help of my team. Suzie and I protect each other from our past and the unforeseen future; we're a team within a team. I guess you could say we're a matched pair of damaged bookends, holding each other up against the life we had and the reality of the life we exist in now.

From the beginning of our partnership, I would re-live the pain and fear of my past through nightmares, not hazy memories, but full-blown scenes of actual incidents that depicted my previous life. With all her nurturing ways, Suzie began to throw herself across my chest to keep me safe when the dreams haunted my sleep. I would wake slowly, feeling the pressure of her protection and soft whimpers smothering me with understanding. Who needs a shrink when they have a protector like Suzie??? I have witnessed her powers and know she would be the best shrink for wounded beings like us. She's wallowed in the same darkness, so she would shrink us from the perspective of someone who's been there.

My dreams still come, but less often as time goes by. I will always have triggers that will send me back, but I have come a long way. No matter how strong a survivor of Domestic Violence becomes, they can't protect themselves from the individual dormant darkness that will rise to seize any opportunity to flaunt the past. The horrors lay in wait to send purposeful reminders of pain that will test their strength and emotions, trying to send them reeling backward. But if they can stand their ground and remember all the hard work it took to find some semblance of peace, they will have the strength to search the shadows for their newly acquired determination, they will hold onto the progress they have achieved and use it to continue moving forward.

Suzie was the first good thing that happened to me after I was set free of my past. And there's no way even to begin to thank her for the unconditional love and support she gave me to start my healing. Because of her, I was able to do more than survive; I was able to work hard and find my way to becoming a survivor. I know first-hand victims can survive horrible acts of violence; I also know that after you survive it, the hard work begins, and it's a long journey. It takes an enormous amount of hidden strength and soul searching to finally step through the shame and pain to believe you will eventually find who you are supposed to be. But, if you can do that, you are well on your way to healing. You can take my word for this because I unwillingly became an expert on the subject. I know the issue, I lived within its darkness, and I know for a fact there's a big difference between *surviving* and being a *survivor*. But, sometimes, thinking of my past and seeing the struggles our newly rescued victims face, I want to flip the bird at the universe and scream, *Come on!!! Are you freaking kidding me???*

Suzie leans her head down and picks up her baby, a pink stuffed bunny, from between her front paws. She always has one with her; it brings the same comfort a security blanket brings a child, but unlike a child, she has no qualms about sharing with others the calming security her pink baby can deliver. She drops it in my lap for safekeeping before she sticks her head back out the window. When we are on a case, she may go through half a dozen babies. She uses them as worry beads to comfort herself when she knows we're heading into, or already in, the danger of dealing with darkness. She licks them intensely for comfort, but all she does is loosen the fur and shred the poor things into soggy pieces. She's always insistent on sharing her baby, especially with anyone she feels needs comfort. She offers it up as a soft, colorful Xanax, then sits back and watches the recipient intently, waiting for the calm she hopes will come.

Suzie can push the damaged pieces of her soul out of her mind, placing them in a silent holding pattern to focus on the present and the job ahead. I'm still getting there, but only because she's showing me the way. My canine protector still finds the good in people and invests her whole beautiful self into helping our victims. She and I are the first contacts a victim will have, and her nurturing nature makes her want to pull all the physical and emotional pain they carry. She wants to absolve them of their damaged souls, and she'll wear that damage until she can shake it off and move on to the next.

She's loyal to a fault and vigilant with the burden she carries to protect me. She's never been able to let me out of her sight without feeling like she's neglecting her duties unless I'm with another team member or in a familiar setting she knows is safe.

Chapter 4

It's a beautiful fall day, and we are heading East from Redmond to Leavenworth. We've been on an overdue outing, seeking an emotional recharge both of us desperately need. I take Suzie out of the noise and turmoil of the city of Seattle as often as I can, and our favorite thing to do is visit a few Assisted Living facilities. Suzie relishes the attention and unconditional love she receives from the residents. It calms her to the point she does nothing but smile when she moves from one room to the next, greeting one resident at a time and all the staff members along the way.

She feels like a princess as she's praised for her beautifulness and lavished with love and affection. Our well-earned retreat started two days ago when we walked out of the Club House, which is a huge hangar located among the hundreds of others, next to the Seattle Airport, into a crisp cold early morning fog. John carried mine and Suzie's backpacks as he followed us out to the car assigned to me by the motor pool. He leaned in through the driver's side window and flicked the bill of my baseball cap up a few inches to kiss me, then told Suzie and me to try and stay out of trouble. And because I know John as I do, there's no chance he'll put himself on a detail outside of the Club House until we're back and safe. He seriously doesn't think Suzie and I can stay out of trouble when we're on our own, and to be honest, more often than not, he's right. But in our defense, we aren't afraid to send up an "SOS" when warranted. So, all I could say was he knew I couldn't make any promises and laughed, but he didn't; he just sent me a warning with his eyes.

He walked around the front of the car and opened the passenger side door. He hugged Miss Suzie and whispered something into her ear; she turned her head and looked at me, then turned back to John and gave him a kiss followed by a significant conspiracy type of snort. I don't know how, but John seemed to understand her response as much as she understood the words he whispered into her ear. They have this weird kind of communication, and for whatever reason, it makes me jealous, after all,,,, she was mine first. *How very mature of me,,,, yadda, yadda, yadda.* I shook my head and started the car, waving out the window as we headed to the outer gate of the Airport Hanger we call the Club House. It slowly began to open as I approached, making me hold back a bit and wait, so I took the opportunity to glance in the rearview mirror to look back at him.

As he watched us approach the gate, a soft smile slowly began to penetrate his usual military stiffness. He looked so yummy with his black boots polished and shiny and his tight black T-shirt stretched taut over his muscled chest and arms. His tan cargo pants looked starched to the point of uncomfortable, and again I asked myself, how could he possibly need that many pockets in a pair of pants. But as I've come to realize, you can take the man out of the military, but in some cases, you can't take the military out of the man. Our eyes held each other's gaze via the rearview mirror while I waited for the gate to slide open completely, and I suddenly had an overwhelming urge to jump out of the car and run back for a hug. But I'm still getting used to the new me and our new relationship, so I just smiled into the mirror and continued. Once the gate was open, I headed to I-5 North, wanting to leave the city of Seattle behind me before the commuters were out in full force. I usually don't mind the traffic, but I was anxious to see the transformation in Suzie when she realized what we were going to do.

Abby, John's mother, makes all the arrangements for us before we head out as she has contacts everywhere acquired from chairing numerous medical committees and charities. She and her sister, Michelle, lost their parents as young adults, leaving them to handle the family fortune and holdings.

After Michelle's death and her husband's life sentence handed down, her entire estate was bequeathed to Abby and John. Because of that, their financial worth is enough to buy a couple of small countries ten times over. *I know right,,,,, it blows the mind!* But those massive amounts of cash are how we started Mickey and have everything we need to try and save lives, including, *wait for it*, a private jet. She's an intelligent money guru who took that family fortune and made it grow immensely and continues to make it grow into an obscene amount. She keeps us privately funded and in contact with entities all over the country, which is crucial as we never know if a case will cause us to reach out for their help. We have individuals and resources from every walk of life; we have cultivated relationships with unlimited professionals who possess unique skills sympathetic to Mickey's cause. They understand their role and are committed to helping us keep our organization hidden. They know how crucial it is for our safety and security, as well as theirs. They're a tremendous asset and intricate cog of our modern-day underground railroad; if we didn't have them, we wouldn't be as successful as we are.

The third and final facility we are going to visit is why we are headed to Leavenworth, and it's relatively new to us; we've only been affiliated with them for a few years and have already used their help twice in that short amount of time. There are times when a current rescue has a loved one who resides in a like facility and needs to be moved and kept safe from the victim's abuser while we perform our extraction. The facility's Director is a huge supporter of Mickey and welcomes us to lend help or just for a visit.

Abby contacted me earlier in the morning, asking us to deviate from our route home to stop there. She received a call from Deloris, the Director, who told her she had a feeling one of the residents could use our help for his daughter.

Deloris is the only person at the facility who knows what we do, and her discretion is paramount. Security is our main concern for all involved; it provides the safety my team and myself need to accomplish our goal as well as protection for the employees of the facility. If we need to place a family member of a victim with her, the staff has no reason to believe they're not new residents. And the guardians we send for their protection portray themselves as family members, so nothing seems out of the ordinary.

I knew Suzie wouldn't mind the detour because who couldn't use more kisses and hugs. Besides, if we were going to be involved in a new case, Suzie deserved all the happiness she could get before she began to worry another litter of bunnies into nudity. Which reminds me, I need to check with Abby concerning the supply of babies we have on hand and make sure the cache is pink only. I still laugh to myself when I remember a few orders ago, Abby decided that Suzie needed a rainbow of different colored babies consisting of blue, green, yellow, and pink. Well, it didn't take us long to realize that Suzie could tell the difference in colors. I know dogs are supposed to be primarily colorblind, but Suzie somehow knows a pink baby from any other colored baby. She even went to the extreme of showing her disappointment in Abby by picking up a green baby and dropping it into the wastebasket by the nearest workstation. And she continued to duplicate this behavior every time she received a replacement baby, and it wasn't pink. *I told you she was special.*

I don't mind the detour either, because it's fall in the Northwest and my favorite time of year. It's too bad we weren't going to be here for fun because people come from all over the state to throw themselves into the Bavarian Village setting that encompasses the town center of Leavenworth. Christmas is a fantastic time to visit with all the holiday lights glowing, and it's beautiful when the whole town receives a blanket of snow. But even without snow, there are unbelievable wineries to peruse, and the beer flows freely to enhance all the social activities. But for this trip, we'll have to be satisfied with the view in front of us and the feeling of freedom one gets when traveling through the Mt. Baker-Snoqualmie National Forest. This time of year, it's an unbelievable sight with the early afternoon sun sending some warmth, mingling harmoniously with a slight breeze. There are multi-colored maple leaves, the size of dinner plates, riding the wind, dancing softly to the ground. It won't be long before all the leaves have enjoyed their ride in the breeze with the sun's rays warming their descent. Soon the rain will begin, and the snow will start to fall, making Winter my favorite season. Then Spring will be my favorite season, and then Summer, well, you get the idea. I know it's silly, but I'm free to think on my own now and enjoy anything I want to, in any way I want to, no matter how simple or silly it seems. I was robbed of the simple and silly for too long.

There are no other cars on the road, so I let up on the gas a bit and roll down my window so I can feel the warmth of the sun and ingest the distinct smells of the forest. The scents of Alder, Cedar, and Fir trees, to name a few, are overwhelming for my senses, so I can only imagine what the mingling of those scents is doing to Suzie's. The Maple leaves that hit the road before I came along are forcibly dispersed to the right and left as my tires roll along the blacktop, sending them into the ditches that hug both sides of the road. Their presence discarded so effortlessly from the scenery by round spheres of intrusive rubber. They reluctantly clear a path for my car, leaving them to wait and watch for more of the clan to be released from the trees, to ride the breeze and take their place once I've passed. I stick my arm out the window and let my hand float along with the wind, suddenly realizing I'm smiling and enjoying the freedom as much as my co-pilot.

Suzie begins to bark into the forest, letting it know she's arrived while being overwhelmed with excitement. We're both enjoying the ride of contentment,,, and who knows, maybe I'll follow Suzie's lead and start barking into the trees myself.

Suzie can hardly contain herself when she realizes where we are and that she's in for more lavish praise. Once I park, she gives off her happy bark and leans into me with thanks, licking my face to seal the deed, then grabs her baby softly and waits. "Thanks; I appreciate all the slime on my sunglasses, Suz." I place them up on top of the bill of my cap where they will stay because I no longer hide behind the dark lenses. In the past, I would have worn them into the facility, thinking by keeping them on, I could hide from my past. But I don't hide anymore; I wear the face from my past and look everyone in the eye. My scars show where I've been; they don't hamper who I am now or where I'm going.

John saw the real me before I did. Before I gave myself the chance to hope and set aside what I thought was my twisted destiny. He never showed me pity; he fed my strength when I didn't even know I had any. I had been hiding behind my physical and emotional scars for so long he understood why I believed I was damaged to the point of no return. He was the one who finally convinced me that my multitude of scars didn't define me. He saw past them to show me tenderness, all the while praying I'd let him love me.

Every time I look at him, I see decency that exudes from every pore in his body. He is an impressive man that bleeds integrity and wears dignity and honor like the military uniform he wore as a soldier; he is a true patriot. He wears a different uniform these days, but his commitment to our team and the relentless fight for those who need his help will never waver.

I am humbled and proud to have him in my life; saying he's a good man doesn't do him justice. Someday maybe I'll be able to find just the right words and phrases to describe him, but until then, I can only carry everything about him close to my heart.

Chapter 5

Suzie and I walk through the door and are immediately greeted by Deloris, the facility director I mentioned earlier. She makes her way around the reception counter and into the lobby with a wide smile. Suzie and her baby receive a royal welcome fit for a Princess; the praise never stops. She then turns to me and extends her hand, but I wave it aside and step in for a hug. She's surprised and delighted by the progress I've made in my journey and acknowledges my growth by returning the hug wholeheartedly.

She remembers that a year ago, I would have backed away and made sure my sunglasses were covering my eyes, and that the hood of my sweatshirt was pulled up covering my head to wear as armor. Deloris's smile is genuine as she steps back from our hug, portraying her understanding of how far I have come, and I am so grateful that she recognizes it.

"Well, the two of you look rested; how was your drive???" I fill her in on the past two days as we follow Suzie; with the proper distance, one follows royalty, of course, to begin her visit by entering the first resident's room she sees. "Let her visit as long as she needs Reggie, but please come by my office when the Princess has made her rounds," she says with a laugh as she walks away.

As I follow Suzie down the hall to the first room, I notice she favors her front leg more than usual. I made a mental note to have Doc Shoemaker take a look once we're back at the Club House. All

I have to do is call the crotchety, old geezer day or night and he comes running because he loves her too. Her left front leg never healed correctly from a fracture she endured in her past, and the paw is missing a couple of toes. Because the break never healed properly, it gives her trouble sometimes. The old Doc told us arthritis has started to set in and will act up more and more as she gets older. But I try not to even think about her slowing down; it hurts too much. So, pushing aside the inevitable, I continued to follow her, stopping at the door she entered, and peeking inside. I see her sitting with her head on the lap of a resident; her baby cradled softly within her mouth, where she is accepting all the attention she craves. No matter how many times I see this, it's comforting to see her in her element. She gives the residents every ounce of love and understanding she has, and at the same time, soaks up the attention they, in turn, give back. To the residents, she plays the role of child, grandchild, and every kind of family member or friend they may need. Life is hard and busy; that's just reality, so, unfortunately, older family members get placed in the, *I'll visit next week category* by loved ones. Please don't get me wrong; I'm in no way saying their families and friends don't love them; it's just another harsh reality of life.

I leaned against the door for a few more minutes watching the interaction between the resident and her canine angel, reminding me again that we don't always have to walk in darkness. For the longest time, I was jaded by the dark, only seeing human interaction in shades of evil and levels of pain, but again, that was the old me. I push myself away from the door, knowing she has just begun her rounds, so I'll be hanging out for a while. And with that knowledge, I seek out one of the many comfortable couches in the common area and call John.

"Hi," I say as soon as he answers, suddenly feeling connected and grounded.

"Hi yourself, how's it going in Leavenworth?"

"We just got here so Suz will be awhile, she's in her first room now and there's twenty-five more," I say with a quiet laugh. "I haven't got the details from Deloris yet on the resident she wants me to talk to, but when Suz is done we're going to meet in her office."

"Mom said Deloris sounded quite sure he needed our help, but of course she didn't say anything to him about us. She knows the drill and is leaving it all up to you to handle."

"Of course, but I won't know anything until I talk with him."

"I want coms on when you meet with both! I've got Marco and the tech team here and on alert for your transmission."

Of course, you do,,, I think to myself. "Absolutely!! I'm hoping to be back tomorrow, but that will depend on what I find out after I talk to Deloris and the resident," I say into the phone, suddenly feeling a little home sick. "Um John,,, I miss you..."

"I miss you too Babe," he says softly, "I hate sleeping alone. Please be careful and remember the coms."

"I will, talk to you later."

I check my phone to make sure the com-link to the Club House is ready to be keyed up. Then, all I have to do is push the link to begin transmitting my conversations with Deloris and the resident.

27

This way, John and the technical team can listen in real-time, giving us an advantage.

The sooner we can acquire some initial intel, the better. The team will pull every little thread that stands out from the real-time recording and use it to dig up information and check facts now, giving us a head start on the process.

I see one of the staff members rolling a coffee cart down the hall, and just as I catch a whiff of the dark aroma, she suddenly turns the cart around and heads my way, asking if I'd like some. Of course, I accept, grateful for the offer and the smile. Sipping my coffee, I see Suzie walking beside a wheelchair transporting a female resident who's clutching Suzie's baby. The woman can't praise her and her baby enough or stop petting her through the whole journey down the hall. Suzie gives me a quick look of ecstasy as she goes by, and like a proud parent watching a child, my heart fills with so many emotions I can't distinguish between them.

I watch her pass by, giving her the freedom to visit on her own without me following her. So, I can stay right here for the rest of the day and know she won't be getting into any trouble. And she, in turn, knows we are safe here, so my protection doesn't need to be her number one priority for a short time.

Chapter 6

During the next three hours, I consume three more cups of coffee and a delicious turkey sandwich from the facility's kitchen while waiting for Suz to come to find me. When she finally comes around the corner and trots over to me, she instantly drops her baby into my lap as she eyes the tray from the kitchen before turning her gaze back to me. She has perfected the art of piercing me with her signature *stink eye*, which she delivers powerfully. Her meaning is translated so clearly with a look of, what,,, you couldn't wait for me?! I started to laugh and reach out, removing the napkin from the tray, revealing another half a sandwich. "Enjoy it, sister, because our vacation is ending today along with all your bad eating habits."

We find Deloris in her office just as she's finishing a phone call, and she waves us in. After we entered and closed the door behind us, she indicated with a delicate hand, for me to take a seat. Then, from behind her desk, she looks at Suzie and asks if she had fun. Suzie responds by placing her baby in my lap and letting out a quiet bark. Then, she gives her best smile before proceeding to lick some left-over mayo from her nose. She's got so much class, my Suzie.

"Excellent, I'm going to take that as a yes," Deloris says as she sits back in her chair, folding her hands into her lap. "Ok, Reggie," she says with a sad sigh, "let's talk about Bud Ainslee."

I can see the concern on her face matches the tone of her statement, so I get comfortable in my chair while Suz grabs her baby from my lap and plops her butt on the floor at my side.

"Bud was placed with us about three years ago by his family, or I should say by his son-in-law, after an accident he sustained at the DuPree Lumber Mill. Because of his condition after the accident, he's now confined to a wheelchair. And I just learned this recently; the son-in-law's father, Darwin DuPree, owns the lumber mill. The situation has always felt very strange to me, but I've never been able to put my finger on it, even though there were many red flags. Bud doesn't want or need to be here; he wants to live with his daughter or on his own, which is entirely within his capabilities. But Dempsey DuPree, that's the son-in-law won't allow Bud to live with them and Bud doesn't have the financial means to find a place of his own. You see, the DuPree's pay for all of Bud's care here."

"A little over a week ago, I walked down the hall and noticed the door to his room was halfway open. So, I thought I would pop in and say hello but, I heard him talking on the phone. I didn't mean to eavesdrop, but his voice rose as he spoke, and he sounded so upset. I overheard him scream Dempsey's name into his phone, telling him he wanted to see Amellia, that's his daughter, and that he had no right to keep her away from him."

"After he slammed down the phone, I knocked on his door and asked if he was alright; he just shook his head and looked at me with such sadness and resignation in his eyes. He said no, he wasn't okay, his daughter was in trouble, and there was nothing he could do to help her, and it was all his fault. I then asked him if we needed to call the police, and he said it wouldn't do any good because he was the police. He, meaning Dempsey DuPree. I guess he's the Sheriff of the DuPree Police Force."

Following John's orders, the coms on my phone are open and sending every word to the Club House. I can picture John and the team listening intently, recognizing that this situation will be highly dicey if we get involved. The combination of an abuser/law enforcement officer would be dangerous, and it's not just because he would be proficient with weapons. It's all the other training he would have received, plus the vast resources at his disposal. We've known from the beginning that if we can open a back door to acquire information, so can an abuser, especially one connected to a Law enforcement agency. As we've learned through the cases we've taken on, abusers don't fit one mold; they infiltrate every aspect of society, hiding in plain sight among all professions. They walk among the rich, the poor, and all the demographics in between, not discriminating against genre, age, or color. They seek out the prey that interests them, and once found, the smooth work of seduction begins. They're like snakes with glistening scales that slither in on two legs to mesmerize them with tender actions and soft, enticing words, all the while working to manipulate and mold the victim into submission. But once the dance of emotional seduction is complete and the I-dos exchanged, they shed their glistening skin to show the evil inside. At this point, there's no more tender actions or soft words, just reality, a harsh reality that proves to the victim it's too late for retreat.

Pulling herself back from the dark side, Reggie hears Deloris say, "that's when I took it upon myself to call his daughter, but the contact info in the file was to the DuPree Police Department. I

31

thought that was strange, but all I could do at that point was leave a message for Sheriff DuPree. That was a week ago, and I haven't heard from him.

"I've only seen his daughter twice; she's tall and slender, long straight dark blonde hair, and incredibly quiet. I missed her the last time she was here, and my staff told me that it was more than three months ago. But the phone conversation I overheard was last week. The morning, I called Abby asking for help, I'd just had a follow-up conversation with Bud. He said the last time Amee was here, her jaw was wired shut, and she couldn't even talk. He also said something I dismissed at the time, thinking it was just him being upset."

"What did he say?"

"He said he was sure that someone here was spying on him!"

I was still digesting all the facts I'd just heard when her last statement sent my senses into overdrive, pushing me to the edge of my chair. And, at this point, Suzie and I realize our vacation could be over. She leans into my leg, and I place my hand on her back, which comforts both of us. But the comfort is short-lived; my heart beats with the knowledge that most likely we'll be sitting in our usual seats on the same dark train we've ridden countless times before, with the same faceless conductor screaming!!! *LADIES AND GENTLEMEN,,, NEXT STOP,,,,,, HELL!!!*

"How long did you say he's been here?"

"A little over three years, as soon as the Rehab facility released him."

"Have you hired any new employees since then?"

"Of course, turnover in this business is high. Why?"

I continue to run my fingers up and down Suzie's back, feeling the soft coat as it passes between them, thinking of how to best digest the situation she has brought to us. Suzie continues to hold her baby softly within her mouth, seeking additional comfort as she continues to sit erect and steady, with a concerned look on her face.

"Deloris, I've been chasing abusers for a long time and lived with one even longer. I wouldn't be surprised if Bud is right."

One thing I've learned is abusers are deranged persons who run full tilt with a need to terrorize and dominate, which proves to me they're one of the most horrible flaws plaguing humanity. They deliver their need to prove they are an Alpha in many ways and relish the darkest ones. They don't just cause physical pain, they tap into emotions as well, and they love to play mind games. There are many colors and layers of Domestic Violence, many facets of pain, and levels of fear an abuser uses to continue to feed his need to dominate. They use any trick they can to try and stay one step ahead of their victim, and in this case, it sounds like Bud is a victim as well. It wouldn't be a stretch in any way; to find out someone here is watching Bud and feeding info to DuPree." I could tell by the look on Deloris's face that the picture I just painted for her was a frightening one, but sadly, she wasn't shocked by it.

"How can you know for sure? I mean, if there is someone passing information onto the Sheriff, how can you figure out who it is?"

I sit back in my chair, my mind racing down the same cruel tunnel it's traveled hundreds of times. I need to get my hands on the employee's names and addresses. But I know she won't be able to hand over that information without her Human Resources department having an ethics aneurysm, spouting employee records are confidential, and such. If she did, she would not only lose her job but jeopardize the facility's federal funding, not to mention losing their license. Soooooo,,, I need to get the information another way.

"Deloris can you point me in the direction of the employee parking lot?"

"What,,, why?" Obviously my changing direction of our conversation caught her off guard.

"Because my team and I are going to do some digging, hopefully, we can find out if Bud is correct and someone is watching him," I say with confidence as I stand up. "We'll go check out the employee parking lot and then go have a conversation with Bud. Thank you, Deloris; I know Abby will be in touch soon to keep you updated. Bye, for now."

Chapter 7

After I leave Deloris's office, I head to the employee parking lot. Standing at the edge of the lot, I bring up the camera on my phone and start snapping pictures of the employees' cars. Once I have an image of every vehicle and plate in the parking lot, I send a text to the Club House asking if they received them. Within seconds, Marco responds, saying he had them and was dispersing the information to his team. As I said, we are incredibly good at what we do and have the best people to do it. And just so we're clear, we don't have a conscience when our help is needed, and we don't apologize that our morals hover in the gray area because that's where we do our best work. So, we do whatever it takes to acquire information that will help us do our job and keep everyone as safe as possible, even if it means hacking into a government agency, which is an everyday occurrence for us. We like to think of it as using our powers for good, to defeat evil.

With that done, I head back into the facility and look for the sign that will direct me to room B2. I see the information immediately on the wall in front of me when I come through the door; an arrow instructs me to hang a left. The hallway is narrow and room B2 is only two doors down on the left. Once Suz and I are standing outside the closed door, I knock softly.

"What???" I hear an impatient, scratchy voice bark from the other side of the door.

I slowly open the door just enough so Suzie and I can stick our heads inside, there are no lights on in the room, so it takes a few seconds for my eyes to adjust. Sitting by the window is a slight man in a wheelchair with his back to the door. His shoulders slumped forward slightly, and all I can see is thick curly gray hair sticking out from underneath a camo, colored baseball cap. He turns just enough to peer back at me with angry eyes, exposing a grizzled face with days of white whisker growth on sunken cheeks. The man I see has wrapped himself in a blanket of defeat, fighting against his physical limitations with his emotions sitting at attention at his feet. Suzie and I stand on the threshold and wait for an invitation to enter, but all we get is a hard stare followed by silence as he reaches for the wheels of his chair and turns to face us. So, I decided to slowly open the door wider, taking a chance on entering the room. Once inside, his greeting is harsh, his question direct.

"Who the hell are you?" The man demands from his wheelchair, leaning forward, trying his best to look intense and menacing.

Suzie gives off a slight whine and looks up at me with questioning eyes, pleading with me to let her do her thing and share her baby. I give my permission, and she moves closer to the man in the wheelchair, where she immediately drops the magical baby in his lap. Her senses are hyper-sensitive, and her body dances with the need to absorb all the sadness and turmoil he carries. She wants to get close enough to draw it all out and take the burden from him. That's what she does; that's who she is. He continues to stare at me for a few more seconds, then drops his eyes to his lap, where Suzie has placed her head alongside her baby. I know damn well she'd climb into the chair with him if she could. But, instead, she patiently waits for his eyes to focus on her. One hand slowly petting her ravaged head, and the other holding the baby, not realizing her gentle ways, and the magical bunny vibes have started to calm him.

"My name is Reggie, and that's Suzie," I say quietly, moving a little further into the room. I quickly glance around the sparsely furnished space, hoping I will find a small semblance of a home, but the only personal item I see is a picture of a young woman, who I assume is Amee. "Out of concern for you, Bud, my friend Deloris asked us to come and speak with you about your daughter. I hear you're concerned about her and the situation she's in."

He lifts his head to look at me again, and I find myself wishing that statement could pull him from his physical and emotional prisons, is the possibility there? But, instead, there's an awkward silence between us as he wonders what my motives could be. I can see the deliberation on his face as he tries to figure out if I'm a friend or an enemy. I can tell he's cautious but curious. But there's something else I see, an emotion that is worn just below the surface, a physical tick of sorts,,, showing the deep burden, he carries. I know trust is hard to give under the best of circumstances, but for victims of any abuse, it's a million times harder. So, I wait in the silence that permeates the room for him to make his decision, looking into his eyes and wishing I didn't recognize his pain.

His existence harbors anger and emotional darkness, heightened only by the knowledge he can't protect his daughter from the treatment she's enduring, making all those emotions even worse. He carries tremendous guilt for being stuck in a chair, believing if he could walk, he could turn the situation around and keep her safe. But the reality of the chair only causes him to feel demoralized and weak. Understandably, he'd put up walls to guard what's left of his dignity, to try to hold the feelings of defeat and helplessness as far away as possible. But there's a sad reality taking root among the emotions he tries to keep hidden, the reality that because of his disability, he's as much a victim as his daughter is, and that defeats him even more.

"Did your man do that to you?" he asks harshly while pointing at my face, cutting into the silence.

"Yes!"

"He dead?"

"Yes!"

"You kill him???"

"No, I didn't have the pleasure," I state flatly. Sorry guys,,, my moral character hovers in the gray area most of the time, but there are instances when it takes a dive into the deep end of the dark pool, and I'm okay with that because I learned to swim a long time ago.

He looks at my face again and shakes his head with a deep silent rage. "Yes, Deloris is right; my daughter needs help," he states with sorrow, "and I can't help her." I watch his emotions consume him, the pain being so transparent I can see the restriction squeezing tighter and tighter. The display is so heartbreaking it lends me the courage I need to press on.

I step over to the corner of the room and retrieve the visitor's chair. I place it on the other side of his wheelchair and sit down close to him so that I can make eye contact on his level. I'm sure the team is not only hearing all the interaction between us, but they're picking up on the internal turmoil Bud carries as well. Suzie shifts closer to Bud's chair and whimpers her understanding, picking up her baby from his lap and offering it to him again.

I place my hand on his gently, silently showing my understanding of his and his daughter's situation. No matter how pain is delivered, whether it's brutally physical or emotionally twisted, it's a horrible extension of our gruesome reality. It's hard to suddenly open up to someone about your situation, mainly because the shame you feel for letting it happen cuts so deep and is so relevant.

"Why don't you tell me what's going on Bud," I say softly. "I think my friends and I can help you."

"Why should I trust you?" he says and pulls his hand away from mine. "For all I know you're here to spy on me for that bastard too!"

"I think you know deep down inside you can trust me; you realized it the second you looked into my eyes and saw the damage to my face. Bud, I've been in the same situation as your daughter, and this is the result," I say, touching my cheek. "Helping victims that find themselves in dire situations is what my team and I do. If you trust us to help Amee and you, I promise we will do everything we can to keep both of you safe." I let my words sit for a bit while he dissects everything I've said; it needs to percolate for a bit so he can decide if he should put his daughter into our hands for safekeeping. He finally comes to a decision and looks intently into my eyes. I see glistening tears reaching for hope as they roll down his cheeks, the realization becoming more apparent that it may be possible to help Amee after all. He's made his decision; it's evident in the slight nod of his head and the difference in his posture. His shoulders lift slightly as the massive weight of helplessness begins to teeter, and he sits up taller in his chair. He feels like there could be some hope to end their nightmare, even if he can't physically make it happen himself.

Chapter 8

"Bud, tell me about your daughter; where is she?" I ask after he's composed himself.

"Her name is Amee DuPree. Well, her real name is Amellia, but she's always hated that name, so she goes by Amee," he says with a sad smile. "She lives in DuPree with her husband Dempsey DuPree, who's the Sheriff of the Key-Stone Cops there," he laughs bitterly.

"So, the town is named DuPree?"

"Yes! Dempsey's daddy, Darwin "Big Daddy" DuPree, owns it and everyone in it," he states with anger. "No one can fart in that town without Big Daddy knowin about it. I'm surprised he hasn't figured out a way to tax the ass gas. His granddaddy started the town by establishing the DuPree Lumber Company and then added the DuPree Sawmill. Next came his private financial institution, the Bank of DuPree, and from there everything else. Like the DuPree Med Center, the Dupree Market and Gas Mart, and the DuPree Diner. Well, you can see the pattern; Big Daddy DuPree owns every business in that town."

"There's the Darwin DuPree Elementary School, but not a middle or high school; those kids are bused here to Leavenworth. Every citizen of that town is a DuPree employee working in one of the businesses, which is why I say Big Daddy owns every person in that town."

Once Bud got started, his thoughts and anger seemed to have a mind of their own, seeing a way to escape from the confines of his mind, suddenly feeling liberated from their silence.

"He holds all the mortgages on everyone's home and never lets anyone sell to move out of town. The mortgage's small writing states that the mortgagee can't leave town until their mortgage contract is fulfilled or the holder has the gall to die. If they die, the property goes right back to him, and if they pay off the mortgage, they can't sell it to move on. All they can do is walk away with nothing, and again, Big Daddy gets the property. But if they somehow manage to pay off their mortgage and are willing to walk away, their home isn't the only thing they sacrifice for their freedom; they also lose their DuPree pension."

"From day one of their employment, Big Daddy takes a percentage of their pay and invests it in what he calls a pension fund. Hell, he's just pulling that money from their paycheck to put it back into his pocket. The same goes for our mortgages; basically, all the people work for free because any money earned ends up right back in his hands to feed the DuPree economy. The sad thing is, no one questions the process at first because it all sounds so good. They land a good job and get a new home, and all it takes is a signature scrawled above a dotted line. But what they don't realize is by signing on that dotted line, they sold their freedom to become nothing more than a slave who ends up pocketing a small allowance disguised as a paycheck at the end of the week."

He sits silently for a few heartbeats, relishing the ability to voice his thoughts before continuing. "When my wife became sick and passed, I thought it would be best for Amellia and me to sell

42

and move, you know, to get away from the memories. But Big Daddy showed me the mortgage contract reminding me of the minuscule writing which stated I couldn't leave until I paid my mortgage in full, or up and died. So, I told him to keep the damn house and that I would leave if I wanted to. He then looked right at me and said I should re-think skipping town because of my family and the health issues that could arise from trying. That was the most blatant and scary threat I had ever heard. At first, I couldn't figure out how he could get away with all his high-handed crap, but then I realized the only way he could do it is to have local and government officials in his pocket. I bet he greases outstretched palms daily, with cash from his private Ponzi scheme."

"I'm telling you there's an underlying threat for silence that blankets every resident in that town; Big Daddy has a hold on them and every aspect of their lives. I know for certain a couple of people have tried to leave, thinking they could contact outside authorities and bring Big Daddy down; one was a good friend of mine. After he left, I tried to reach out but couldn't get ahold of him. Then about three days after my last attempt, everyone in town got an anonymous email showing his dead body with a bullet hole in his right temple. It was a message that scared all of us shitless, a very subtle reminder that we needed to stay in line because he was always watching. The only reason I got out is because of my accident," he says, pointing to his dead legs.

"What was your friends name Bud?" I ask, knowing Marco's team will be ready to dig into this once we have the information.

"Gregory, Gregory Fairchild," he says sadly.

"Do you know where he was from before settling in DuPree?"

"Oregon, I think it was Salem or Eugene, somewhere around there."

"Can you remember anything else about Gregory? Did he have family in Oregon?"

"He did, a daughter, but she passed away in a car accident about a year before he moved to Dupree. He said that was the reason for the move; he couldn't stand the reminders anymore. After my wife passed, I knew all about reminders; that's why I wanted to leave DuPree." He seemed drained from being able to lighten his burden, at last. His face showed fatigue and suddenly became blank as he looked down to his lap, where he was unconsciously stroking Suzie and her baby.

Lifting his gaze from his lap, he started again. "Reggie, I was one of those wide-eyed people that fell into the same trap as everyone else when my wife and I settled there. I had accepted a foreman position at the Sawmill, thinking life couldn't get any better, but what did I know? A year later, Amellia was born, and I found out things can always get better." He said it softly with a fleeting smile, which was replaced immediately with sadness when all the past sorrow crept into his chair to sit a stone vigil with his broken heart. He had been a man of substance and honor, a protector and provider for his family. Now he battles festering guilt from his decision to move to DuPree and fights with his inability to protect his family every day.

"Bud, how old is Amee, and how long has she been married to Dempsey?"

"She's almost twenty-two, and they were married right after my accident at the mill, three and a half years ago." He looks at me and decides to go all-in with the trust thing, hoping he isn't making a mistake. "Reggie,,, I don't believe my accident was an accident."

"Why do you say that Bud? Tell me what happened," I press softly.

"Ok, he says," locking his eyes with mine as he leans in and lowers his voice. "I was working the day shift at the time, so Amellia and I would see each other in the morning before I left for work, and she took off to school. Her senior year was ending, and she couldn't wait to get the hell out of there and leave DuPree behind. Her words, not mine," he says with a sad smile. "She always had a mind of her own and knew what she wanted as well as what she didn't, and she didn't want DuPree, the town, or the man."

He looks down into Suzie's brown eyes, taking a deep breath before continuing, his hand placed lightly on her head. "Did your man do this also?" he asks while touching her head where a nonexistent ear used to sit. He runs his finger gently across the damage, touching scar tissue and bare skin, muttering disbelief to himself.

"No,,," I state flatly, as the all too familiar hatred I carry inside for Suzie's abuser turns my stomach. "No, some other bastard did that, and I've never been able to track him down."

"Too bad," he says, picking up Suzie's baby and wiggling it in front of her nose, eliciting a soft whine.

His mind travels back to the past as he continues to explain his thoughts on his accident. "The morning of the "accident," he says with air quotes, Amellia came into the kitchen and told me that Dempsey expected her to marry him. He didn't ask her to marry him; he told her she was going to marry him."

"She was so pissed when she told me that, but then started to laugh as she dramatically informed me what her response to that sorry excuse of a man was. In her words, and I'm quoting now, she said,,, I couldn't possibly marry someone with balls smaller than mine!!!! I remember just sitting there with my mouth open, not because I was surprised by what she said, oh God no, that's my Amellia, or that *was* my Amellia before he destroyed her spirit," he says with hatred. "Anyway, this was coming way out of left field, because as far as I knew, she had only been out with him a few times. A few weeks after their second date, she had told me that she didn't even like him. She said he was arrogant and a bully, not to mention irrationally possessive, and she didn't want any part of that, so she was going to break it off."

"Now, this is where it gets interesting, so listen up," he says as he leans his head even closer to mine, maintaining the intense lock on my eyes. "That same morning when I arrived at the mill, Dempsey was there, leaning against his car that was parked a few spots down from my assigned space. When he saw me, he laughed and told me to have a nice day, which should have been my first clue that something was up."

"It wasn't fifteen minutes later, as I was heading up the stairs to my office that the second step from the top slipped out from under my foot when I put my weight on it. I was sent flying backward, trying to grab the railing to catch myself, but ended up falling twelve steps to land on the concrete floor. We had just had a safety inspection two days before, and I know for a fact that the stairs were solid. So that's how I ended up in this chariot," he says, slapping an armrest of his wheelchair.

"Was Dempsey the Sheriff then?" I asked, not breaking the eye contact he had initiated, afraid I would lose the connection if I did.

"Yes, but it hadn't been that long. Dempsey had joined the Army the summer before Amellia's Senior year but ended up back in town after a few months because he had nowhere else to go after they gave him the boot. He hadn't even made it through basic training at Fort Leonard Wood, Missouri. From what I've heard through hushed whispers of gossip, he assaulted a female soldier, raped her, and put her in the hospital. I wish we had known that when he first came back to town with his arrogant smile, setting his eyes on my girl. The soldier was afraid to press charges; she was terrified of Dempsey and what this would do to her military career. So, along with no charges filed, rumor has it, Big Daddy paid a hefty fine to someone at that fort to stamp the paperwork giving Dempsey only a Dishonorable Discharge. Then he came back to DuPree and, once again, became the town bully. That Bastard struts around that town like he's untouchable, and that only makes him more dangerous; that boy is a full-blown psycho!"

"This is unbelievable; how did someone like that land a job as a cop? Doesn't he have a felony record? Or, in the very least, the Dishonorable Discharge should have stopped him from being accepted into the police academy. I mean, there is no way he could have passed a psych eval."

"Big Daddy knew Dempsey wasn't going to be able to do anything because of his tarnished military record along with his reputation of being a bully with no brains. So, handing him a career that would be interesting enough to keep him focused was the only option he had left. Big Daddy knew his son would be a problem if boredom were to set in, so the job needed to be one that would keep him engaged. That was his thinking when he built the DuPree Private Police Department, placing Dempsey into the highest position of Sheriff. He knowingly handed that maniac son of his, the law of DuPree, and the firepower to terrorize the whole town."

Still reeling with disbelief, I finally ask, "how many officers are in the Department?"

"Three, including Dempsey. One officer handles the front desk, his name is Stanley Woodard, and he's the scrawniest little shit I've ever seen. He can't even tighten his belt enough to keep the big-ass weapon he has strapped to his hip from falling around his ankles; that guy isn't very threatening, and I've always wondered if he can even shoot. The other officer is David Tack, and Dempsey uses him as his driver. Now that piece of crap is scary; he's glued so tight to Dempsey's backside that if he stopped suddenly, he'd get Tack's head stuck up his ass. Tack has and will continue to do whatever he's told because he craves the power that stems from licking Dempsey's boots!"

I thought to myself, oh man this is outrageously perfect, if that's even possible. It's a police force made up of two tiny maniacs following the big maniac, and just because they sound like a joke doesn't mean they are. I could only imagine what John and the team were thinking, especially since most of them were ex-military and served under John in Iraq. In my head, I knew Hell wasn't the best way to describe our destination on this one, but it was going to be the last stop after a dangerous journey. We wouldn't be extracting one victim, but two, all the while colliding against one of the Devil's most prized creations, not to mention the two boot lickers ready to follow alongside him blindly. UGH,,, we are going to have to dig deep on this one and stay even more vigilant while we diligently work to survive and accomplish our goal. And that train to Hell I mentioned earlier will feel like it's traveling on slicked rails. It'll send us gliding forward while exhaling buried screams, the steel tracks sending us sailing around dark curves into the all too familiar. It will force our emotions to stay focused, and our power will come into question as we try to stay upright, fighting the momentum, its only goal, to throw us into our past nightmares.

Chapter 9

From my chair, I watch him continue to interact with Suz and her baby. I tune myself into the comfort he's pulling from her nurturing, witnessing the strength he's feeling for the first time in years. He's moving forward already, just by voicing what he's been hiding for so long. I needed to ask something now, and I hoped it didn't upset him because it could sound like I was accusing him of failing his daughter.

"Bud, why didn't you try to stop the marriage, especially after you knew how Amee felt about Dempsey! Didn't you question it?"

"WELL, I WOULD HAVE IF I'D KNOWN ABOUT IT!!!" he shouts, exploding into my face. He lowers his head, shaking it violently, and begins chastising himself for the outburst. "I'm so sorry, Reggie, that was uncalled for, but every time I think about the marriage, it reminds me it happened because of me and my so-called accident," he says with air quotes again. "You see, by getting me out of the way and disabled, he could swoop in and tell her they would take care of me. I was in a coma for about three weeks after the fall, and when I woke up, I found out they were married."

"In my heart, I know she married him because of me and what he told her about taking care of my medical needs. After I came out of the coma, I began to ask questions of the staff taking care of me, and from their answers, I was able to piece a lot of this together." So it wasn't long after I woke up, they shipped me by private ambulance, and I'm guessing with a butt load of money, to the hospital here in Leavenworth."

"I get sick to my stomach every time I think about her sacrifice for me, and it's all because of Dempsey's setup in the first place. He plays such a good mind game, threatening her by stating he'll stop paying for my care here. He tells her I'd have nowhere else to go, and I sure as hell was not going to live with them. He'd just let this place throw me out onto the street. And he threatens me by showing me what he can do to her. It sickens me so much but lends truth to the fact he set this up. The broken jaw isn't the first act of violence toward her. When he does allow her to visit me, it's always with a new bruise or new stitches, or worse, probably administered just for a visit. At some point, he did something to her ankle because she wears a hard, plastic brace that hits just below her calf muscle, causing her to walk with a limp."

"What hospital does she go to when he hurts her?"

"She doesn't go to a hospital. Instead, Dempsey takes her to the DuPree Med Center, where Big Daddy's highly paid Doctor and nurse patch her up and keep their mouths shut. He even has Surgeons and Dentists he can pay to perform services quietly. They slink in at night, under cover of darkness when called, so no one sees them selling their souls to the big man for money and favors."

"Do you remember any of their names?"

"No, I was never treated by any of them."

I can't help but see the correlation between Darwin's mode of operation and ours. The Club House's medical bay consists of every type of medical equipment imaginable and staff of the highest caliber with extraordinary abilities. The only difference is, we use our operation to keep all of us safe while lending aid to victims and their families, whereas DuPree uses his for control over the town's residents. But, even with such a contrast between our motives and goals, maybe this will work in our favor somehow.

"Do they have any children?" I asked, holding my breath for the answer, hoping it was a no. Not just because no child deserves to witness or receive horrible acts of violence, but because Suzie can't handle seeing a broken child. She gives too much of herself; she ages by hours, then days, when trying to comfort one that has had to accept these acts as an everyday burden. She doesn't have enough babies to lick into nudity for that. It takes weeks for her to recover after we finish a case that involves children.

"No!" Bud states sadly. "About eighteen months ago, Amellia went into labor, and delivered a stillborn baby boy. That's when my girl disappeared for good; she just gave up after that. I miss her on so many levels and feel so guilty each time I think about her. My heart breaks from the losses she has endured because of me, not to mention the horrible existence she's stuck in."

"I'm so sorry to hear that, Bud," I say. My mind begins the rewind to the past and my loss of a child and how it left me unable to have another; even after all this time, emotional pain still sits on my shoulder, as strong as ever. I push the pain down where it's supposed to stay, trying to focus on Bud, but I feel it emerge again to reposition itself onto my other shoulder, reminding me this is a hurt that I'll never be able to forget. Once again, I find myself seething inwardly with the knowledge that life can be cruel; it takes it upon itself to suck the happiness out of some of us, leaving our souls empty to feel our losses so profoundly.

Finding my voice again, I ask, "do you think she would accept our help to get her out of there if we offered?"

"I wish, but I know she wouldn't do anything to jeopardize my safety and care to save herself; she just wouldn't!"

"What if we could assure her that wouldn't happen because we can get you out of this mess and keep both of you protected. We have the best medical care out there and free of charge."

His expression is one of initial doubt, hopeful surprise, and finally gratitude, and he nods his head in understanding. "In that case, I know she'd at least listen to you. But how could you do that without Dempsey finding out about it?"

"Why don't you let me worry about that," I say quietly, giving him a wink. "I have a team of extraordinary people who do incredible feats of this type daily, but we'll need as much help from you as possible. Is there anything you can think of that would help me be able to talk to her undetected? Someplace she would feel at ease enough to listen to me?"

"I'm not sure," he says. "The only way I can think of is at the DuPree Book Store; she runs it and is there all day. Big Daddy built it after Dempsey and Amellia got married. I think Dempsey thought she needed to keep busy, but it had to be someplace where he could watch her every move. He has a phone app to check on her anytime he wants, because he installed cameras all over that place. She once told me the only area she couldn't be seen, besides the bathroom, was in the far back corner where she keeps the Science Fiction titles. That could work, couldn't it?"

"Possibly, but what about when she's not at the bookstore, maybe when she goes shopping or to the post office? Something normal like that."

"There *is* no normal in my daughter's life, if she's not at the bookstore she's locked in at home. I wouldn't be surprised if he has damn cameras in the house too. As for shopping and anything else, Dempsey has his lackey, Deputy Tack, drive her around to do her errands, and she isn't allowed to have a cell phone."

"Okay, Bud, I'm going to have you write Amee a note telling her you sent me, and she can trust what I tell her. But first, we need to talk about one more thing."

"Which is?"

"When I first came into your room, you asked why you should trust me. For all you knew, I was here to spy on you also." I didn't tell him that Deloris mentioned he had said he thought someone was spying on him, "why would you think that?"

"Because of the late afternoon phone calls from that Bastard. He calls to ask me if I enjoyed my lunch. He says things like; didn't you want your pudding today? I thought you liked chocolate. How did he know they served chocolate pudding that day, and how did he know I didn't eat it? Or he will tell me I really should eat both halves of my sandwich because he's paying good money to feed me. Shit like that, now how would he know those things if somebody wasn't telling him?"

54

Inwardly I agree with him, instinctively looking up and scanning the ceiling for anything out of the ordinary but see nothing. "Does he only talk about lunch, or does he call after dinner also?"

"Just lunch!"

"Does the same staff member deliver your lunch each day?"

"No, it varies," he says, looking confused. "Sometimes, it's a different person picking up my tray than the one who delivered it."

"Do you eat in the dining hall sometimes?"

"Yes, now and then."

I hope the team is following my train of thought on this. We need to look into the day shift employees for any connection with the town of DuPree or Dempsey, and we need to look beyond the person who delivers or retrieves the lunch tray. Any staff member can check up on him during that time, and we won't know until we do some digging. Once we've narrowed down the list, we need to pull their financial records to see if one of them is making a recurring deposit of any kind besides their paycheck. Hopefully, there will be a money trail, but there's always the chance that the payoff is in cash, or instigated by intimidation on Dempsey's part, making our job harder, but not impossible. Remember, we're incredibly good at what we do.

"Bud, it's most likely someone is passing this info onto Dempsey, information he can use to taunt you and keep you in line. Did he call you today before I came to see you?"

"Yes, right before you knocked on the door, that's why I was so angry when you came in," he says apologetically.

Thinking back, it's a good thing Suz, and I hadn't entered the building yet after taking the pictures in the employee parking lot. It must have been a shift change because we saw about five employees coming through the door and heading to their cars. If we had been inside knocking on Bud's door as they went down the hall to the exit, we would have been in plain sight. And one of them could be Dempsey's spy, and there's no doubt in my mind that we would have been reported if that were the case.

"It's a good thing we came in late then because we don't want our visit passed onto him. Don't worry, we'll find out who it is, and Bud, I need you to act like nothing has changed for the next week or so, especially when Dempsey calls. It is so important for you to keep this visit and our conversation to yourself; it's too dangerous for you and Amee, as well as my team, understand?"

"I understand completely, no need to worry about me."

"We'll need to put a plan together before we can get both of you to safety, away from DuPree and Dempsey's hold."

My mind wanders back again to the night we lost Jennifer, but all I can do at this point is push the memory and the horrific scene back into the box where I keep it. I wish I could tape the box shut and never have to relive the tragedy again, but it will be some time before that will happen for any of us. As we've learned and witnessed too many times, all scenarios are subject to change at a moment's notice, adjusting to outside influences and unforeseen circumstances. Even the best plan to meet our objective can

56

instantly become the worst plan due to circumstances out of our control. All we can do at that point is jump to the next plan and hang on, hoping to succeed.

Pulling herself back to the present, Reggie looks down at Bud, "the only thing you need to worry about is this! When Deloris tells you it's time to go, you don't question it; you don't pack anything; you just follow her lead. I don't know which team member will do your extraction at this point, but like I said, just follow Deloris's lead."

"Got it," Bud says.

"Okay, give me directions to DuPree and get cracking on that note to Amee."

Chapter 10

Suzie and I are almost to my car when Toby Keith's song, *"We'll put a boot in your ass courtesy of the Red White and Blue, (The Angry American album)* blares from my pocket. I roll my eyes for the hundredth time, thinking I should never have let John pick his ring tone. Since we both know who this is, we stop in our tracks and look at each other with resignation, knowing we can't ignore it. This phone call will not go well because without even talking to me, John knows that Suz and I will head to DuPree on our own. He's constantly telling me I make split-second decisions that aren't always safe, and for the most part, it's true, so I know I need to listen to what he has to say. I don't think it will change my mind, but I'll listen because I've learned to pick my battles. Mainly because I know he loves me and can't stand the fact I'm going to head into a dangerous situation by myself. But if he thought about it, he'd know that isn't exactly the case because I've got Suzie.

Ever since John and I have moved from friends to lovers, he thinks my rank in the team has changed. It hasn't; the only place my rank has changed is the position I hold in his heart. He's never been my boss, we have always piloted the ship of Mickey side by side, but now it's hard for him to continue with the original protocols because of how we feel about each other.

He knows I'm still going to carry out my job description the way I always have, but it's hard for him now, so I let him rant and rave about my safety. We're still figuring out our new relationship and how the change affects how we work together, but the bumpy road will flatten out soon with many concessions from both of us. He tries to think like I'm a fellow team member when it comes to a case but at times it falls short because now there is too much at stake personally. So, because of that, there are moments when he wants to protect me, not give me a logical order like he would the other members of the team. But most of the time, he tries to tread lightly with Suz and me. He remembers he can't become overbearing or demanding and in no way attempt to control me because that's the mess I escaped from. He's trying to figure out how to be sturdy and protective while continuing to help me cleanse my past as best he can. But he drew the short straw when he fell in love with me, the straw that put him face to face with the broken and guarded Reggie. He's stood back and watched as time and this team's dedication have turned me into the new version of me, the stronger me that refuses to take any shit. Lucky him!

I look down at Suzie, and we share a look of surrender as I answer the phone.

"Hello,,, who is speaking please?" I say sweetly, dripping colorful sarcasm while smiling down at Suzie, waiting for it, waiting for the voice to come booming into the night, and here it is...

"You know damn well who this is," he barks into the phone, and I can't help but notice today he forgot the whole concept of treading lightly.

I hold the phone out in front of me and place it on speaker mode. Suzie and I are content to listen, mainly because we know he is going off out of love, so the least we can do is let him go all commando and wear himself out. But, instead, his voice hits a pitch I'm sure is straining his throat muscles, and I can't help but cringe as the tirade heightens with new emotion. I hear his words blare through the phone in disjointed rants, catching every third word or so as it spits through the line, which everyone in the Club House is hearing as well as Suz and me I'm sure. "Reggie,,,,,,,,,,,, don't,,,,,,,,,,,,,,,,, hell,,,,,,,,,, butt back,,,,,, what about Suzie??"

"Wow, now that's a new one, using you as a guilt tool," I say and look at Suz. She cocks her head closer, using her undamaged ear as a satellite dish to pick up every word as if she can understand him. She can, however, hear as the anger in his voice begins to change to concern causing her to whimper softly, feeling sorry for him.

"Are,,,,,,,,,, I'll be there,,,,,,,,,,,,,,,, don't even,,,,,,,,,,,, dangerous,,, you,,,, need backup!!!"

Eventually, the strained voice on the other end of the line drops a few notches on the soundbar, leaving a heavy resignation to travel through the line before the tirade fades out completely. "Damn, Reggie!" He says into the phone from his end after what seems like ages.

"Are ya done?" I ask softly.

"Yes,,, I know everything I say is falling on deaf ears anyway, except for the ears of all the team members!" he shouts strongly, and I can only imagine the looks he's giving the surveillance team.

"Roger that Boss!" They all yell in the background, some even daring to laugh.

"Are ya sure?" I say, laughing into the phone as well. "I'm going to stay in Leavenworth tonight and head to DuPree in the morning so that I can catch Amee at the bookstore. We should have Marco see if he can worm his way into the camera feed while I'm there. But if not, I'll have coms on, of course. It sounds like the directions Bud gave me are pretty simple; it shouldn't be hard to find the bookstore once I get there. Don't worry; I don't want to mix it up with that psycho until we have a plan. In the meantime, you guys do what you do, so we'll be able to put a preliminary plan together if we do end up moving forward. If I determine she will be on board, I'll leave one of the burner phones with her. Hang on, and I'll get the ID number for you to pass onto Marco; he probably has it, but better safe than sorry. I reach into my backpack and pull out the disposable phone turning it over to see the number. It's XX2SS902; pass that onto Marco, okay?"

After a slight pause, I resume, "John, we both know that Suz and I will turn enough heads in that little town as it is. So it will seem like too much of a coincidence if you send in even one guardian, not to mention two. At least this way, it's just Suz and me who are compromised, just like it's always been. And I need to state this again; if you send backup, it will just be another unfamiliar face that can't hide in plain sight; they would just attract more attention. And as we've learned, if the guardians can't blend in, they can't protect. This first contact will not be our norm, so we don't need to make it any harder from the get-go. Amee needs to see my face, and I need to look into her eyes to see how far gone she is. The protocols for first contact haven't changed. But this time, we need to adjust and adapt to a situation we haven't faced before," I say with determination, hoping common sense can override concern for a minute. I stand my ground waiting for a response, mentally adding a checkmark to his side of the concessions board.

"I need to talk to her," I hear Abby say in the background!

"Babe, mom wants to talk to you. I hear what you're saying, and I agree the circumstances are different, but I don't like it. You need to keep a lid on your little self, and if pushed by anyone, don't push back, damn it! Keeping yourself and Suzie safe is just as important as the face-to-face you need to do! Got it???"

"Roger that Boss!"

"Boss of you,,, as if! You're such a smart ass," he says, handing the phone to his mother.

"Reggie," I made a reservation for you at the Leavenworth Inn for the night; I pretty much figured you'd be staying and heading off to DuPree in the morning.

"So, you heard the dialogue between Bud and me?"

"Yes, yes, I was in the Club House listening to the coms-link; I think they need our help."

"I agree, I know Bud is on board but it's all up to Amee now."

"And if I know you, she will be. Reggie, you be safe and come back to your family as soon as you can," Abby whispers into the phone with motherly concern.

"I will Abby, and you try to keep you know who calm until I get back, Ok?" I say choking up from Abby's words. I'm still getting used to the concept of a family, mainly because I never had a real one due to growing up within the system.

Chapter 11

Suzie and I walk into the Inn and make our way through the lobby, heading toward the counter to check-in. Suzie is on her best behavior because not everyone accepts dogs, even if they're self-proclaimed royalty like she is. The young man behind the counter welcomes us and acts like seeing a woman with a jagged road map across her face, accompanied by a seventy-five-pound German Shepard with one ear, favoring a front leg with missing toes, is an everyday occurrence.

"You must be Beth Trumball," he states.

"Yep," I say placing my arms on the cool, granite countertop.

"Can I see your Identification please?"

I hand over my Beth Trumball driver's license and watch him compare my face with the picture on it.

"Thank you," he says with a smile handing it back across the counter once he's satisfied I am who my ID says I am, *wink, wink.* "I see your stay has already been taken care of along with room service this evening if you choose," he informs me looking up from his computer screen. He then turns his smile and attention down to Suzie. "What about you," he says jokingly, "can I see your ID as well?"

She looks up at me waiting for the approval nod. Once I give it she gracefully stands on her back legs and places her huge front paws on the counter flashing her most demure smile, she's such a flirt. Caught off guard by Suzie's size once she is standing, the young man takes a second to wonder if he should have thought this through more carefully. But he doesn't deliberate his decision long, sensing he is safe, he leans in a bit closer so he can read her dog tag, which is actually a military dog tag. It was a gift from the extraction team and she's immensely proud of it. Her beautiful face is engraved onto the silver tag and embedded into the steel alloy is a tracking device that can be triggered remotely from the Club House if need be.

Every member of the extraction team wears a like pair of tags, but ours are engraved with an insignia of the American flag. It was a necessary action and sad event the day the tags were handed out, a silent ceremony showing individual devotion to our cause. An acknowledgment of the need to protect ourselves from the dangers we encounter, because we never know what we'll face once we blast through locked doors, chasing the madness. But for the ex-military members of the team, it felt like they were replacing a part of themselves, the part that made them into the individuals they are now.

The actions that day caused the air in the room to turn thin and still, allowing the silence to begin suffocating their bond, pushing the devastating loss into their souls. To watch John and the four members who served under him overseas slip their original military tags, that represented courage and country, from around their necks made my understanding of serving together in hell that much stronger.

As they stood there staring into their hands holding pieces of metal that bound them together for ever, only they could hear the silver alloy scream; *you will always be a soldier!!!* Then, one by one, they placed that part of themselves carefully on the table in front of them, as if saying goodbye to a fallen brother. It was the ultimate sacrifice in motion, and to watch them shed the real dog tags they had worn for so long, was inspiring and selfless. Those tags were a promise to protect this country with bravery and blood, they shaped their lives and made them the individuals they are today. They did not voice their emotional acknowledgment to each other; their eyes said it all, darting from one to the other as, in unison, they slipped the new tags over their heads, silently taking an oath to continue to fight. They acknowledge the war they fight now is different, and the enemy puts a new spin on sadistic, but they will never falter in their dedication.

I am still in awe of their dedication to our team, the unwavering reserves they seem to find to keep on fighting the battle with evil. But they all realized it needed to be done, for their own safety. The military identification could put them and the team in danger if the devil got his hands on it.

"Welcome to the Inn; it's nice to meet both of you," he says, smiling. "You're on the bottom floor, room 15," he informs us as he passes the room key across the counter. Abby has been handling arrangements like this for a long time, and she would have requested the ground floor because it's the fastest way out if we need to run. Even though we aren't involved in a case for sure yet, it's always possible our past could come screaming down on us, so we take precautions and work diligently to protect ourselves.

"You just pass through the lobby there," he points with his right hand," and take a left into the hallway. You can also access your room from the outside if you wish. Do you need help with your bags?"

"No, we just have the two backpacks I'm carrying. But thank you," I say and head to the hallway that will take us to our room, turning only a few heads along the way. While traveling the hall, I took a second to look at the falsified ID I still hold in my hand and can't help but think of Jennifer again and how our protocols have changed since her extraction failed.

The first change to our protocols was: each individual in the extraction team is issued a different car from the motor pool with every new case we take on and continues to use it until we move on to another. Inside that vehicle is a fake insurance card and vehicle registration that matches the temporary ID we will carry. The fabricated identity includes our picture, a phony name, address, and date of birth, and for those members that carry a concealed weapon, they are issued a fabricated 'UTAH' permit as well. This permit allows the extraction team and all our Guardians in the field to carry in most states.

So, no matter what agency, silent entity, or hacker runs the name and address, or name and DOB from our identification, we won't be compromised. And in this game, being compromised could mean the worst kind of defeat for us and the victims we are trying to help. Even if someone uses back channels through the web or facial recognition software to try and find us, our system's firewalls will grab the inquiry and channel falsified info back to whoever is trying to identify us. In addition, the fabricated identifications are scrubbed and replaced continually as an added precaution per our new safety protocols. I have no idea how all this stuff works, and I don't need to; all that matters is we are safe and can trust the tech team to have our backs 24/7.

Mickey's organization encompasses different sections with multiple functions, and every individual within each department holds important and demanding responsibilities. The areas consist of mechanics, medical personnel, technical surveillance, and of course, the financing, which I explained earlier.

In addition to the extraction team, there are teams consisting of Guardians. Once a victim is out of immediate danger, the case doesn't stop there. They and any family members are watched 24/7 for any pushback from their abusers. This protection stays in place until we decide it isn't needed anymore. Sometimes this protection continues for only weeks, or it could be years; either way, it doesn't matter because we will always be watching. It's just as important to monitor the past as it is the present, that's why we have people in the field that stand guard until we deem it isn't necessary any longer.

Several different technical surveillance teams monitor the extraction team and the guardians in the field, but their duties encompass much more. They also monitor chat rooms and social media for any signs of abusers we've confronted in the past. Unfortunately, we've encountered monsters who didn't take Mickey's warning to heart and continue to try and find the victim snatched out of their control. Most of the time, the women we have helped have disappeared to a location of their choosing, supplied with a new identity and all the financial help they need to start building a new life. Even now, we can still be blindsided by how resourceful some of these monsters can be, hence, the continual monitoring.   There have been a few instances that our techs combing through social media have identified a victim who needed our help, and we could reach out to offer it. But it isn't like we need to troll for victims, there are so many out there, and unfortunately, we're just one team.

John and I head up the extraction team, which consists of ourselves, one huge ex-Merchant Marine, three elite ex-military composed of two men and one woman, along with a young man who just found his way to our doorstep. Not all of us are ex-military, so not all of us served under John overseas, but we come together now, as a hard-hitting effective unit trusting each other blindly with our lives.

After I make the first contact with a victim and feel we can move forward, the extraction team formulates the plan for the initial snatch and grab before it's too late to make a difference. We stand up to the dangers of the case from start to finish. Once we have completed the extraction and have begun to help the victim see a new life, we also dole out the warning message to their abuser; we intend to make them understand we will always be watching. The message is harsh, messy, and beyond cruel from the abuser's point of view, but we take the point of view of the abuser's victim, finding it hard at times to stop before it goes too far. And still, we move forward to the next case without guilt or regret; we stand behind our actions because hopefully, we have shut down one more of the Devil's minions. But sadly, there are times we find out the message should have been clearer or more ruthless, because as I mentioned earlier, some of them just don't surrender. That's why safety protocols are so important.

From the surveillance techs to the motor pool mechanics, the whole team of Mickey is dedicated to procuring a positive outcome and keeping everyone safe. When on a case, we come together on a dark battlefield, where we push forward through the muck we have become used to, determined that our actions will make a positive difference. Mickey consists of exceptional people whose abilities are unprecedented, making them the best at what they do. Suzie and I put our lives in their hands every day, and I am so grateful to every one of them.

Chapter 12

After John hands the phone to his mother, he silently walks away to our glass-walled conference room. He can feel the eyes of his team follow him intently, they'll hold off for a bit to let him get a grip on his emotions, and he's grateful. They know it's vital for him to try to detach himself from his personal turmoil to oversee the case that lies ahead logically, so they allow him his solace.

As he enters the room, he automatically turns on the low lighting he prefers and begins to pace around the long oval table. He tries to manipulate his fears for Reggie into a calm resignation but can't seem to do it; there's no clear path from protector to spectator, and it's eating him up inside. He's watched Reggie walk into danger too many times to count and also watched her walk out of it. And each time he looks for the darkness he has no doubt tried to resubmerge itself within her. For John, it was so much easier commanding troops in Iraq than watching the woman he loves step back into the sadistic realm of her past. A past he is continually helping her to fight, not only personally but professionally as well.

He looks through the glass walls, taking in all the activity as every team member he sees is performing their duties with due diligence. He is so proud of the team they have put together and knows everyone is there to do nothing but help. They will work toward a positive outcome and not judge themselves on their actions to make that happen. Every member of Mickey will do whatever it takes to get the job done. They'll push through the gray areas, knowing that darkness waits as they swim through the filthy waters of past and present abusers, using whatever means necessary in the process to gain the upper hand.

These people watch victims come to grips with what humanity's worst flaw can dish out, and they know it's because they've done their jobs. So they don't question their resolve to fight, they don't regret or apologize for their actions, and they don't lose sleep at night.

He looks up and sees his mother enter the conference room, closing the door softly behind her. She leans back into the solid glass and watches him as he slides into the chair in front of him, placing his head in his hands. But she knows her son, so she waits quietly, leaving him alone with his tortured thoughts.

Finally, she speaks, "it's hard, isn't it, John?"

"What is?" he says with a tired sigh before dropping his hands from his head and leaning back in his chair, waiting to be enlightened.

"Feeling so powerless and vulnerable because of the love you feel for another person. The love overwhelms you, and it feels like your heart will stop beating every time you're apart," she says, sitting down across from him, marveling at the man he's become. A quick flash of a little boy in his Super Man pajamas runs through her mind, and she smiles inwardly at the memory. But she realizes there's nothing she can say to change how he feels, all she can do is watch him struggle with his heart as it assaults his reality. "Why is this one affecting you so hard, John?"

"I don't know for sure; maybe it's because I know this DuPree is ex-military, well, almost ex-military, and that's enough to make him more dangerous. I think about what he did to get that dishonorable discharged, and I want to wrap myself around Reggie and keep her out of harm's way."

"This guy is violent and will hide behind his father and fake badge while he abuses anyone that pushes him. And you know if he confronts her, she'll push back, and she'll push hard because she won't be able to help herself," he states sharply, slapping an open palm onto the table. "Mom, Reggie has never been up against someone like this before, someone who has the law on his side, so he can be open with his abuse knowing no one can touch him. Hell, Mickey has never been up against a mentally unstable maniac like this before! Jesus,,, this was so much easier before," he says with a lump in his throat.

"Before what?" his mother asks softly.

"Before she became my whole world. Mom,,, I truly can't breathe without her!"

She looks at him for a few seconds, taking it all in, silently watching the emotional struggle he feels before she speaks. "Well, now is where you need to rely on the team. Get Pixie, Matt, and Dominic in here and start strategizing like you were still in that god-forsaken sandbox; you guys have dealt with thousands of different kinds of evil!" She says it harshly while pushing her chair back and standing abruptly, giving him a stern look like it should be easy. But she knows it won't be, all she can do is hope he isn't going to lose his ability to lead his team in the right direction. She finds herself hoping he can place his emotions on the sidelines so he can run the next play safely. She'll have to rely on the whole team, not just his military brothers and sister, who have done battle with him before. She'll have to trust every member of Mickey to help him keep his head on straight.

"He's not just an abuser, Mom; he's also a god damn RAPIST!!!" John says with anger, like she doesn't get the situation.

"Exactly John,,, so keep your head on straight and get to work. You're already ahead of him because, you *know,* he's a god damn RAPIST!!!" she says, raising her voice to mimic his. But, unfortunately, all she can do is stand there as her words bounce off the walls to land harshly in the middle of the conference table between them, hoping she didn't go too far as she waits for his reaction.

Starring at her in surprise from her outburst, he tries to slow his heart rate before asking quietly, "has Dad ever seen this side of you???"

"Of course," she exhales with relief, waving him off with her hand in the air. "I'd like to say he appreciates my ability to get to the point, but I can't," she says with a soft laugh.

Still looking at his mother, he says, "I always thought you and Dad had a special kind of connection," he states knowingly. "But I also thought that kind of connection was too rare to ever happen for me, but that woman grabbed my heart the minute she walked into my life. I saw what could be, not what had been, so I waited, and it was the hardest thing I've ever done."

"John, what do you need from me?" she asks, walking around the table to stand in front of him.

"Well,,, apparently I need you to give me a good kick in the ass every once in a while. But really, all I need is your love, Mom, just your love," he whispers as he stands and reaches out to hug her. "Thank you."

Abby has tears in her eyes as she pulls away from the embrace, making her way to the door, leaving her son alone to think about what's to come and the best way to proceed.

"Whatever you need, John!" she says before opening the door and stepping out.

After he watches her walk away, he picks up his phone and dials, waiting as the phone rings twice on the other end before it's connected. "What's your ETA Pix?"

"I'm still about forty-five minutes out. Um, Boss,,, she's going to be pissed, isn't she?"

"Affirmative, but it won't be you she's pissed at."

"Copy that!!!"

Chapter 13

Suzie's dog tags clank out an agonizing tune, hitting the side of her food dish as she finishes the last morsel. Once she finishes with her food, she moves over to the deep-water bowl and shoves her whole face into its coolness. From there, a shower of water flows heavily across the room like an out-of-control oscillating sprinkler, the wet spray landing on every dry surface as she shakes and snorts. She's definitely royalty of a different breed.

I grab a towel out of the bathroom and begin the process of drying everything off but stop when she gives a little bark and looks at the door. She knows there's someone there even before a soft knock proves her instincts are correct.

I knew it wasn't room service because I hadn't ordered any, so I moved to the door picking up my aluminum bat on the way.

Most of the extraction team members carry concealed weapons, but I prefer to rely on the same weapon that destroyed my leg. It's the only thing I took from my past life. The softball field was my only home in many ways, and colleges were looking for talent, which I had in spades. At one point, it was my future and represented what I could have achieved if given a chance. But now, in my hands, it's a weapon, the one I choose to move forward, not the symbol used to cause the wreckage that shattered my life. It reminds me of what my life could have been and what he took from me; it was my future, then it was my nightmare, and now it's my strength. It helps me protect myself when the job sends me

75

traveling toward the dark perimeter of insanity, sending me running into horrific situations to try and beat the evil of man time after time. It helps me stand my ground; it helps me remember how far I've come to retrieve and retain the *me* I'd lost; it's a solid comfort in my hands. I know you're thinking it would be the last thing you'd want in your life, a constant reminder of how it destroyed your body, but don't judge me too harshly because the only person it needs to make sense to is me.

So, holding the bat and standing close to the door, I ask who it is, not feeling threatened exactly, but engrained diligence prevails. Suzie pushes her body in front of me, placing herself between me and the door, *her* engrained diligence taking over as well. I have a relatively good idea it's a friend; I just don't know which one.

"Reggie,,,, put the bat down; it's Pix," she says through the door.

My shoulders involuntarily slump with resignation, but I do as she says before pushing the handle down to open the door. All I see once it opens is a small hand waving a white rag in the opening, then Pixie's elfin face appears around the door frame.

"Just following orders, sister," she says hurriedly, putting both her hands in the air dramatically.

"Hell, I expected one of you guys about half an hour ago," I say, acknowledging the fact I knew John wouldn't compromise fully. "What took you so long?" I ask, delivering the question with sarcasm, a butt load of it.

All I can do is open the door wider and wave her inside. After closing it behind her, I reach out and grab the rag she still holds in her hand as a weak peace offering and throw it in her face. Turning away and walking deeper into the room, all I can manage to say is, "so you drew the short straw,,, lucky you!" As I turn around, I notice she's got a hiker's backpack draped over each shoulder, with hiking boots secured to the frames. "So, what's the plan?" I hope you're not going to suggest we hike to DuPree from here."

But before she can even say anything, Suzie is wagging her tail and circling Pix with excitement. "Hi, sweet girl," she says, kneeling to accept all the loving Suz has begun to lavish on her. With her canine welcome completed, Pixie pulls both packs off her shoulders and stacks them against the wall. She then removes her coat before dropping her tiny butt into one of the chairs situated around the small table in the corner of the room.

"So, how pissed are you on a scale from one to ten, with ten being, like SUPERRRRR PISSED?"

Reggie tries to glare at her and give a harsh retort, but she has this way of fixing her face into this cute little cherub lip pout. She's shorter than Reggie's 5'4", with short blonde hair cut close to her head on the sides and back. The hair on top of her head is brushed forward into long bangs that fall forward, brushing across her eyebrows to mingle with thick lashes encompassing her huge, beautiful blue eyes. Her name is Pixie, but John and his team gave her the nickname "Pix" when they were overseas. She handles a snipper rifle better than any man in the military, and she saved their butts more times than they can count. Hence the nickname Pix, from her love of *"picking"* off the enemy one by one from an incredible distance. She looks like she belongs in a mystical fairy tale, surrounded by elves and trees with tiny moss huts built on the limbs, the scene enhanced with fireflies zooming from one hut to the other like tiny traveling solar lights.

The last thing you would think of is her eating sand and tolerating extreme heat with a sniper rifle in her hands fighting overseas. Now she's a Registered Nurse who works with Michael, John's dad, at the hospital and Xander in the Med Bay at the Club House, but one thing's for sure, she's an asset in whatever role she plays. And because of her military training, she's an indispensable member of the extraction team as well. John has trusted her with his life and the lives of his men, so who am I to doubt her abilities just because she looks like Tinker Bell.

"I have a few ideas," she says, flashing a smile of white teeth, "but before we discuss them, let's hit that mini frig in the corner! I know there's a chilled bottle of Chardonnay in there because you never leave home without it." So, before Reggie can comment, she heads to the frig and opens the door, pulling out a bottle to prove her point.

"True, that sister, you know me too well, and apparently so does Abby because it was in there chilling when I checked in," Reggie says taking the bottle from her, flashing her own smile.

While Reggie opens the chilled bottle of her favorite beverage, Pix steps into the bathroom to grab two plastic glasses. They meet at the table in the corner and sit down across from each other. Suzie is happy to lie at the foot of one of the two Queen size beds in comfort, trying to pay attention, but her eyelids are getting heavy. She does her best to fight the exhaustion from the wonderful day she had, but it doesn't take long, and she's snoring into the room with all her lady-like royalty.

They begin to discuss what options they have for entering the town of DuPree, knowing their faces will turn heads the minute they arrive. Pix heard everything Bud Ainslee had said through the coms about Dempsey's character and what got him a Dishonorable Discharge, causing her to fight back lingering nausea from her time in the military. She knew this guy was dangerous, and that shit could hit the fan so quickly it would make your head spin. Pix relayed her knowledge to Reggie of what a woman could expect while serving her country because, unfortunately, she had seen first-hand what went on at the hands of scum like Dempsey DuPree. Fortunately for Pix, John and his men took her under their wings from the get-go, and she never experienced anything like most women did in the ranks. She was always protected from that brutality and respected, even before she saved their butts in combat. Having that first-hand knowledge was upsetting, especially because they wouldn't physically be there to protect her and Reggie against the potential danger of a horrible act from a wretched animal disguised as a human being. But they're both strong women and having the intel they did so far and the additional they'd get by morning from the team, she was hopeful they'd be able to stay one step ahead of Dempsey.

So, Pix continued to relay her eyewitness accounts bluntly, no sugar coating or icing over the cruelties and double standards, because Reggie wouldn't want it any other way. Besides, the atrocities this woman has lived through and seen aren't any less severe on the brutality scale. On more than one occasion, she's felt that fighting a war overseas was just as brutal as the war they fight on Domestic Violence here at home, especially if you lived it as Reggie had.

FROM SURVIVING TO SURVIVOR

Pix looks across the small table at Reggie, once again consumed with respect for the strength and fortitude the woman carries. She was mentally destroyed and physically broken at one time but has worked her way out of the darkness, managing for the most part, to leave the shadows of her previous self behind. Yet, Pix can't fathom how Reggie wakes up every day harboring the knowledge that today could be the day. The day where just a simple word, song lyric, smell, or someone's mannerisms could trigger a mental floundering, sending her back through a time warp of pain demanding her return. Where the toxic memories crawl and scatter within; taking up residence inside her soul as they send her reeling toward her past where they think she belongs, sending her back to the place from which she had the insufferable gall and courage to escape. The mission of the triggered memory is always the same. It is to seek her out and wake up her past nightmares, letting her know the darkness still lurks within her and is tired of waiting for her to return home, demanding its expectation of her immediate surrender and obedience profusely.

Pixie has seen her fight her demons, watched her battle against an evil that commanded and consumed her past. And like every member of Mickey, each time she makes her way back to them, their respect for her grows even more. Every time she lands on her feet, Mickey stands in awe, not missing a step in their current assignment. As always, she thanked them for their concern for her well-being, promising with a strong insistence she'd found her way back once more. No, there is no limit on the respect you can give where Regina "Reggie" Reynolds is concerned.

80

Chapter 14

It's getting close to sunrise, and the Club House is buzzing like it always is when working a new case, and without a doubt, John knew they were going to be doing just that. He could tell by the tone of Reggie's voice when she called to rip him a new one for sending Pix to cover her ass. He also knew it was her turn to deliver one of the concessions she was always talking about, which would keep the scoreboard pretty much even by his calculations. So, after he let her rip him, *"said new one,"* she did concede to his play, and they talked well into the night, leaving him feeling confident he made the right call.

The team was working hard with the information they had, and he was optimistic that in a few hours, he'd be able to give Reggie and Pix more intel concerning all the players they'd most likely run into when they entered DuPree.

He stands at the core of the Club House, acknowledging the operation they have built. He's proud and saddened at the same time for the need of its existence and the importance it plays concerning the war they fight. For the umpteenth time, he envisions himself and the team sitting down to a Q&A with the devil, and he has satisfying visions of how that face-to-face would end, and his team wouldn't be the ones eviscerated.

His elite security firm takes up a small corner of the football field size hanger located next to the Sea-Tac airport and I-5. The regular access door into the firm's office lends to the realism of a security business, but it's used chiefly now as a cover for what the operation houses, which is Mickey.

90% of the security techs and field agents listed as employees for the security business work for Mickey, 40% of those take up their posts at the core of the Club House, making it the heart of the operation. Its soft lighting hangs from open rafters and metal pipes, mixing their soft glow with the harsh lighting from colossal computer screens. The screens hum with real-time info, alerting the dedicated techs standing vigil with second-by-second updates. The protocols and monitoring techniques used by the techs to follow all parties involved before, during, and after an extraction are major.

A current Rescue needs to believe she is safe as she spins on a carousel of fear and life-changing decisions. She needs to have confidence in our team to make those decisions and accept the assurances that we will be there to continue her safety for as long as we think necessary. We all know the unrelenting dedication of our techs to the safety of the new and past Rescue victims is the foundation they need. They need something to rely on, and the knowledge they're protected gives them a well-earned sense of security. It gives them what they need to feel safe and comfortable moving forward. Being able to pull strength from that sense of security enables them to work hard to pursue a new life, and of course, once they've achieved the new life, be able to hold onto it.

The next section of the hangar houses the motor pool and numerous vehicles used by the extraction and surveillance teams. Then at the far end of the motor pool is Mickey's private jet, they used a bunch of the zeroes on the spreadsheet to acquire it, but it didn't take his mother long to replenish all those zeros and add more.

On the other end of the hangar is a Medical Bay, consisting of an Emergency room and Surgical Department equipped with everything you can think of, including a staff comprised of doctors, nurses, X-ray techs, PT specialists, and most recently, a Trauma specialist. In addition, the ER department is staffed 24 hours a day, not only for the extraction team and the security details but for all the team members that work within the other departments here at the Club House.

Finally, there's a workout area for strength training and physical therapy, used by the team members and the Rescues. His eyes wander to the corner of the workout area where a batting cage sits, which was Reggie's only request when they drew up the plans for the Club House. She uses it to keep her muscles toned and to work up some full-blown cardio. She says it keeps her focused on the war they fight and as physically healthy as possible due to her leg and knee limitations. And she made it clear from the start that the bat helps her work through the emotional therapy she needs, keeping her mind and soul on the same page. He doesn't care what it does or how it works, as long as it helps, and like she always says, it only has to make sense to her.

There's a well-stocked kitchen and laundry room equipped with the latest appliances, along with a large Bunk House with eight beds plus a bathroom and a shower. The team works 24/7, 365, so it's a comfortable home away from home for the techs and members of the surveillance teams to grab some sleep and a shower. About a year ago, he made a renovation, cutting down the number of beds for the team members from twelve to the current eight, so he could wall off one end and make it into a small private residence for Reggie and himself. And on the other end, there's a private bedroom and bathroom for the current Rescue.

Just past the Bunk House entrance is a flight of metal stairs leading up to a jogging track that circles the inner perimeter. The members of Mickey use it to stay in shape, and the Rescued are encouraged to utilize it as well, to add cardio to their PT when they're strong enough. They have many decisions to make, but they need to become strong physically and mentally before deciding where they want to go and what they want to do.

It had been a while since he stood in the Club House and focused on each section that makes up Mickey, and as usual, he remembers the horrible reality that caused them to put this place together, and it sickens him. From this high-tech location, they pursue an entity that has had the human sucked right out of them, and in its place is a festering virus of pure evil. After all this time, the battle against this black plague still rages on, one pursuit after another with no cure in sight. There's no way to be proactive in this fight, no way to chase and stop a monster before he slithers in to present himself to the victim of his choice, especially when there's no way to know who the victim will be.

"Boss, you ready?"

"Boss…" Matt says as he passes him heading to the conference room. "We have some intel, Boss. You okay?" he asks, stopping a few steps ahead of John and turning to see what the holdup is and why there was no response to the question.

"Sorry, Matt, right behind ya."

Chapter 15

John follows Matt through the door of the conference room. The air feels heavy and still, and the only movement in the room comes from the eyes that follow him to the head of the table. His exhaustion mirrors theirs as he greets them in turn with his own red, gritty eyes. Everyone here has worked all night to acquire as much information as possible. Finally, they're ready to deliver what intel they've compiled, which is a significant amount because there is no firewall or sophisticated hacking deterrent to stop these people. They can bounce around the dark web, leaving no breadcrumbs, as easy as your mother can download a recipe from the Betty Crocker website.

Marco, the lead computer/surveillance tech, sits at the other end of the conference table, bringing up his laptop to sync with the large monitor mounted high on the wall directly behind him. Matt sits to his left next to John's parents Abby and Michael, with Dominic and Oscar-D sitting to his right, and all eyes are on John as he stands at the head of the table.

"Has anyone heard from Mountain? I don't want to start until we're all here," John says while massaging the back of his neck with strong fingers, trying to soothe a few raging muscles.

"Right here, Boss," Mountain's deep baritone voice precedes him through the door waking up the members sitting around the table. His build is like a slab of granite, and he's tall enough to make even a tall man look small, which is displayed when he must duck his head slightly when coming through the door. However, his heart is just as big as his presence, and the team knows that the scowl worn is just for show. He has ridden a motorcycle his entire adult life, and even now, it's his only personal mode of transportation, rain, snow, or shine. His face is weathered from the elements adding to his look of fierceness, but it's just camouflage hiding the real man. He wears his long hair tied back in a ponytail, and a leather vest like most biker's wear, but this one shows no club affiliation. Instead, a baby Panda Bear is intricately stitched in a multicolored pattern on the back of the vest, leaving the people who don't know him to wonder at the contrast. "Sorry I'm late, Boss," he says while taking the chair next to Oscar-D.

"No worries, Man," John says, leaning down to shake hands. "Let's get Reggie and Pix dialed in before we start," he says to Marco while taking his position at the head of the table again. Marco hits a button on his keyboard sending out the communications link to Reggie's laptop so they can join the group via a high-tech zoom meeting. The monitor mounted on the wall behind Marco's head is suddenly lit up with Reggie and Pixie sitting side by side in the motel room, each clutching paper cups of coffee. Their eyes, raw and puffy showing they hadn't slept much either from their all-night strategy session.

"Good morning," Reggie says, yawning at the screen while running a hand through her thick dark mane of hair. "It's a wonderful day in the neighborhood, isn't it?" she says but realizes immediately from the look she's getting from John that his neighborhood was far from wonderful, and he wasn't in the mood for silliness this morning.

"Reggie,,, Pix,,," John says, returning the morning greeting, minus the silliness, "as you can see, the team is all here, and they're ready to pass on their initial intel."

A crisp, agitated bark attached to a furry presence emanates through the screen as Suzie pushes herself between Reggie and Pix to place her nose so close to the computer screen she will leave heavy DNA smeared across it. In no uncertain terms, she lets everyone know she's beyond insulted by the fact the morning greeting didn't include her, causing everyone around the table to respond to the reprimand.

"Good morning Suzie," they all say guiltily, responding to the cold snout scolding they've received, suddenly feeling like children who have been disciplined by a parent, leaving them to wonder how long they'll be grounded.

"Marco, you're up!" John says after Suzie snorts into the monitor, looking appeased.

Chapter 16

"Okay, Boss," Marco says while his fingers fly across his keyboard. He manipulates the monitor, so Reggie and Pixie are displayed within a small square up in the right-hand corner. By doing so, they will see any images Marco sends to the screen just by looking into the laptop in front of them. He clicks a few keys on his computer, sending multiple images up for display for everyone to see. "These documents explain how Darwin Dupree acquired his wealth; apparently, it's inherited family money. By searching from the present backward, I was able to find out how he acquired his wealth. His great, great grandfather, Rupert Darwin DuPree, was one of the lucky few to hit a huge vein of gold during the Klondike Gold Rush during the late 1800s. He was among the thousands of individuals who migrated into the Canadian Region heading to Skagway Alaska." Marco clicks on a document to enlarge it. The paper shows the name of a ship and its passenger manifest dated April 23, 1897. He then highlights the entry showing Rupert DuPree. "He was only eighteen years old when he stepped off the ship in Skagway." Marco then puts up another document on the screen showing the recording of his claim with the Mining District Recorder on August 27, 1900. "The next day on August 28, 1900, Rupert boards another ship heading home," Marco says, tossing up another ship's passenger manifest to be viewed behind him. It displays, just like the previous one, the name of the vessel and the passengers.

"Rupert died in 1942, and it was amazing how he was able to hold onto his wealth through the depression to pass it onto his son, Jacob Darwin DuPree, Darwin's Great Grandfather." With another click of a button, Rupert's Death Certificate pops up on the screen.

"So, Jacob Darwin DuPree took up the reins. He was young and not book smart but had the intelligence to figure out what the country needed as we entered WWII with the Nazis breathing down our necks. He took the fortune and invested it in his country, and by doing so, he infused the family's fortune.

"Some Arms factories needed to be up and running, along with Ironworks and shipbuilding," the information is displayed as a result of more clicks, sending documents up on the monitor. "Sadly, the DuPree family fortune grew immensely during one of the most catastrophic events of survival in our history."

The room is quiet as everyone understands the meaning of war, the losses are always too great, even if on the winning end. But the American men and women who fought in WWII met the challenge head on with the mindset that failure would deface what our country was built on and what it stood for. They knew with every fighting breath they took, the outcome, if they failed would be the apocalypse of our freedom, doomed and obliterated. Every soldier that died in that war did so to keep us from having our freedoms annihilated, and to keep the American people from being forced into Socialism with the English language being replaced by German. The men and women who fought in that war were from the greatest generation to date. And it's unconscionable that their sacrifices and what the importance of winning that war meant to our country has been forgotten, the meaning left out of history books to be replaced with *"new"* history. It's a slap in the face to every true American and fallen soldier who sacrificed their lives so we could remain free.

Marco continues as the faces around the table depict mirrored thoughts of outrage for the sacrifices forgotten. "Jacob Darwin DuPree died in 1958, passing the fortune onto his son Chester Darwin DuPree, Darwin's, Grand Father. Are you guys seeing a pattern here with the names?" Marco says sarcastically, sending another death certificate up on the screen. "Anyway, moving forward, Chester kept the same line of thinking as his father when it came to reaping profits from the death and destruction of war. He renewed the contract for arms production with the US Government when President Kennedy sent our troops into Vietnam, but soon saw an additional opportunity. He got heavy into the opium and heroin trades and soon realized there were so many hands in government that could be greased and so much money in which to grease them, there were never any repercussions, just butt loads of money to be passed around and coveted. He had to have pants with extra, large pockets in order to accommodate all the officials that wanted to jump in."

"Chester died in 1976 passing the fortune onto his son, Jasper Darwin DuPree, Big Daddy's Daddy, along with the list of officials who protected him. The list had been narrowed down of course after the Viet Nam War ended in 1975, and drugs were no longer in play. Jasper knew he would need to concentrate on the local and state officials in order to accomplish what he saw for the future now. Jasper was the one who actually had the vision to build the town of DuPree so there would be a legacy for many more

FROM SURVIVING TO SURVIVOR

generations of DuPree's to come, and he would need the local officials to help him hurdle right over the red tape. But eventually, due to failing health, Jasper realized he needed Big Daddy to be included in all the initial planning because it would be up to him to complete his dream.

Jasper schooled Big Daddy up on what he needed to know about the players in his pocket and how the money was distributed among the upstanding officials. So immediately after the town of DuPree was envisioned and drawn out on paper, Darwin began clearing all the land adjacent to the newly established Sawmill. He wanted his father to at least see the beginning of his dream come together. Jasper was only able to see some of the town he'd envisioned before his death in June of 1987, but as we've learned Big Daddy was already running things by then."

The monitor on the wall was filled with the history of a family who produced not only a town of prisoners, but a deranged predator to police its streets and citizens. The possibility that the end result may have been incredibly different if just one of those men hadn't had a son, the chain on the road to producing the dark violence they will be chasing could have been broken.

Marco closed all the documents on the screen before continuing. "I was able to worm my way into the dark web," he says with a smile, "and retrieve all the financials for Darwin and the town of DuPree; that's when I handed everything I discovered over to Abby to do her thing with the info and decipher what she could."

"Well, I don't know-how, especially on such short notice, but you've done it again, Marco," Reggie praises through the coms link.

"Piece of cake, Miss Reggie, but it's nothing compared to what Abby was able to dig up."   And with that, all eyes around the conference table turned to Abby.

"Boss," Matt interrupts while looking at his watch, "I need to share my intel before Abby begins; I've got a skype session scheduled with DuPree's rape victim from Fort Leonard Wood. I reached out to an old buddy there and picked his brain a bit; he was a Sergeant when DuPree was there for training, and the incident took place. He told me he would contact her and ask if she was willing to speak with us about DuPree, and she agreed, but the time is now because of her circumstances. She's part of the platoon President Trump sent when he ordered the drone strike that killed Iran's; you know who, and she's still there." Matt turns to Marco after receiving the go ahead from John and says, "make it happen, brother."

Chapter 17

After a few silent seconds, the monitor on the wall zoomed in to focus on Sergeant First Class Amber Taft. "Good morning," she says crisply, her years of military training resonating from her speech. She sits with her back straight in the chair, her eyes scanning the monitor taking in the team. "Sergeant Sims asked if I was willing to speak with you concerning the incident at Fort Leonard Wood." Her body language didn't waver or give away any emotion as she spoke into the monitor, but her face couldn't follow suit. There were cracks in her facial armor that portrayed, and probably always would, the momentary breakdown of strength for even the most disciplined victim. She nervously reached up to touch her hair, making sure every strand was tight and in its place within the regulation bun resting just above the collar of her army fatigues.

"Yes," that's correct, Matt says into the monitor. "First, we'd all like to thank you for your service, Sergeant, and we promise not to keep you from your duties for long, but we're hoping you can provide some insight into Dempsey DuPree. But before we begin, I'd like to give you a quick introduction of all the faces attending this inquiry." He introduces Reggie and Pix by pointing up to the corner of the monitor, and the Sergeant acknowledges them with a stiff nod, Pix returning it with her own. He quickly moves around the table with short introductions before turning to the left and gesturing to John, "and this is the Boss Man…"

"No introduction needed," she says intently, her eyes roaming over the faces she sees through the monitor before focusing on John. "The Lieutenant has a reputation over here and is gravely missed, along with his team. I see some members of his command sitting at your table, and you as well, Matt."

"Thank you for the words, Sergeant," John says, clearing his throat, "but I'm just the Boss Man now, and this is my team," he interjects with a quick nod around the table. He knows she can't be away from her duties for long, so he doesn't waste any time and pushes forward, "what are you able to tell us, Sergeant?"

Leaning closer to the laptop in front of her, she drops her voice and begins telling these strangers the worst moments of her life. She shares every second of shame and pain she felt as it was delivered through an act of fierce strength, using its dominance to do nothing but cause terror and fill a sexual need. She didn't blink or fold while relaying her experience through the non-personal channel of a computer screen. Her eyes travel into their space, resonating with the horror they've all become too familiar with; she describes the actual moment she met the devil and began to believe in hell.

Her eyes shimmer with hate as she continues to explicitly deliver the worst moments of the act that almost destroyed her. She inhales deeply, sucking air into her lungs so she can continue, revealing the instant she knew she couldn't win. But she manages to swallow the putrid humiliation to continue. She shares with the team the overwhelming sense of shameful acceptance she felt the instant her mind told her body she couldn't win and had to succumb to the inevitable. Darkly she admits her disgraceful defeat by acknowledging DuPree had the power, and she had no choice but to endure the act and live with the scars left by the animal.

Mickey is used to dealing with Domestic Violence, has seen the mental carnage, and touched the physical outcomes of broken bones and blood because of it. They've watched the victims fight their mental horrors day in and day out. But now, the team is being enlightened as to the violence of rape. The act itself and the brutal mechanics of rape are a distant cousin to domestic violence in many ways, but just as close as a loving sibling in others.

Rape is just another short-term form of dominance and unbelievable cruelty. If a victim is lucky, they won't suffer physical damage, but everyone suffers the mental issues of the act.

Reggie sits in the motel room glued to the computer screen in front of her; she feels a kinship with the shimmering eyes resonating through the small screen. She can feel all the emotional pain still hiding there, the pain that this woman refused to let beat her. She removes her eyes from the Sergeants and quickly glances around the monitor to see all the faces set in sorrow as they try to understand her never-ending emotional toll.

But Reggie suddenly feels the intrusion of the team is out of line because she knows the mental consequences could be too much. Within her heart, she carries a feeling of deep sorrow. They had no right to call on this woman, prompting her to share all the gory details of DuPree's game of violent dominance.

"STOP, SHUT THIS DOWN NOW!!!" Reggie shouts into her monitor as she stiffly stands agitated and appalled within the small box in the corner of their screen. Pixie instantly stands as well and reaches out to her, laying a gentle hand on her arm. In addition, the outburst has unnerved Suzie's protective instincts, causing her to pace around Reggie's legs in her all too familiar dance, trying to calm her down. But the calm refuses to come because Reggie knows with every beat of her heart that Mickey has no right to invade the Sergeant's story, no right to dissect every black nuance and terrifying minute of her hell.

"Sergeant Taft," Reggie says with sorrow, "we have no right to ask you to relive your horror. It sickens me that we would allow you to slip back into your nightmare, causing you to have to fight all over again to regain the strength you've achieved. We have no right to dissect your soul or dig around picking and choosing what horrors we could use." She's breathing heavily now, standing there staring into the monitor with clenched fists, hating their intrusion. She knows how easy it is to stumble backward and how hard it is to regain the mental footing you've achieved. There is nothing but silence in both rooms as Pix slowly pushes Reggie back down into her chair, where Suzie places her baby in the familiar lap for comfort. The silence is so smothering that no one can catch their breath, but the Sergeant manages to grab some air and addresses the monitors.

"I appreciate the concern Ma'am, but I need to finish this so you will know what to expect from that man. And believe me, this is how I will gain all that ground back and more in the future. Besides, I sit here and look around that table, and I have a feeling that I will get my justice; I just hope what I'm sharing with you helps."

Once she described the actual event in all its dark details, she continued without any prompting to lead them down the path taken and explain why she'd chosen it. Her decision pointed her toward the only scenario she felt she could live with. She reached inside herself and dug up a deep, hidden strength DuPree hadn't stomped on. She found the act of digging into every available scenario the first step to healing. It was liberating maneuvering through the lesser of her options, discarding their absurdity, while flipping the brass the bird. She was determined to succeed and do it on her terms.

"I came damn close to shutting down and running back to the small town of Walterboro, South Carolina; it's my home." As soon as she mentioned where she was from, she felt connected to something real, something good that gave her the strength to continue. Talking about her past life seemed to calm her. Because of that, a beautiful transformation took place before the team's eyes as a southern drawl came pouring out of her mouth, laced with the honey that all Southern Bells learn at a young age. "The Army," she shifted her gaze to Reggie and Pix, "well, all military branches have come a long way to try to protect women soldiers, just now accepting us in the ranks. I know they dealt with DuPree quietly because all he got was a dishonorable discharge.

But I was so bitter," she says, pounding her fist on the desk, "I wanted a trial, I wanted him punished for the predator he was, and probably still is... He needed to be locked away; shipping him home just gave him a bigger hunting ground, but no one would listen to me. So finally, I told the brass I was willing to testify in court, but they said it would raise too many red flags, warning me my career would, not could, would be in jeopardy. At that point, they offered me the standard 'ODPMC,' but that just pissed me off and enraged me, so I decided to stay and fight, not only the memories of what happened to me but battle the brass as well."

Curious, Reggie leans into Pix and asks, "what's an ODPMC?"

"It's an acronym for; Other Designated Physical and Mental Conditions Discharge. You wouldn't believe how many times that is offered when there is an incident the military just wants to make go away," she whispered.

"I guess they thought I was going to fall apart or something. But the minute the brass threw out the offer, I just felt rage that DuPree would win, and all the others would see me as weak. So I decided then that while my physical bruises were healing, I'd send my wounded mental fitness back to find the strength I pulled from in basic training. It came down to two choices. I could fold up within myself and run or use the rage the situation instilled in me to heal. I decided to use the memories of DuPree's actions to stimulate my healing and help me focus on achieving respect and protect my career. It hasn't been easy, but I know for a fact that if I had run back home, he would have beaten me in here," she said, tapping her left temple, "and I just couldn't allow his actions to destroy me."

"We commend your strength, Sergeant," John said, standing to his full height, locking his intense eyes onto hers. "And just like Reggie voiced earlier, we had no right to put you through this nightmare again, but we felt you'd have some insight into DuPree that would help us take him down."

"Take him down, oh my god, he's still at it," she says, feeling sick with the horrible realization. "So, there's more victims out there, I'm guessing?"

There was a pause in the conversation as all parties shifted in their seats, but then Reggie replied, "Two victims that we know of for sure," she said. For the next twenty minutes, Reggie delivered the team's situation, painting a sad picture of Bud and Amee.

"As you have probably figured out by now," John picked up where Reggie left off, "we battle a horrible darkness that spreads throughout society. This team dedicates itself to helping victims of domestic abuse when their lives and the lives of loved ones live in fear with no hope of escape. We work in the dark, stepping in before it's too late, to fight and rescue victims who are in dire situations."

"That man is not human!" Sergeant Taft exclaims into the monitor. "I saw it in his eyes as he held me down, spitting his self-importance into my face, getting all revved up to claim what he thought was his right. His eyes bore into my soul, and I saw a byproduct of hell! He's not only dangerous but a psychopath, and it's obvious he won't be stopped by the law; it's clear there are powers at work that protect him. Unfortunately, I can't lend any insight into his domestic abuse except to say it all comes down to his lack of humanity; he lives to dominate by violence. I can't even imagine having to live with someone like that. I had one altercation with him, and I'm still finding my way back, but to have to be subjected to his violence and control day after day is unfathomable to me. So I hope I have helped at least a little bit, and I'm glad you reached out. I had no idea there were organizations like yours out there; I commend your work and compassion," the Sergeant says into the monitor.

"About that Sergeant," John interjects, "we are the only team of this sort that exists but have long arms stretching across the United States. So,,, the only way we are successful is because of our anonymity and diligence toward security; we must stay dark to protect all involved. So we hope we can count on you to understand that this conversation never took place. I can't stress enough how important it is that we stay under everyone's radar. Can we count on your discretion, Sergeant?"

"Copy that, Lieutenant," she says, slipping back into her stiff military stature. She takes a moment to make eye contact with the team and thank them for their courage. "I wish all of you success with this endeavor, Taft out."

"Moving on," John says, clearing his throat, gazing up at Reggie as she sits saddened by the painful enlightenment of the past hour. He can read her thoughts and body language through the little square bubble up in the corner of the screen. He can guarantee her soul has shrunk a bit more by the revelation there is another dark twist to the brutality they've been fighting for so long. "Well now we know Bud wasn't exaggerating his fears and his knowledge of DuPree's past. Matt, with someone like DuPree, we can pretty much bet his tendencies for rape didn't just develop when he entered the Army. Work your magic and do some digging into his high school days. I'd bet from everything we've learned so far, there are sealed files and dismissed charges stacked up somewhere just waiting for you to get into."

"Copy that, Boss."

Chapter 18

"Mom, what did you find out about Darwin's financials?"

Abby pulls herself from the shroud of disbelief that heavily cloaks her heart after listening to the Sergeant's story. She looks down at her laptop, fighting to hide the visible cracks that have somehow etched themselves into her usual porcelain features. Slim, elegant fingers find their way to the keyboard in front of her. There's a thickness in her throat, and tears are threatening to fall because of heavy eyelids. But she won't blink because that would cause them to fall, and she's determined to be strong and deliver her findings. But, as hard as she tries, she can't hide the visible shaking of her hands, and her fingers seem to have a mind of their own as she forces them across the keyboard.

"Sorry, sorry, ah damn," she spits at her screen because she has to keep backing up, deleting her incorrect keystrokes.

"It's okay Honey," Michael whispers close to her ear, while placing his hand on her thigh underneath the table, "you got this." She takes a breath, a quick peek into his eyes and agrees, yes, she does have this.

Once composed, she begins. "Well, I found his money or at least a big chunk of it," she says, feeling stronger with every second that passes. "Marco was able to point me in the right direction, which helped me find one financial breadcrumb after another," she says and directs everyone to look at the screen behind Marco. "I'm no forensic accountant, but I was able to follow the numerous

101

money transfers, which eventually landed me in the Cayman Islands. Luckily, he funnels his fortune through dummy corporations and LLCs, but with low-security firewalls, so I was able to shadow my way in and have a look around. Whoever set this up for him was just as arrogant as he is or just wasn't too savvy where security is concerned. Maybe his lawyer?" She throws the possibility out there but continues to think of other scenarios as well.

"Here are his financials from the money institution in DuPree," she says, sending a spreadsheet up on the screen. "As you can see, he keeps a large number of reserves on hand for various projects he's funding and plenty of cash flow to run the town. But this is what caught my eye; These are BLACK FILES, at least that's what the financial world calls them," she says while enlarging what looks like account numbers with a different letter of the alphabet attached to each one. A, B, C, D, etc. "From there, I was able to dig deeper behind the flimsy walls of security and found a hidden ledger, which looks like it's connected to this information. She waits with electric anticipation for the reaction she knows is coming and isn't disappointed when it arrives. With a large knowing smile, she says, "HOLY CRAP is right!"

The information on the screen listed elected officials starting at the local and state level and continued up the political ladder to our high-ranking government officials as well. Each name listed has a corresponding letter of the alphabet, which connects it to an account number. One member of the team let out a high-pitched whistle that screeched off the walls of the conference room, which in turn encouraged everyone to start talking and reading the names out loud, muttering their disbelief.

"This bullshit right here is why I don't vote," shouted Matt as he swiftly circled the perimeter of the room, ending up in front of the monitor, casting a rigid shadow. "It doesn't make a damn bit of difference because right there in black and white is the proof that corruption is just as big a reality and as widespread as Domestic Violence, and I can only handle one reality of bullshit at a time. Jesus, look at those names, especially the last one,,," he shouts into the room. The list was utterly jaw-dropping and took a while for everyone to read through it.

All Matt felt was a steely rage as he stepped back into a corner of the room, jamming his hands into the front pockets of his jeans; this was no time to voice personal issues; he knew he had to calm down. His eyes automatically drifted to the corner bubble where Pix was trying to convey her understanding, hoping he could draw some calm from her.

At first glance, you wouldn't see ex-military when you looked at him, but when his training needs to kick in, there is no doubt. Un-like John and Dominic, he chooses not to wear the stiff cargo pants and black lace-up boots they prefer; he likes a more casual dress since returning home.

He wears jeans, white T-shirts underneath unbuttoned cotton shirts, hiking boots, and his dark hair is a bit longer than the regulation military cut.

"Is he going to be alright?" Reggie asks Pix from their little corner of the screen.

"Yes, he just gets so ramped up about politics lately. But, he'll be fine," Pix assures her.

John stepped back from the crowd and stood in front of his military brother and trusted friend, feeling the same rage at what this list represents. "Matt, don't worry, once Bud and Amee are safe, and this case is over, we'll deal with every name on that list. It won't solve the problem, but that's how we roll man, every battle we fight is uphill. We'll figure out a way to take them down as well, but right now, I need your head in the game, no distractions. My girl is out there, and so is yours; feel me?"

"God damn political parasites," Matt mutters from his self-imposed time out in the corner.

"I feel ya, Boss."

John heads back to the table, his eyes glued to the screen once again. Then, raising his voice to be heard over the outrage of the team, he asks, "exactly what do these "black files" mean, mom?"

"According to the entries, I believe these are the officials Darwin has in his pocket," she says, pointing at the ledger, "and these entries are most likely payoffs."

"Well, that would explain how he has no restrictions or hoops to jump through to run the town or expand it, for that matter. No financial audits would take place because of name number four up there," he says and waves at the screen. "No permits or inspections on building because there are outstretched palms for that as well," John sighs, stating the obvious.

There's a name on that list connected to any issue that would stand in the way of Darwin's progress, and one of the biggest is law

104

enforcement. I'm guessing that's what happened with Bud's friend Gregory Fairchild; I bet he ended up in Leavenworth and thought he was safe when he walked into the local Sheriff's Office. I see the Sheriff's name on that list," Dominic states harshly, his European accent becoming thicker, and his intense dark eyes grew even darker from scanning the evidence of corruption in front of them. "It's obvious we can't be asking any law enforcement agency questions about Fairchild because we don't know how far down the chain the corruption has spread, and we don't want to give Darwin a heads up. I'm glad we saw this intel before morning because that's where I was going to start digging."

"Marco," John says, "have you been able to find out who sent the intimidating e-mail to all the residents of DuPree showing Gregory Fairchild's body?"

"Getting close, Boss, it appears the security connected to the IP address of the sender is thicker than the security set up around Big Daddy's finances. But don't worry, I'm close."

The list was long and unbelievably frightening. On the local level alone, it listed all the County Commissioner's names, several high-ranking law enforcement officials, and four out of five county judges. But the list seemed never-ending because it listed more prominent players that held the same positions on the state level. And by looking at the corresponding payoff amounts, they were being paid for huge favors.

"There's another page," Abby says, adding it to the large monitor screen. "I don't recognize any of these names, though."

"I do," Michael says dejectedly, "well, at least two of them. One is a General Practitioner out of Tacoma, and the other is a General Surgeon in Leavenworth. I bet the other names are in the medical field also. Abby and I can do some quiet digging using contacts we have from the numerous medical boards we sit on, and Xander might also recognize a few of the names. If not, there's always a quick Internet search. It explains why Amee never went to an emergency room; as Bud said, these guys just come running to patch her up after Dempsey beats the crap out of her. It's one thing to turn your back on your Hippocratic Oath, but *this* betrayal to a patient is deplorable," he states with anger.

"Thank you Dad, let Marco know if you need any help going forward."

Michael nods rigidly, and with his jaw clenched tightly, he sits back in his chair, and as always, his eyes seek out Reggie's. From a brutal beginning, they share a sorrowful understanding that has forged a bond between them the rest of the team will never understand. He came close to being destroyed by the numerous acts of violence he had seen before the formation of Mickey. Reggie had been destroyed by the same violent acts, enduring them for years. It was the last act of brutality she received that brought them together. He asked for her trust, asked her to endure more physical pain at his hands to put her broken body back together. She didn't want it, fought it, didn't think she deserved it, but finally relented, accepting his kindness and obvious concern. She nods her head through the monitor, just a slight move of her head that only he would see. She understands how hard it is for him to see the everyday cruel and brutal acts from monsters, but this atrocity touches home, touches him personally because it darkens his calling.

Sighing deeply, John moves on, "Dom, what have you been able to dig up on the two Deputies?" He wanted to give Reggie and Pix as much info as possible because they would most likely be interacting with them in one way or another when they entered DuPree.

Chapter 19

Dominic looks at Marco and lifts his chin to the monitor behind him, indicating the intel he has compiled so far on the Deputies to be displayed before he begins his narration.

"This first picture," Dom says into the room, "is Deputy Stanley Woodard. He was born and raised in DuPree, and from what I have been able to grab onto, he's never left. He was a mediocre student in high school, so college wasn't in his future, and there are no traces of him attending a trade school or any police training. So I have no idea what put him on that police force unless Dempsey wanted a lackey who never asked questions handling the front desk. Looking at what Bud told us about the big gun this deputy wears, I searched for registered firearms under his name. I found nothing but plucked some interesting information from the search; every weapon used by the DuPree Police Force is registered to Darwin."

"And since he has most of the law enforcement in Northern Washington under his thumb, there will never be any repercussions from any acts involving one of his weapons."

"All those payoffs and the obvious corruption crap is making me homesick," Oscar-D says sarcastically. "My old man's hands are just as dirty, and he's just as controlling and arrogant as that piece of shit Darwin is! You can bet Big Daddy," Oscar-D says with a knowing disgust, "used those dirty hands of his to beat the crap out of Dempsey when he was a boy because that's where a lot of this behavior starts!" As the room quiets from the young man's revelation, the team members realize this is the first time Oscar-D has given them even a hint of his past.

All eyes turn in his direction with surprise, wondering if they will get more of his story, but they get nothing, nada. "Oh, sorry, Dominator, didn't mean to interrupt ya, continue, man." And just like that, the small glimpse of the hidden Oscar-D is gone, and he's not going to share anything more.

Still looking at Oscar-D, Dominic hesitates before continuing. Oscar-D is the kid who has always been a thorn in his side, a royal pain in his ass, not to mention the guy who drives him absolutely mental with his antics. Oscar-D sits there next to him in his usual dress, brown hoody, boots, and camo shorts which he wears all year long no matter what the weather. He no longer sports magnificent dreadlocks because he lost those to a pair of clippers attached to Dominic's hand, but that's another story. A chain hangs from a belt loop on his shorts, connecting itself to his wallet, which sits in a back pocket. All this time, Dominic thought the kid was just naturally wired with crazy, but now he realizes there's a reason for it. So, the kid didn't just show up accidentally as he led us to believe, proving once again that we all have a story.

"Okay, moving on," Dominic finally says, turning back to the monitor where Marco has put up another picture.

"Now, David Tack is a whole different story. He tried to take the Police standard entrance exam three times and failed each time, and you only get three chances to pass that. He did, however, pass the fitness and interview/assessment portion each time. He was born and raised in a small town in Indiana by his grandmother,

Elizabeth Tack. He stayed with her doing menial jobs around town until she died in 2000. After he collected her life insurance, he took off. Unfortunately, there isn't much information on his whereabouts between his grandmother's death and 2002 when he applied for a Washington State driver's license and started taking the police exams. I can't find anything else so far, but I'm still working on it. I don't think he's anyone to mess with if he has a hero complex towards Dempsey; I wish I could find the connection or how he ended up in DuPree."

"Okay," John says to the room, "this is what we have to work with for now, but I want everyone to keep digging and filling up the holes. Good work, everyone." With that, he heads for the door, but as he opens it, he hears Dominic's deep voice.

"Boss, a word, please."

Sighing tiredly in Dom's direction, John knows what this is about so, he steps out of the way, standing back to let everyone leave before he closes the door behind them. Then, looking exhausted and not in the mood to have a debate, he says, "I vetted the kid myself, Dom! We've all got a story; that's why we're here; Oscar-D just gave us a short synopsis of his."

"Boss, I was just going to suggest he might be too close to this one."

"Dom, every case we take on resonates with one of the team members in some way," he says, wearing his exhaustion heavily as he looks out at the activity in the heart of Mickey. "Sadly, each case is a plagiarized version of one of our individual stories, that's why we're here, and that's why we're so good at what we do. So don't overthink it; I'm telling you the kid is solid on that front! Anyway, I don't think he's fully recovered from surgery yet, and he won't be doing anything until he's released." And with that, John opens the door and leaves the room, letting Dominic know the discussion is over.

Chapter 20

The room is quiet as Reggie and Pix begin to gather their things. Suzie watches intently as her bowls and food get slipped into her backpack, along with a few treats she wasn't able to guilt Reggie into giving her. *I'm not getting fat; I'm getting attractively thicker* Suzie says to herself while licking her lips. Both women are still trying to process all the information they acquired, each one coming up with silent scenarios as to how they should proceed, but when it was time to leave, the original plan they had discussed the night before was still the best option.

"If we're going to roll into town under the pretense of going hiking, I think we should find out if we need any permits. I'll get on the phone to Marco and see if he can find anything out; it would lend credibility to our ruse for sure if we're questioned," Pix says.

"Good idea; while you're doing that, I'll go to the front desk and check out. Then, I'll see if I can get any info; maybe there's a brochure table showing all the trails and information. If they do, I'll grab some, and we can throw them in the car to make it look good."

They had decided to use Reggie's vehicle and leave Pix's rig at the Inn, where a retrieval team would be dispatched from the motor pool to grab it later today. So, with all their belongings loaded and Suzie sitting sentry in the back seat, they were on their way. They turned left, coming out of the Inn parking lot, and made their way to US-2, heading back to Seattle, "Bud said there is only one small sign announcing the town of DuPree, and there is no warning that the turn off is coming up."

"It's like they don't want any visitors stopping by. He said the road into town is a dead end, people must do a U-turn to leave."

A few minutes into the drive, Pix reaches up and grabs the brochures Reggie had found in the lobby of the Inn and begins glancing through them. "These pictures are amazing; I'm always in awe of the beauty around here. Maybe one of these days, when we have some downtime, we could get the guys to come out here and do some hiking. This one," she says, holding up a pamphlet, "is in the Alpine Lakes Wilderness; it's called the Icicle Gorge Trail. It says it's an easy hike and only about 4.5 miles. I think the Princess in the back seat would love the river and all the animals she could find."

"I'm sure she would; it's good for her to know she can chase something other than human filth. But, I agree, we need to be finding outlets to help us remember there can still be peace and beauty in this existence of ours," Reggie says, smiling sadly in her direction.

"Oh look, here's another one called the Icicle Ridge Trail located in the Okanogan-Wenatchee National Forest, that's not far from here, and it's a moderate level hike about 5.5 miles.

Look at these scenery pictures," Pix says, holding the info out for Reggie to see.

Reggie watches Pix peruse the brochures in her hand and decides it's time to do some sharing. "Pix, have you ever wondered how the flaw of Domestic Violence even got started? I mean, how could the creation of man have happened without some guidance as to forming humanity. I think there should have been a how-to manual provided with step-by-step instructions as to the forming of morals and a conscience," she says passionately, glancing at Pix trying to read her expression. "I think about crap like this all the time. For some reason, it's important to me to figure out where this flaw came from and where the creation of humanity failed, not that it would make a difference now, I just need to know. I've envisioned many scenarios while standing on humanities ledge, letting my morals hover closer and closer to its edge trying to dissect this twisted reality we chase."

Laughing softly, she says, "I just recently came up with this one, and it could be it. I know I'm grasping for an explanation, and I know it won't make our jobs any easier, but I still think and search for anything that could make sense. I think Domestic Violence may exist because the creation of humanity got dropped into the laps of a bunch of cave-dwelling Neanderthals."

The whole conversation was taking a path Pix never saw coming, and even though the question was a serious one, she found herself belly laughing. The vision Reggie was painting was hysterical, so she asks, "do you mean a manual something like; How to Create Humanity for Dummies?"

"Hell yes, it's as good as any," Reggie says, becoming animated as she squirms behind the wheel, explaining her vision concerning the creation of humanity and the slugs/men that produced its flaws. "It's like the creator dropped the two-legged pea-brained thugs down and just left, saying something like, *ok, you're on your own now, go forth and create humanity!!!* There were no instructions, no guidelines to follow, and to top it off, no contact information for the Imperial Wizard who left them. So, I believe being left to their own devices is how humanity got created.

They did the hunch back knuckle-dragging walk into the mouth of their cave with a lot of grunting and spitting, followed by a bunch of disgusting ass scratching. Once inside the space, they gave the little women lewd gestures and stern grunts demanding a meal. There they would sit gnawing on mastodon and mammoth bones, belching and farting, grunting to one another as they voted on another flaw to add to the creation of humanity."

"Stop laughing at me," she says, beginning to laugh at herself as well, realizing how silly it all sounded, but continued. "So, one thug..."

"Oh, come on," Pix says dryly, "not the,,, so one Thug walks into a bar and grunts to the other Thug joke!!!"

"No, just listen."

"So, one Thug demands more grub from the woman he has claimed, but she doesn't move fast enough from the corner she was squatting in picking at her fleas, waiting for him to throw her a morsel. So, he jumps up with his club in one hairy hand, grabs her by her long flea matted hair, and pulls her outside kicking and grunting with fear, where he proceeds to beat the crap out of her."

After exhaling with enthusiasm, Reggie waits for Pix to react to this scenario, but she seems to be tongue-tied, so Reggie continues. And with a wave of her hand and an embarrassing smile, she continues to look at Pix, "and that, Sister; is how humanity got Domestic Violence."

Pix takes a second to look into Reggie's eyes, trying to relate to her thought process but can't, so she responds with, "does the Boss know you're this weird?"

"Yes, Reggie laughs, turning her head to the road, "I had to ask him how to spell Neanderthal."

"Oh,,,, shut up!"

After the laughing stops, the inside of the car becomes quiet until Suzie's demeanor in the back seat becomes edgy, causing her to pace back and forth behind the two women. Reggie puts down a window for her, and as soon as she can, Suzie sticks her head through the opening and lets out a horrible whimper while scanning the tree line to the right. Finally, Reggie begins to slow down so they can figure out why Suzie is in such a state, and as soon as they do, they see a gray and silver wolf bound from the tree line, landing in the ditch up ahead. It lifts its head and points its nose to the sky, letting out the most lonesome of calls, resonating with a deep sorrow that fills their hearts with the sadness it lets loose. And in turn, Suzie sends forth a deep-seated call of the wild she inherited from her wolf ancestors, communicating her understanding with the ageless rhythms of canines.

Reggie, reacting to the movement in front of her in the ditch brings the car to a stop. All the occupants inside the car can do is stare at the animal in front of them, assuming if they take the slightest breath it will bolt. But to their dismay, the creature stands its ground, never taking its eyes off Suzie.

The car sits idling and still, close enough to the animal to see its multi-colored fur in shades of gray and silver with tan

116

highlights. It looks healthy, portraying its natural strength, and its coat glistens in the sunlight supplied by the orb sifting through the trees. Suddenly, it becomes agitated and tosses its head from side to side with wild eyes scanning its surroundings. The eyes show a sorrow laced with fear, a primal fear.

This behavior continues for another few minutes before racing towards the car. Suzie sticks her head out the window, pushing her muscled chest into the unwavering barrier of the door, whimpering seductively, drawing her ancestor closer. The wolf stops a few feet away from the door and looks longingly into Suzie's eyes, never blinking, just communicating through an ancient primal connection before dashing off into the forest. Suzie's saddened eyes show a longing to follow, she fights her ancient heritage sending out a call through the wild to her distant sibling relaying her desire to help, but her duties of protection for Reggie will always come first. But knowing she's needed here doesn't change the pack mentality that still floods her veins, pushing her canine instincts to the max with a desire to join her distant cousin on the quest she chases.

"Um, Reggie???"

"I know!! Holy Crap!!!"

Chapter 21

Just like Bud had said, the little sign indicating the town of DuPree just appeared out of nowhere, giving them approximately the length of a city block before the turn. And they were lucky even to see it, as their minds were still reeling from the wolf encounter, not to mention the tree limbs that were playing peek-a-boo with it in a teasing manner, as the breeze shuffled them back and forth.

As they came closer to the town of DuPree, the smell of sawdust from the sawmill began to assault their noses with the mingling scents of Cedar, Alder, Maple, and others as they hung heavy in the air. The noise of machinery from inside the mill let out high-pitched screeches as the Sawyers fed logs into the colossal steel saw blades. While outside, workers drove forklifts and ATVs around the yard in what looked like a well, choreographed routine of organized mayhem. They continued to move forward letting the high-pitched whine of machinery fade into the background. They hadn't traveled too much further before they reached the town of DuPree and began to slow down. Looking up ahead, Reggie sees the DuPree Police Station and a gas station on the right, and across the street was the DuPree Book Store, just as Bud had described. It was rustic, looking like every other building in the town, with its milled Cedar plank siding, making it look inviting.

"I'm going to pull in and get gas before going to the bookstore; sound good?" Reggie asks, turning her head to Pix then glancing in the rearview mirror to check on Suzie.

"Didn't take long for us to attract attention," she says, nodding out the window of the car. "I feel like we're in an episode of the Twilight Zone with all these heads turning our way. It feels like we just drove into another dimension, went through the Twilight Zone mirror, and landed on the dark side of Mayberry USA," Pix says dryly. And she was right; with whiplash speed, heads were turning in their direction, looking at them through guarded eyes before quickly turning away and going about their business. Then, as Reggie pulls up alongside a gas pump, Pix declares, "I'm serious right now; if I start seeing doppelgangers of the team, I'm so out of here."

"And you think I'm weird!!!"

Before Reggie has a chance to turn off the car, a huge Ford F350 comes barreling up to the aisle next to them, stops beside a diesel pump, and cuts the engine. They sit in their car in disbelief because staring them in the face is an enormous wolf strapped to the hood of the massive machine. The animal is so big it is splayed across the hood from the front passenger side fender to the driver's side fender with heavy-duty ratchet straps. Its head is closest to them, displaying dead eyes that were full of life not too long ago, surrounded by a beautiful face of multiple colors of fur. Its mouth is open, and its once moist, pink tongue now hangs exposed and dry. It's beautiful, muscular body lay in its own sticky blood on the hood of the truck where it's cruelly secured. The animal had been thrust up there before death, leaving the flood of its remaining life's blood to flow darkly from its body. With every agonizing pump of its failing heart, its life's elixir ran down the grill in crimson streaks until it had drained, and its heart stopped beating.

119

Suzie becomes lost in her canine sorrow from the back seat, letting out a pitiful call of connection, making her feel so overwhelmed she starts to shake uncontrollably, accompanied by heavy drool that falls soaking into her muscled chest. Heads turn their way as Reggie leans into the back seat, grabbing the stuffed bunny. She begins to murmur motherly reassurances while trying to give Suzie her baby for comfort. But the normal calming reaction didn't come, and Suzie continued her manic behavior in the back seat.

The truck door opens and deposits the sturdy driver onto the cracked cement alongside the fuel pump where he stands looking their way, unable to take his eyes off the strangers. Reggie opens her door and slides out of the car, trying to keep Suzie quiet and contained while she does so, meeting the man's eyes after turning her head in his direction.

"Hey," the man says to Reggie, "best keep that dog under control! She looks too much like a wolf and could wind up as a hood ornament on some other truck," he says laughing with no remorse, pointing to the hood of his truck where it displayed the once breathing wolf so unceremoniously.

Reggie stands rigid in place, making eye contact with the muscle-bound idiot but gives him no reaction; then, after many tense seconds, she turns to the gas pump and begins to pump her gas. Standing there in disbelief, she peers through the back window of the car, keeping her eyes on Suzie, who is mournfully eyeing the wolf displayed so mercilessly across the hood of the gigantic truck. Suzie's body absorbs the viciousness of the act, and she can feel every painful second it endured before it had succumbed to the inevitable, its death.

All she can offer through the confines of the car are hysterical whimpers and low sorrowful whines. Reggie tries to stay calm while standing outside the car, watching the pathetic reaction of her trusted friend, and mutters under her breath; *aren't wolves protected in Washington State?* Then, forgetting the question she posed to herself, she starts to think about the wolf they encountered on the drive-in and can't help but feel there's a connection between the two.

It feels like hours instead of minutes for the gas pump to shut off, and as soon as it does, she can't get back in the car fast enough. Once inside, she immediately calls John and asks for a snapshot of Dempsey to be sent to her phone. Dominic didn't include his picture in the briefing earlier this morning like the Deputies photos were, and she has a feeling she just stood ten feet from him.

But the picture sent isn't the same man, leaving Reggie with a hard lump in her stomach because she knows, without a doubt, there are more dangerous entities to watch out for in this town than just Dempsey and his two minions.

"Damn,,, that's not the guy I just saw. Things are bizarre here John, I'm looking at a huge truck with a dead wolf tied to the hood, and we encountered a live wolf on the road in." She takes about five minutes and relays what has happened so far, even Pix's Twilight Zone theory. He listens intently and tells her to make sure they both have their coms on from here on out. She agrees with no back talk and then asks, "aren't wolves protected in Washington State?"

121

"Yes, they are, but that doesn't stop the backwoods idiots who hunt them for sport. And as we've figured out, even if the bastards from DuPree get caught, they're more protected than the wolves are. Not only that but from what I understand, wolves also mate for life, so that could explain the bizarre encounter with the wolf in the ditch. You said the dead one was a huge male; maybe he was its mate."

"Brutal bastards!!! But that makes sense because you wouldn't believe her behavior with Suzie, and Suzie with her, in an unexplainable way that wolf was communicating its loss." She pauses for a second in thought, facing the reality of viciousness once again that humans can inflict. It electrifies her resolve, and she begins to feed on the saddened adrenaline she feels to help Amee and Bud escape. Her determination starts to kick her senses into overdrive. She finds herself, once again, face-to-face with the fact there are no boundaries for cruelty and pain, and as if her sorrowful reality needs a reboot, she glances at the hood of the truck and looks at the horrible proof. "Okay," she says, suddenly feeling her body begin to tingle with energy and determination, "we're heading across the street to the DuPree Book Store now. I need Marco to pause the observation feed in the store, maybe make it look like an internet glitch or something?"

"I'll get him on it right away, but play it out as if they're still watching, just in case he can't block the feed."

"Of course," she says lightly, trying to lift her spirits. Looking out of the window of her car, a feeling of unease climbs into the driver's seat with her. "I feel the same dark Twilight Zone vibe Pix

122

does," she says to John. "She's actually looking for doppelgangers of the team right now."

"What,,, doppelgangers, are you kidding me???"

"Nope, not kidding, apparently she and Matt watch the SCI-FI channel. I just hope we go through the right portal when we leave here," she says with a strange laugh looking over at Pix, whose nose is pressed against the window just like Suzie's is.

"Amen to that, Sister," Pix whispers.

Chapter 22

After they both make sure their coms are on, Reggie starts the car, and as hard as they try, the three occupants of the vehicle can't help but take one more morbid glance at the once-living animal strapped to the hood of the truck. As they drive across the street, a violent chill dances up Reggie's back; its icy presence bites its way around her body zeroing in on her chest, freezing each heartbeat and heightening her awareness off the charts. Her fingers tremble on the wheel as she makes her way to the front of the bookstore, taking the first parking space she sees.

The door to the bookstore opens, and a delivery girl pushes her empty dolly through the opening and heads to her van, which it turns out is parked a couple of spaces away from their car. Reggie turns her head to the delivery van and reads the logo painted in bright colors on the side; *Jack's New and Used books.* She grabs her phone and snaps a picture of the van and its logo, sending it to the team. You never know what piece of intel could be crucial down the road.

Reggie is parked directly in front of the door to the bookstore; she sits behind the wheel of the car, gathering her strength for the physical scars and mental traumas she knows she will face once she enters.   The store is newer than the rest of the surrounding buildings; its Cedar siding still holds its healthy natural glow and adds to its rustic feel. The store itself looks inviting to the eye, with its large clean windows displaying posters of new and old titles. In one of the windows, there is an advertisement for an online book club indicating what titles are featured this month. Cedar flower boxes sit on each side of the door, adding color to the invitation to enter. Potential customers would never suspect it holds a captive within.

This is a prison, the walls constructed to keep Amee wandering between bookshelves, trapped within the rows because of her love and commitment to family. She's a caged animal, at the mercy of a psychopath who invades her thoughts and reaches into her beautiful core, destroying any sense of herself. She's lost and shamefully dependent on her jailor; he controls every aspect of her life, only allowing her out of her cage when supervised. She's just a possession, a human pet in a dressed-up cage watched by the eyes of her possessor through the lenses of small surveillance cameras.

Customers can't see the invisible bars of the cage, the displays in the windows look like warm, welcoming invitations to enter. They suggest there's a story inside the walls that will allow their soul to seek anything it needs to exist in another world, even if it's just for an afternoon. And their soul is promised millions of choices to pick from to feed its desire of the day. It may want to read about love by grabbing a tear-wrenching romance or become the hero in a spy novel; maybe they want to find a children's book that sends them back to a childhood innocence for a few precious hours.

Reggie can imagine Amee taking advantage of the only freedom she has, the ability to teleport herself to fantasy lands held secretly by hardcovers and bindings. In these lands, there is no brutality, no broken bones or tearing of flesh; these lands are void of pain, cruelty, and heartache. In these fantasy lands, she controls every aspect of her life. She decides the who, what, where, and when of her existence. She holds a secret freedom, a strong defiance and unwavering will to be happy.

Reggie sits in the car staring at the entrance, fighting back a rage so deep it feels like it will bleed from her ears. It saddens her that this inviting building full of fantasy, fiction, and facts is just camouflage; the books with bright covers and bindings play their part blindly, unknowingly hiding their real purpose. And that purpose is to confine and control a possession, a human possession, where he can wield dominance and cruelty on a whim.

There are pages and pages hidden behind new and well-worn covers on the shelves that mirror the horrors of her existence. So many stories of others that found themselves existing in the same world of domination she does now and all of them would break your heart. These heartbreaking stories are bound in dark colors, and scream their written testimonials of this cruelty, the words depicting lost souls that ended up in its darkness. But occasionally, a bright binder will push its way to the edge of the shelf, its bound words laced with promise describing a miraculous adventure of escape.

Sadly, there are plenty of printed words concerning the many thicknesses and layers of this dark sludge. The writings describe numerous levels of pain as it was inflicted, and they intensify the feelings of shame one carries once they let it consume them. Believe me, I know, I've not only lived them, but hell, I could've written them.

It's one thing, a horrible one thing, to describe the many years someone lived and suffered while being locked in a cage of fear, but just because the freed victims are now able to tell the millions of cruel stories of their past, they also need to be able to share what their day-to-day life is like now. They can't just tell part of the story making the reader think it's over and all that's left moving forward is roses and sunshine. The books can't stop there because the stories never end. There needs to be a follow-up to the individual biographies, one that depicts their future with brutal truths that may or may not hold a happy ending.

A sequel needs to be included with each individual truth splayed among the pages of a horrific fight for physical and mental freedom. It needs to portray what the victim's journey entailed after their escape. It's the reality that the victims who physically escape their cages learn all too quickly; they begin to understand they left one battle behind but came face to face with another as they began to move forward.

They become aware that even though they're not the victim in a locked cage any longer, they will always be a slave to the past horrors that creep in and try to regain their property. The stories need to be honest, and the victims need to tell what came next, what they endured, and continue to endure every day now that their cage door is open. They need to describe the excruciatingly painful amount of hard work it took to finally find some peace. They need to relay the fortitude required to dig deep and grab onto a past strength they thought they had lost. Readers need to be able to follow the journey and literally feel the swirl of emotions the victim felt when flooded from every direction. Explaining that shame, fear, and hopelessness are just a few. The list of hurdles to jump is never-ending; as their story continues, and they prepare for what comes next. The first hurdle they face is to forgive themselves for what they thought was weakness. This act is hard to comprehend and even harder to accomplish because it doesn't make sense that what they thought was a weakness was really a survival mechanism.

The sequel needs to hold chapters full of words explaining that physical freedom is so much easier to obtain than emotional freedom because the residue of their past horrors will always be a constant companion in one way or another. Reality dictates they will always be a victim to some extent. The words within the sentences need to be precise, the sentences within the paragraphs need to be clear for the chapters of information to be read and retained. Finally, they need to express how they prepared for another long, exhausting fight and what it took to see they deserved better and accept offers of help.

We can't afford an incomplete edition with missing words or mistakes because current victims and readers deserve the truth, which clearly explains what the future will hold. The words will help them understand that a victim will always be a victim, physically caged or not, because, for the rest of their existence, they will live on the edge of a contorting abyss of; *when will it happen.* When will the next similar face or physical appearance send you running in the other direction to find safety while you break down? Will today be the day that a certain Fleetwood Mac song comes blaring through the speakers of your car, sending you into oncoming traffic? It could be a specific smell, TV show, or hell, just a brand of mayonnaise that will send you back into the darkness where the memories are stored. And let's not forget about the suffocating nightmares that will invade your sleep, happy to remind you of your past torment. There needs to be a heads-up about the courage it will take to just get through the day while fighting the stress of waiting for the inevitable to happen, because it will.

The writing needs to depict that as miraculous as it is for a victim to survive an abuser by escaping their physical bondage, the road to becoming a SURVIVOR stretches to infinity. The realization will soon become evident that breaking free was just the beginning, because at the end of every day, moving forward, victims will realize that surviving brutality and eventually getting out was, in fact, the easy part.

"Are you coming?"

"No, I'll stay with the car and watch your six," Pix declares opening her door and stepping out, but before shutting it she leans down and sticks her head back in the car. "I'm telling you there is something really strange about this town, I can feel it."

Reggie nods in agreement before opening her door and stepping out, all the while scanning her surroundings with a trained eye. She's been punched with the unexpected too many times not to listen to her inner self when something feels off, and Pix is right, this town definitely feels off. She opens the back door of the car, reaches in for her backpack, and sees a pink bunny hanging below two beautiful orbs of concern trained on her every move. Usually, her four-legged protector's concern calms her, but she finds herself on alert and can't shake the same feeling that Pix has; it's like the whole damn town is watching their every move.

She closes the car door after Suzie jumps out and tells her to sit, then bends down on her good knee and whispers in her ear, "anything?" Suzie stiffens her body and tips her head back, sniffing the air, and lets out a snort. She then scans the area observing and analyzing everything around her, looking for any possible threat. After a few minutes, Suzie's body releases its tautness; and she emits a slight whine while dropping her baby into Reggie's hands for safekeeping. She then delivers the; *it's all good* kiss to Reggie's cheek.

"Are ya sure?" Suzie's response was another wet kiss, before she leans into Reggie to retrieve her baby. "Good enough for me," Reggie says standing, but she can't help but do another scan of the area before looking down at Suzie saying, "ok, let's go meet Amee!"

Chapter 23

The door of the bookstore opens to the inside, and Reggie hears a bell ring as she steps across the threshold, drawing her attention to the little bell hanging above the door. It brings a small smile to her disfigured features, portraying the fact that her soul has regenerated itself enough to enjoy the smallest of pleasures. Over time she has managed to find new avenues to travel. It hasn't been easy, but her mental growth and a new self-awareness have helped the cleansing process of her past. She can figure out more and more these days how to bypass the nucleus of trouble and avoid the muck, instead of wading through it up to her knees and emerging on the dark side where it waits with another level of sludge.

After Suzie follows her in, she lets go of the doorknob and hears the overhead bell tinkle softly again as the door closes behind them. After her eyes adjust to the soft lighting, they hear a voice from the back of the store, "be right there," it says.

Suzie sits anxiously by Reggie's side, her baby held softly in her mouth with her; *'can I do my thing now look,'* plastered clearly on her concerned face. Suzie can hear the years of sobering infliction in the woman's voice; the intended cheerfulness falls short as it fights through a shroud of pain. She's tuned into the pitch of the woman's voice as the words ride among the damaged emotions from the shadows, and she drastically feels the need to comfort her.

"Go ahead," Reggie says, nodding in the direction of the voice. And just like that, a canine version of the *FLASH* streaks to the back of the store.

"Well,,, hello there! Where did you come from?" Reggie hears the voice ask. At this point the woman still hasn't shown herself, but Reggie can hear Suzie connecting with the woman, using her slight whines and usual comforting manner. "What have you got there? Is that your baby? It's beautiful, oh,,, oh,,, and you want me to hold it?"

"Suzie girl, have you had enough time to introduce yourself?" Reggie asks from the front of the bookstore. As she waits, she glances around the store nonchalantly, hoping Marco could cut the feed, but just in case, she plays it cool for the cameras. Each corner had one, and they were pointed at different locations around the store, setting Reggie's rage off again. She adjusts her pack on her shoulder, then reaches into her back pocket for Bud's note while she waits for Amee.

"Coming," the voice says from the shadows, as Suzie makes her way back to Reggie.

The owner of the voice steps out from the back of the store, maneuvering around a bookshelf leaving the shadows behind.

"Hello," the woman says, "can I help you?"

The woman who walks toward Reggie does so visibly defeated. She's about 5'7" but appears shorter because of her slumped shoulders, a classic sign of physical and mental abuse. So, this is Amee, or what Amee has become. She looks too thin, and her once athletic frame now walks with a noticeable limp due to the stiff plastic brace on her right ankle. Her dark blonde hair is pulled back into a messy ponytail that rides limply below her shoulder blades. Her face shows signs of past beauty, but its symmetry is lopsided because of the broken jaw Bud mentioned. Her left eye sits lower than her right, just by a millimeter, but it's enough to be noticeable. The dark pigmentation surrounding it makes her look like she had tied one on the night before, but more likely, it's a fading black eye. Below it, her left cheek is hollow and looks like she has lost too much weight, but only on the left side of her face. Her smile is genuine but lacks the strength to touch her eyes, and Reggie has the feeling that at one time, those eyes would have lit up with a happy sparkle. Sadly, it's apparent this woman has sacrificed so much of herself, and Reggie's rage is ignited again, her will to help boiling over.

"Yes, I'm looking for this Science Fiction title and am wondering if you carry it." Reggie hopes her acting is convincing enough for the surveillance cameras watching from the corners of the room; it's possible, but not likely, that Marco wasn't able to cut the feed.

Amee scrutinizes her customer intently, knowing deep down inside they share something no human should have to, the pain of abuse. The eyes looking at her are the same eyes she, herself, sees every time she looks in the mirror. She acknowledges this fellow broken soul, relating to the depth of darkness and pain behind the physical scars. There's no need for the scars to scream for notice because they're as prominent as a neon sign, and as permanent as an intricate tattoo.

She clears her throat as it has become dry and finally finds her voice. "What's the title of the book you're looking for?"

Reggie hands Amee the note from her father as if it's the information for the book. "Don't react for the cameras," Reggie whispers, "just take me back to the Science Fiction section." Amee nods her head, confusion evident on her face but turns in the aisle and walks back to the Science Fiction titles. Along the way, they pass a small bathroom and what Reggie believes is a back door next to it; she whispers the intel into her phone; it could be important down the road.

Once in the back corner, Amee unfolds the note from Bud, her eyes begin to water producing painful heavy tears when she realizes what she's holding.

"How did you get this?" Amee whispers desperately, obviously agitated. "Who are you???"

"My name is Reggie, and this is Suzie," she says pointing to her sidekick. "Please, just read it Amee; I'm guessing we don't have a lot of time."

After another questioning look at Reggie, Amee begins to read from the slip of paper in her hand.

My dearest Amellia,

We have lived a horrible existence for far too long now. But I want you to know that this woman and her friends have offered us their help. She will guide us out of this hell; we need to trust her and not question the process. If we don't do this now, it will only become more dangerous for us, for you, than it already is. Enough is Enough, Amellia girl; I have confidence in the helping hand offered to us and believe we have a way out now. Please follow Reggie's instructions, know that I will be safe, and we'll both be free from this nightmare soon.

You will no longer sacrifice yourself for me!!! I can't carry this burden any longer.

All my love, Dad

"I don't understand," Amee says guardedly, "how did you find out about my father and me?"

Continuing to speak in a whisper among the shadows, Reggie answers the question. "My friend Deloris is the manager of your father's facility, and she has helped my team in the past with situations like this. She overheard a phone conversation between your father and Dempsey and noticed how upset he got. It took a little coaxing on her part, but he revealed enough to her that she felt my team and I could help. My partner here," she says reaching out to pet Suzie's head affectionately, "and I met your father yesterday and had a very in-depth conversation about your circumstances. He believes he's the reason you married Dempsey and are excepting of this physical and mental brutality, which is something I know all too much about," Reggie says pointing to her face.

"Unfortunately, that's exactly why I married that monster," Amee says, massaging her left upper cheek with her fingers. "I certainly didn't love him then, and I don't love him now; I just had no choice. I had no way of paying for Bud's care, and Dempsey knew it. I even believe, like Bud does, that his fall down those stairs wasn't an accident. But of course, no one investigated it, the employees at that mill are too terrified to speak up, and the only law to investigate an allegation like that would be the person who caused the "*accident*" she says with air quotes, to happen in the first place. The only way for me to make sure Bud's taken care of is to pay with the pain that Bastard dishes out.

"Yes, that's what Bud told us," Reggie says, trying to keep the conversation moving away from what she already knew so as not to waste time. "Listen, Amee, I know this is coming out of left field, and what I'm offering you is scary and overwhelming, but we want to help. And if you let us, I promise that you and Bud will be in the best hands and kept safe for as long as is needed, even if it means years."

The back corner they're standing in is dark compared to the rest of the store, but Reggie can see the questions swirling around in Amee's sad eyes. "But what about his medical needs, I still can't take care of him financially. I've never had a job except for this one, and I don't even get paid here. I do it because I'm told to, if I don't, another piece of my body gets beat to hell and then Dempsey takes me to see Bud. It may be *my* physical pain, but it's Bud's torment," she says massaging her cheek again for a few silent seconds.

"Listen Amee, I know you are having trouble trusting what I'm telling you, but look at me, it's obvious we share a past. Let us help you gain a future with no worries concerning Bud's medical care, or your financial needs. All of that will be taken care of by my organization for as long as needed. This is what we do, unfortunately there's a need for people like us because there's trash like your husband."

Amee looks at Reggie, silently deliberating, asking herself if this could really be true. "You'll get Bud out first?" she asks, wanting to be assured of his safety. She's still having trouble accepting the olive branch that just minutes ago walked through the store's door. She struggles within, weighing all her options, as her mind sloshes through the all too familiar slurry of fear that has become her norm. Do I go, or do I stay, she asks herself as her fingers continue to massage her upper jaw. Her mind begins to reel with a slide show of the dark consequences her actions will inflict if she's caught. But the most important thing is Bud's safety and care, she would endure anything to protect him, and has.

Through the low lighting she looks into Reggie's eyes, then slowly traces the jagged road map of a scar down her face. As strange as it sounds, those scars show her the possibility of freedom. They begin poking at her damaged soul from all directions, and it's just enough to make her want to find out more.

"I don't think you realize how dangerous this will be for you and your team," she whispers desperately. "Dempsey feeds on fire and craps a kind of torment no one deserves. He breathes hate, wearing it like a suit of armor, and he won't just direct the results at Bud and me; he'll hurt anyone who threatens his power!"

"Amee, give us the chance to put the power in your hands for once, let us help you and Bud to start over, we will protect both of you for as long as necessary. Financially you won't have any worries, and we have a medical staff that surpasses any hospital in the country. All you have to do is let us get you out of here, and from that minute on, both of you will have guardians protecting you 24/7. We'll make sure you and Bud are safe and financially sound, even if it's for the rest of your lives!"

"I want to believe you, but I know he'll come after us, and it won't matter how long it takes; he won't give up!" She's fought against the claustrophobic pain her entrapment delivered so many times and endured the hot ooze of her beaten soul as it dripped like smooth Whisky from the faucet of her being. Her existence has been burned by its fire leaking slowly through the drain into the septic's darkness, not allowing it to grab for purchase along the way. Eventually her life had no choice but to surrender to the stagnant debris waiting below, and once there, her soul had no choice but to add a little bit more of itself to the festering mix. She sees her pathetic life floating on top of the sludge. She watches it swirl around to mix with the Whiskey, where it has existed for so many years. So, it's no wonder she's having trouble believing that a ladder has suddenly appeared and is being lowered down into the drain, giving her the means to emerge from its darkness, one rung at a time.

The tears begin to fall now, dripping heavily from her eyes drop by drop like the rain from a clogged gutter. But once the emotional meltdown is over, she re-reads Bud's letter and can allow herself to make this life changing decision. Believing Bud will be safe, she's ready to fight the man who claimed her, the man she never loved or wanted to marry, and she decides this is a chance worth taking.

Chapter 24

Once Amee decides to put her faith in Reggie's and the team's hands, she feels a renewed strength start to creep into the damaged soul she carries inside. Reggie can see her inner strength fight to emerge, it's a clear transformation sprouting before her eyes, the woman is beginning to awaken from her constant dream of painful isolation to feed on the possibility of freedom. Reggie witnesses Amee's transformation in awe, as she begins to paint a picture with deliberate brush strokes of emotion, using bold colors to acknowledge her renewed strength to cover the canvas with a blossoming determination. The colors begin to rise and encourage the fire deep within, feeding the possibility of freedom. The flickers are small at first, dancing on the edges of the canvas, as they reach out and tease the darkness with their warmth. Eventually the darkness begins to surrender but promises it won't go without a fight, because the man who caused it won't allow it.

The team has executed many extractions since the formation of Mickey, but this one is going to be different and not just because there are two victims. Amee didn't fall in love with her Prince Charming; she didn't dream of a beautiful kingdom to live out her days with her Prince. She certainly didn't dream of a castle full of little Prince and Princesses that would carry the name of DuPree. No, Amee didn't want Dempsey or this life, but she loves her father unconditionally and has done everything to keep him safe and cared for. Amee didn't fall in love with her husband; he claimed her. And being only nineteen years old at the time, she wasn't wise to the alternatives to their financial situation. So, because of that, Amee felt the only choice was to marry the monster that exploited her love for her father and dedication to family. But now that she knows Bud will be protected and cared for, she's determined to escape, and there won't be any second-guessing her decision, no matter what the cost may be to herself.

But let's flip the switch to victims who had no idea they were going to become victims, the ones who actually believed they were going to get their fairy tale because they were marrying their Prince.

Among the apparent dangers that could befall an extraction, the act of a victim second-guessing their decision to escape is one of the most challenging and dangerous obstacles Mickey must face. Because in most cases, the victim didn't know she would be a victim in the years to come, she married for love and took her vow thinking he did the same.

But for domestic abuse to even begin, the perfect victim needs to be found. So, the hunter starts his long-awaited quest to acquire his prize. Once the hunter/monster finds the perfect woman, all the searching he'd done becomes an elixir to what lies ahead. So, he disguises his inner predator with a smoke screen of lies to ensure his manipulation; he begins the courtship ritual by playing to her fantasies of love. He will use chameleon ways to hide his inner snake by making himself look honorable and sincere, sucking in the chosen one by playing to her emotions and dreams. The game of seduction is fun to the monster; he remembers his training as he forges ahead. He rolls the dice in his sick game, advancing the tiny plastic replica of himself to the indicated square on the board; it tells him to put in the time by slowly seducing his chosen one to fall in love with him. He will worm his way into her being and push the buttons of deception, making her believe they will live happily ever after. But once they say their I Do's, the man shows his true self, this is where he sheds his camouflage, and her world starts to fall apart.

Once her life has landed as deep into the sludge of his world as is possible and the fairy tale obliterated, the abuse begins to escalate and escalate; that's when Mickey steps in. The initial contact with a victim could go either way; the victim either believes the team can help them or is too broken even to consider accepting their help. The hardest part of Mickey's job is to educate a new Rescue on what lies ahead and hope they can comprehend the significance of their actions. The team needs to trust that they are all in and willing to do whatever it takes to help with their escape. But even though their mind tells them they have the chance to escape, and they take it, their ingrained fear will tighten and constrict with an all too consuming pull that sends them running back to hell. Their minds will replay the continually spewed threats on an automated loop, and they will un-vail the canvas showing the years of abuse inflicted on their bodies. The voice in their head slithers in and out, tormenting heavily with the promise that she will regret this decision.

Unfortunately, there have been instances where the team has lost victims to the overpowering memories made up of threats and the consequences they will endure if they don't come home. Fear pushes and prods them to run back, suggesting their punishment at this point can't be as bad as if they're hunted down and drug back. But almost all of them find out the old discipline has evolved, and yes, it can be worse. Because of this, the team has devised protocols to protect its identity when this scenario plays out. It's dangerous for all involved, and all the team can hope for at that point is they don't see another tragedy described on the nightly news.

But it does become a tragedy more often than not, because Mickey wouldn't have stepped in to help unless the abuse was escalating, and the woman didn't have much time. So, sadly, it just gives the smiling blonde anchor bimbo one more chance to report to the world; *yes, folks, this is such a tragedy, but tune in after this break for Chuck and his dancing pigs.*

"Ok Reggie," Amee responds with a renewed look for hers and Buds futures, "what do you need me to do?"

But before Reggie has a chance to answer, her phone begins to vibrate in her hand, a text is coming in.

Pix: Heads up, a deputy is heading into the store!

Reggie reads the text and looks at Amee, then the bell above the door begins to chime. Reggie quickly shows Amee the text and reaches down to place her fingers around Suzie's muzzle, their personal signal for quiet. After reading the text, Amee looks at Reggie and mouths; "I've got this."

She heads around the shelving making her way to the front and Reggie can hear her say, and not too friendly, "what do you need Deputy Tack?"

From the dark corner within the Science Fiction section, Reggie can watch the interaction through a small crack between the books

142

on the shelf in front of her. She sees the Deputy remove his sunglasses and look around the store, "I thought I saw a woman and a dog come in here."

"Is that a question or an observation," she asks irritably. What is it you need Deputy?"

"Just wondering what she's doing in here is all."

"Well look around you Deputy Tack, this is a bookstore, and the woman is a customer. I'm helping her find a book, because that's what we do here Deputy, we sell books."

"Well, I don't like the looks of her friend out there," he says pointing to their car through the front windows at Pixie, "she seems to be loitering from what I can tell."

"She doesn't like to read, so she decided to enjoy the sunshine a bit," Reggie comments from the back, hoping it will appease the uniformed douche bag.

"And what about that dog, I hope it has all its shots! Ma'am, I think you should come out here so we can have a chat face to face."

"Not necessary Deputy, we'll be leaving as soon as I finish up here. Oh, and concerning the shots for my friend, she's good. I hope you can say the same." Oops, Sorry John, my vomit filter failed again," Reggie whispers into her phone.

The deputy was caught off guard by the woman's sarcasm and lack of respect too his badge but didn't quite know how to respond, so he decided not to push it. "Well, just make sure you do Ma'am, we don't want any trouble here!"

FROM SURVIVING TO SURVIVOR

"That's enough Tack," Amee scolds, massaging her left cheek. "She can browse as long as she likes, now go harass someone else," she says pointing to the door.

"I don't think you should be sassing the Sheriff's right-hand man Amee; you know what happens when he gets all riled up," he says while putting his sunglasses back on and heading to the door.

"Hey, deputy!"

"Yes Amee," the deputy responds, turning her way before opening the door.

"When you go tattle on me to the Sheriff will you give him a message for me?"

"I guess I can do that, what's the message?"

"Tell him *you're* an asshole!!!"

Oh boy, holy, holy crap, Amee just flung open her cage door and walked through the opening, sidestepping the moving barrier before its spring-loaded hinges could slam it shut, stopping her escape. Again, Reggie starts to realize how different this extraction is going to be for the team. One thing is for sure; they won't have to worry about Amee and Bud running back to their situation because Dempsey will have lost all his leverage. He won't have any threats to wield or in-depth consequences to describe for their actions because he won't be able to play one against the other anymore. In Reggie's mind, this is good, but on the flip side, the team will have to fight twice as hard to keep all parties safe; it won't just be the enemy himself chasing them; it will be the enemy's backing as well.

After the Deputy leaves the store, Reggie's phone vibrates again.

Pix: All good in there?

Reggie: All good, out in a few.

Chapter 25

After the Deputy leaves, Amee returns to the corner where Reggie and Suzie are waiting for her. "God, that guy is such an ass; it felt so good to tell him off finally," Amee says with satisfaction. "Okay, where do we go from here, Reggie?"

"Well, as much as I enjoyed your display of liberation just now, I must tell you that can't happen again; I mean it, not again!!! I don't know how long it will take us to formulate the plan to pull you and Bud out, so you need to act like nothing has changed. I'm sorry to have to say this, but you need to continue to play the part of victim for a bit longer. I just hope that the outburst directed at the Deputy doesn't raise any red flags with Dempsey. Have you ever talked to him like that before?" Reggie asks, noticing Amee massaging her cheek again and thinking it must be a stress- habit or something; she probably isn't even aware she's doing it.

"No, I never have, but if he finds the guts to tell Dempsey that he let me, and you, for that matter, get away with talking to him like that, I won't be the only one to catch hell for it. So, no, I'm not too worried about it. I promise to continue acting as usual for as long as it takes; I understand the importance, that won't happen again."

"Good to hear, because we have a lot of moving parts to coordinate before you and Bud will be taken to safety. The most important part for you to remember is not to question anything we tell you to do, no matter how out of the norm it may seem. This is for your safety as well as Bud's and my team's, do you understand?"

Amee understood what Reggie was saying, she was also aware of how real this was getting; her thoughts were swirling behind her eyes as she locked them with Reggie's. She suddenly felt her body freeze in the shadows, and all she could do now was wait for the thaw. She couldn't blink, couldn't think, and most importantly, she knew how agonizing it was going to be to play her role and wait, especially now that she knew there was a way out.

"Amee," Reggie says reaching out and touching her arm realizing she'd lost the woman's attention in the dark corner, "do you understand what I'm saying to you? Do you understand how important it is for everyone's safety?" Again, all Amee could manage was a blink; it was barely noticeable, but it was there. The first sign of the thaw, Amee was slowly coming back.

"Yes,,, yes I understand," Amee says softly, her eyes becoming clear and focused once again. "Sorry, the enormity of all this just hit me I guess."

"I understand Girl, no need to be sorry for anything," Reggie says as her phone buzzes with an incoming text.

John: wrap it up quickly; Pix says the Sheriff just pulled up in front of the police station, and I want you out of town before that Deputy fills him in on your INTERACTION!!! 'Understood?'

Reggie: Roger that!

"Alright, Amee," she says as she lets her backpack fall off her shoulder. I'm going to give you a phone; it has the number to my

147

team already programmed in, see." Amee takes the phone and looks at the number nodding her understanding. "I want you to hide it somewhere in the bathroom," Reggie says. "I say that because, according to Bud, it's the only space, besides this corner, that doesn't have surveillance, is that right?"

"Yes, at least I can pee in private."

"I recommend putting it in the bottom of your Tampax or Kotex box; men never want to even get close to that stuff. You can call the number but only in an emergency, and I will text you with updates and instructions frequently, so check it often. Now, is there any time of day or any certain day that we should target for getting you out of here?"

Amee took a few precious seconds to think, "I know he and some buddies are going wolf hunting on the 24th, I think that's next Wednesday. He usually leaves by 6:00 am and doesn't come back until well after dark, but I have no idea where they go."

"Do the Deputies go hunting with him?"

"I don't really know, sorry!"

"That's okay; we'll find out soon enough. Thank you for the information on the hunt. I think we can work with that; it would give us a little over a week to put a plan together," Reggie says into the shadows.

"Again, please try to act as normal as possible and know that we'll be working on a plan to get you and Bud out safely. Pretty soon, you'll begin to heal and regain some of the power you've given up for Bud's care and safety. It won't be easy by any stretch, but I can see you're a fighter, and once you see the win is in your grasp, you'll take it."

Reggie reaches out and places her hand on Amee's shoulder squeezing lightly, hopefully rendering some assurance by the act. "Just think of this chance as the bell to the last round and the round ends with Dempsey going down. And remember once he's down we'll make sure he stays down, our measures are brutal, and our warnings are administered in a manner where there's no misunderstanding their intent. It's time to fight back Amee, and we'll help you do it. Soon you'll be pursuing tomorrow and not even looking at yesterday." Reggie's phone buzzes again with a text.

John: I want you out now!'

Reggie acknowledges John's demand by sending a response, but before leaving the shadows she reaches up and grabs a book off the shelf, it will play into the guise for her visit.

"This will work," she says looking at Amee, "let's go check out."

Chapter 26

John tries to take a calming breath once he hears Reggie leave the bookstore, but he's too keyed up and weary to settle himself completely, it's been close to 24 hours now, and they're just getting started. Looking around the Club House at all the faces listening to the interaction between the two women, he realizes he's not the only weary one. They each have their jobs and quietly do them through tired yawns and gulps of coffee; they need no coaching or encouragement from him to continue. A determined silence engulfs the Club House as team members push themselves forward, working under their cloaks of exhaustion.

But the little boy inside Oscar-D can't help himself and intrudes into the silence of the Club House, insisting on playtime. Gone was the sad portrayal of his past the team glimpsed earlier, and in its place was the happy, irritating Oscar-D they know and love.

"Yo there, Dominator, are you afraid of the Tampax box?" Oscar-D yells across the room at the man he loves to torment, causing the workflow to stop at all the stations. Every pair of eyes begin to dance a familiar waltz between Oscar-D and Dominic, knowing the eruption will come instantly. Oscar-D lives for the chance to push Dominic's buttons, and Dominic makes it so easy that Oscar-D is never disappointed with Dom's reaction. It's been like that from day one; John even had to pull Oscar-D from surveillance details with Dom because the two mixed like oil and water, and he never knew what would happen. But deep down, John knew the two had a friendship, even if it seemed one-sided.

"Boss, I'm begging you, just one bullet is all I need!"

"Not today, Dom, he may come in handy on this one, sorry brother," John says and throws a nerf basketball at the back of Oscar-D's head, inciting tired laughter from the team. "You owe me one kid," John says pointing a finger at Oscar-D.

"Okay, I know we have a lot of intel to play with here, so let's get some extraction ideas on paper, and as soon as Reggie and Pix get back, we can all put our heads together. And remember, this is going to be a double extraction, so timing and coordination are paramount. I want brains engaged and seeking our best plan. And I want each scenario presented with the protocols to follow if all goes to shit. I want," John stops himself and looks around, "hell, you all know what I want," he says with knowing confidence, "So, get to it!"

"Roger that Boss!"

Once John sees the team grasp another second wind, or it could be a third or fourth wind, he's so tired he's lost count; he internally acknowledges this won't be the last burst of energy they call upon and hopes they have an endless supply.

He's still turning that information and gratitude for the team's dedication over in his mind when he notices Matt coming his way. And by the look of determination the man carries, this chat is going to rain down another butt load of crap to add to the festering pile they already have.

"Boss, you were right about Dempsey having a sealed record. It didn't take me too long to find what you suspected, and the judge that signed the order, is on Abby's list of names," Matt says pointing to the highlighted name.

"On me," John says, and heads to the conference room carrying the information Matt had just handed him. The file in his hand burned violently with its hot torment, sending him seething with anger into the conference room, envisioning the battle they would fight. He feels ashamed of what his country is becoming and guilty he can't do more to honor the fallen who ultimately gave of themselves for it. He thought back on the promise he had made Matt earlier, solidifying his remarks with a deep rage. He vowed, even more intensely than before, that every name on his mother's list would feel the team's wrath, leaving them again with an uphill battle.

Chapter 27

As they enter the conference room, John reaches over and lifts one of the switches on the wall next to the door. Just a few low-watt lights come on at the other end of the conference table. Both men head toward the soft glow and grab chairs across from each other. John had only scanned the highlighted portions in the file Matt had given him, and he knew he couldn't delve into it further just now without help. His discouragement on the state of this country and fatigue were too heavy, all he has the energy to do is listen at this point. So, he slides the file across the table to Matt, who looks at him with questioning eyes.

"You dug it up, you lay it out!"

With one last glance in John's direction, Matt begins. "The incident and let me say *'incident,'* falls short when describing what went down that night. It happened in 2010 when Dempsey was sixteen and a Junior at Leavenworth High School. According to the statements in the file, he had become fixated on a fellow female student, Candis Levine." Matt reaches into the back of the file and pulls out a yearbook photo. John accepts it and looks into the happy blue eyes peering into the camera. In an instant, he knew that when Matt was through relaying the information, the girl with the happy blue eyes was going to be damaged in more ways than one.

John sighs and pushes the photo back across the table to Matt, "beautiful girl," he says, leaning back in his chair, bracing himself for what he knew he would hear next.

Matt slowly places the photo back into the file and continues, "It was the Homecoming game for Leavenworth High School, and Dempsey had the best game and put-up numbers the school had never seen before; he was unstoppable, racking up the yards and scoring three touchdowns. I was able to pull a newspaper clipping from the net," Matt says and starts to hand it to John, who waves it off, knowing it would just fuel the fire he was feeling already.

"Okay," Matt continues, "his last touchdown put the winning points on the board leaving the opposition to flounder with shame because of the spread in the score. So, Dempsey, being the brainless psychotic that he is, figured that Candis would want to be with him now since he was a hero and all." Matt lifted his eyes from the folder in front of him and looked across the table at his Boss. He can feel the man's rage as it bounces off the walls of the room, he's seen it before and has no doubt he will act on it.

The unease John feels begins to grow, taking root deep inside his chest, causing him to see red, the color of rage and evil immediately. He watched Matt's mouth deliver a clear picture of the events of that night, leaving him to digest the wicked facts of corruption he would have to deal with after hearing the detailed dissertation.

Matt begins flipping through the papers in the file resting just below his fingertips, and his own rage threatens to devour him as well, but he continues. He begins to read from the police report in his hand, informing John that the events of that night started with the Homecoming game and ended with the dance. Although, he shakes his head, "this is crazy; each statement mirrors the next. Once the final numbers blinked on the scoreboard causing pandemonium on the field, Dempsey made his move rushing to the sidelines to find Candis. The cheer squad, which was led by Candis, was celebrating the win with one final cheer. The statements say that Dempsey makes his way to the sidelines, grabs Candis by the arm, and attempts to drag her away from the crowd. According to the cheer squad, Dempsey had recently been coming onto her hot and heavy, and she kept shutting him down. That's when the quarterback, and Candis's boyfriend, Chad Pomeroy, came charging off the field because he'd seen the interaction between Candis and Dempsey. The two boys threw some punches but did no damage because of the full pads and helmets. The boys exchanged heated words before separating and walking off the field, but witnesses said with all the celebrating, they didn't hear any specifics."

"So, what happened? I know this can't be why the record's sealed," John says, leaning back from the table, crossing his arms in disgust, shooting daggers with his eyes at the piece of paper in Matt's hand as if it was responsible for the event.

"Later that night at the Homecoming dance, Dempsey showed up about 11:00 pm, very drunk, it states here, and started an altercation with the couple. He just couldn't let Candis get away with continually shutting him down; he saw it as disrespectful or some shit like that. He tried to cut in between the couple and take over dancing with Candis but ended up falling on his ass. That's when Candis and Chad decided to leave and headed out to Chad's car in the high school parking lot. Just as Chad was unlocking his car, they heard boots on the gravel and turned to see Dempsey running/staggering toward them. Chad didn't have a chance to defend himself; even though Dempsey was drunk, he got the jump on him. Chad hit the ground, where Dempsey proceeded to beat the snot out of him one blow after another to his face but didn't stop there. Instead, he spotted a good-sized rock under the parked car next to them, retrieving the rock he lifted it high above Chad's head and began smashing it into the kid's head more than once. While Chad is laying there bleeding profusely, Dempsey stands up, opens the door to the back seat of Chad's car, and throws Candis inside, slapping her silly all the while raping her multiple times."

"There's a picture of her taken the next day and it's not pretty Boss!"

"Keep it Matt, we've seen it before," John says sadly.

"Yes, we have, too many damn times I'm afraid."

Candis was able to give her statement the next day even after the invasive medical treatment of the night before. After the ambulance took her and Chad to the emergency department, he went one way in the hospital, and she went another. First, Candis endured the humiliating and painful process of a rape kit so DNA could be collected and cataloged. Then the bruises covering 70 percent of her body were photographed and added to the rape kit as well. Unfortunately, her pain didn't stop there; the Emergency room Doc found two cracked ribs she'd sustained when Dempsey placed his knee on her torso to hold her down in between each rape. But she states the worst part was not knowing how Chad was and if he would be okay. The poor kid suffered so much brain trauma he was hospitalized for two years and then was shipped to a private facility because he will need 24-hour care for the rest of his life. He can't speak or communicate in any way, and he isn't able to feed himself, so his sustenance is delivered by a feeding tube. He can't walk so his life consists of being moved between his bed and a wheelchair. He lives in his own little world which no one can enter, if spoken too he doesn't react because he doesn't know he's supposed to.

Chapter 28

"What charges were filed against this maniac?"

"Charges of rape and assault for Candis and a charge of attempted murder for Chad. But before the DA could hand down the indictments against him, both sets of parents withdrew the charges."

"I wonder how much money it took to make this go away. I mean, we know the Judge is a piece of crap and on the take, and I'm betting Darwin threatened the families somehow to back off," said John into the room. "We need to get all the information we can on these two families; hopefully someone will talk to us," John mutters, looking at Matt.

"Marco and your mom are already digging into it. Your mom says she can study the Black File on the Judge and determine when he received his payoff and how much. As for Candis and Chad, Marco is hoping he can get the name of the extended care facility Chad is in, so your dad and Xander can dig into that using their medical connections. But Candis is a mystery; the only information we can find is her parents' address. It's like she just stopped existing the night of the attack, no employment or financial trail to follow."

"Have them look into the parent's finances also, it wouldn't surprise me if they are being paid off to keep quiet."

"Isn't Xander due back today?" Matt asks, looking up from the file.

"Last I heard, he is. Okay, as soon as you get that info, let Marco, Mom, Dad, and Xander know we need to meet here," he says, jamming his finger into the top of the table for emphasis. "Also," John says, yawning and rubbing his hands over his face, "I think if we decide it's important to talk to Candis, it would be a good idea to have Harley included on the visit."

Dr. Harley Stafford is the newest member to join the team; she is a well-known psychologist and victim advocate. What makes her so good at her role here with Mickey is she was one of their rescued victims about a year ago. She still can't believe that she allowed herself to become a victim with all her education and years of counseling women in this situation. But as we all know, predators are bred by evil to become evil; they can't fight their existence and take to the dark grooming with excitement. Harley was no different than anyone of her patients; she didn't have a chance once her abuser imprinted on her because victims never see it coming, no matter what their education or stature in this life.

"Do you know if Marco found out who sent the email to all the residents of DuPree concerning Gregory Fairchild yet?"

"He has a pretty good idea where to start looking, but he needs to tread lightly because of all the names on your mom's list connected to law enforcement. He doesn't want to tip anyone off."

"Damn, okay I'll connect with him," John says as he and Matt stand to leave the room.

"Hey guys," the smiling, tanned good looks of Doc Xander presented themselves in the doorway of the conference room.

"Welcome back, Doc. We were just talking about you; how was Nashville?" John asks while extending his hand for a welcome back handshake.

"It was hot, exhilarating, noisy, and the best three days of my life," Xander says, grinning ear to ear.

"What was the race called again? Something like Machine Big whatever...."

"No, Matt, the Big Machine Music City Grand Prix, and this was the inaugural race, and the first time Indy cars raced over water. Oh man you should have seen it. The 2.17-mile street track included the bridges that crossed over the Cumberland River with tight turns and various speeds up to 200 mph in some spots, and it was through town, the greatest thing ever. But, of course, it was hotter than hell, so at one point during qualifying, I sat in my room on the tenth floor of my hotel, watching from the window, and could feel the vibrations of the engines as they passed right below me. And you'll like this Matt since you are into football; the Tennessee Titans stadium was just across the parking lot where all the cars and their pit crews were staged. Man, I'm so glad I got the VIP status because every year from now on, I can cash in on all the perks affiliated with the race. The best rooms, seats, ticket prices and so much more."

"So, who won?"

"Not my man Colton Herta, I'm sorry to say. The flag went to Marcus Ericsson; he made an unbelievable run and finish, can't fault him his win."

"What about the music?" Matt asks.

"Yes, there was music but not my thing."

"What are you talking about, not your thing? You were in the heart of Nashville and country music!"

"Funny, I've heard that response several times since I got back. Now, if the Grand Ole Opry had featured ACDC or Queen, I would've been in the front row."

"Well, we're glad you're back, Doc, because we just took on another shit storm, and I have a feeling it's going to be ugly," John emphasizes with a scowl.

"I heard a bit about it wh…"

Before Xander could finish his comment, the Club House emergency red strobe lighting began to beat through the facility, infiltrating every department with its harshness. The distant, familiar voice of a family member began to flood all the departments through the speakers affixed to the walls. The listeners sat and stood, frozen in place, as each one zeroed in on a speaker feeling helpless and inadequate but ready to act when needed.

The entire facility was void of sound except for the voice coming through the speakers; not a whisper was expelled, not a keystroke heard, not a tool clanked in the motor pool; all eyes were on their speaker of choice.

"911, 911 to the Club House," came Pixie's voice through the speakers. "We didn't make it out of town; the Sheriff and his deputy just pulled us over; they're getting out of their cars now and coming our way. The emergency frequency will stay open," she says hurriedly.

"Marco," John screams into the heart of Mickey as he, Matt, and Xander make their way out of the conference room.

"Already on it, Boss!"

"And someone kill the damn strobes!"

Chapter 29

"Listen up the Club House," Reggie says into the emergency frequency on her phone as she watches the Sheriff through the driver-side mirror arrogantly stroll up to her car. "Looks like we stepped in it again, and it's about to get real." She then turns to Pix, indicating for her to slide her phone down between the seats, and she does the same. The emergency frequency will stay open until the Club House shuts it down on their end.

Just as she finishes relaying her thoughts to the Club House and stashing her phone, there is a two-knuckled knock on her window. Turning her head, she sees a vast hand indicating for her to roll the window down.

Reggie complied, rolling the window down halfway, and immediately the car inhabitants heard several sorrowful whimpers emanating from the tree line. The whimpers suddenly turn into a howl, allowing Suzie to track it and lock onto the glowing eyes of warning from the forest. The animal stays hidden in the foliage, watching intently, wishing it could do something to protect the humans and her ancient cousin from the monster. Suzie's anxiety takes over, causing her to pace among the back seat with long entrails of saliva landing on the inside of the windows as she shakes her head. Finally, adhering to the warnings from the tree line, Suzie lets out barks of understanding within the car as she tries to push herself into the front seats to protect the women.

"Easy, Sweet Girl," Pix says, reaching between the seats to find Suzie's soggy baby, hoping what's left of it will calm her. And as she gives the baby to Suzie, she says, "Reggie, just be cool!"

"License and reg..." the Sheriff begins, but he couldn't finish his request as Reggie's damaged face becomes apparent through the window, throwing him off guard. "Damn, girl, looks like you sassed your man one too many times; you need to cover that shit up! Wow!" He declares shaking his head admiring the work her man had done. "Like I was saying, license and registration, and her ID too," he says motioning to Pixie. Once Reggie has the car registration and both IDs in hand she slips them through the half open car window to the Sheriff.

"Was I speeding, Sheriff?" Reggie asks sweetly behind a lump of hot rage, while trying to keep Suzie and her intent to protect them from getting out of hand. Her rage matches Suzie's as she pushes on the dog's muscled chest to keep her in the back seat, fighting the heavy breathing and noticeable quivering taking over Suzie's body. She so wanted to give Suzie free reign to do her thing, but it was too soon. "Calm down, Suz, you'll get your shot, I promise," Reggie whispers into her protector's ear.

Another howl makes its way through the brush from the other side of the ditch. But the two uniformed men don't even seem to acknowledge it as they are so focused on the car and playing with the occupants inside.

"Sheriff, was I speeding?" Reggie asks again impatiently. Her eyes rake over the man standing outside her door, and she is suddenly nauseous. He is tall but not well-muscled, and he seemed to be losing the battle with his expanding waistline, not bad yet, but she could only imagine what he would look like in a few years. Hopefully, she wouldn't have to see it. His dark hair looked like it was cut close to his head, at least from what she could see below his hat.

"No, you weren't speeding, but I should write you up for driving while ugly," he laughs, looking across the top of the car at his deputy who they know is Deputy Tack.

"That's a good one, Sheriff," the Deputy laughs along using his one brain cell, placing his hand on his gun belt, mentally placing his lips to the Sheriff's ass.

"So, we have Miss Beth Trumball, that's Scar Face here," he laughs, holding the Driver's License up to show his deputy, and her little friend is Miss Shirley Rose.

Handing the IDs across the top of the car to Deputy Tack, he says, "go check these ladies out while I get more information from them." He leans down with a leering smile to penetrate the inside of the car; the action meant to intimidate and scare the two women. But little does he know they have fought the blackest of enemies before and won. Yes, they've emerged with layers of mental and physical bruises and swam through torrents of pain. And in Pix's case, she sustained deadly knife wounds and sports the scars to prove it, but they're still standing; they're still pushing. This guy has no idea what's coming his way.

"Now, what are you two doing in my town?"

"We were hike,,," Pix tried to speak before Reggie got a chance to come all uncorked.

"NOT,,, talking to you,,, I'm talking to Scar Face here," he says impatiently in Pix's direction.

"Like my friend was trying to say Sheriff before you cut her off," Reggie begins with no respect to the self-appointed Sheriff, "we were doing some hiking, and on our way home, we realized we were low on gas, so we decided to get some here, which we did."

"Why did you go to the bookstore?"

Reggie couldn't help but stare at the man as her anger grew and swirled within her mind like flames from a campfire, they singed her thoughts and burned through her body. Her hands begin to tremble with an itch she has felt many times before, her fingers punishing her flesh as her nails puncture half-moons into her palms. She takes a quick glance at Pix remembering John's words to not push, or be a smartass, and realizes she can't follow the dark road of anger spurring her forward, she has no right to drag another team member into her game. She has no choice but to keep it together because it's not just her and Suzie's safety this time, so she concedes it's time to engage her verbal filter.

Suzie begins to scratch at the back window with determined paws; then, her huge fangs protrude from her maw as she tries biting into the window. But the man is lucky; the window holds Suzie's inner beast at bay, for now, leaving him to hope the barrier will continue to stand the pressure. She can smell the evil on the monster, like a thick soup of fetid odor in the air, standing only a few feet away and she continues to be mindful of the wolf's warning. But it's not just the warning; there's something about this man that's tugging on her past, memories of a deep voice delivered before the unwarranted cruelty directed at her.

"You better keep that mutt under control," Dempsey says pointing at the back window, "because we shoot dangerous animals around here. Now I'm going to ask you one more time, why were you in the bookstore?"

With a verbal filter breakdown she says, "I understand that backwoods bullies can't read," she lets the comment hang in the air, hoping it wouldn't take him too long on the uptake. But one can only wait so long for a meat head to realize he's being called illiterate, so she sighs through the disappointment and continues. "I'm one of those people who enjoys a good book now and then," and to add credence to the ruse, she picks up the book she purchased from the bookstore and waves it at him. Before putting it back in the seat she silently decides to believe her verbal filter must be broken, at least that's what she is going to tell John. She takes the time to glance over at Pix who is trying to help Suzie to calm down and mouths *'sorry, I just couldn't help myself.'*

"They check out Sheriff," the Deputy says, walking up to him, placing the ID's back in his outstretched hand.

"Where you two from?" he asks with anger.

"You have our ID's," Pix begins to interject hotly, still trying to calm Suzie by giving her the baby which by this time is even more soggy with liquid anxiety and missing splotches of pink fur.

"AGAIN, not talking to you so shut the hell up!"

"West," Reggie answered.

"Don't be a smartass," he warns! "Where you headed?"

"West," Reggie says again, locking eyes with the beast. "We live in Seattle," she says, pointing West just in case he didn't know where 'West' is.

"Step out of the car," the Sheriff says heatedly, pulling the driver's side door open.

That split second gave Suzie just the opportunity she needed to lunge for the front seat and place herself in Reggie's lap. With her entire seventy-five pounds of protection on alert and her body quivering, she waits for the nod from Reggie so they could end this mission right here and now.

Caught off guard, the Sheriff steps back, placing his hand on the gun at his side, "I said to keep that dog under control, because I won't lose any sleep if I have to put it down."

Reggie immediately wraps her arms around her protector and begins to murmur promises into her ear about the carnage she can deliver down the road. Suzie seems to be appeased by the assurances and jumps down to the ground, planting herself between the man and Reggie, who is now climbing out of the car to stand behind her next to the open door.

"Wait just a damn minute, we've done nothing wrong," Pix exclaims as she's being roughly hauled out of the passenger side of the car. Then she finds herself fighting the weapons search by the Deputy, physically and verbally. She tries to swat his clammy hands away from her body and screams, "you can't do this," it's harassment! Hey, watch your freakin hands!" she warns. *Well, who's coming all uncorked now!*

"Look what we got here Sheriff; this little thing is carrying."

"I have a concealed carry permit for that," Pix says as the deputy drags her around to the other side of the car to stand next to Reggie and Suzie. "Let me get it out of my pack."

"I don't care about some damn permit no body carries a handgun in my town except me and my men! What the hell does a little thing like you need a nice piece like this for anyway?" the Sheriff says scrutinizing the Glock in his hand. "This will be a nice addition to my collection," he says with the joy of a kid on Christmas morning after opening the best gift ever.

"You can't just confiscate my weapon, who the hell do you think you are?" Pix shouts in his face.

"Right now, I'm your Daddy, Sweetheart!"

"Like we said," Reggie interjects quickly as to draw his attention away from Pix, "we were hiking, and you never know what you'll run into out in the woods. She brought it for protection!" *Asshole!*

"You ladies got any other weapons in the car I should know about?"

"That's enough Sheriff, I'm tired of this cat and mouse game you're playing, so whatever you got in mind, bring it on!" Reggie spits with the anger she's been trying to keep a lid on, all the while deliberating between does, she really wants to know what's coming or should she just wait for the surprise. Finally, she has joined the ranks of the enraged, her trembling matching Suzie's but not quite reaching Pix's. Because Pix looks like she's ready to pounce and grab her gun out of the man's hand and shove it somewhere most uncomfortable. And Reggie has no doubt she could, without even breaking a sweat. *Now that would be something to see, enjoyable, most enjoyable in-deed.*

Suzie strains against the hold Reggie has placed on her, wanting to lunge forward and take the beast out. She can see eyes watching intently from the tree line; she hears agitated panting and quiet rustling of leaves as enormous paws pace back and forth snapping twigs in the process. Suzie reaches for the ancient connection like a thread to her past. In her mind, she pulls the cord tight, testing its strength because she doesn't want to lose the tie between them. She can feel the wolf's presence as if they share heartbeats, every other beat allowing Suzie to absorb the boiling turmoil her canine cousin carries. It allows her to connect with the wild instincts of the animal who has just thrown her head back and cried into the forest around her, delivering another heated warning. Suzie sniffs the breeze as its chilly October movement lightly skims her face, sending her senses into overdrive. She turns her head to the tree line, searching for the piercing eyes hidden within so she can send her thanks and acknowledgment of the warning.

"Deputy, I want you to search the vehicle for more weapons." The Sheriff barks. "Give him your keys," Dempsey demands of Reggie, not taking his eyes off the animal baring its healthy white canines at her side.

Obliging the demand, she leans into the car to retrieve the keys and whispers into its interior, "Club House I have a feeling this is going to go sideways."

Once the deputy has the keys, he releases Pix, telling her to stay right where she is, and begins his search. The trunk is first, and he begins to rifle through the hiking packs and Reggie's go-bag. Smiling sickly, he grabs a pair of dirty multi-colored panties from Reggie's backpack and puts them to his nose, inhaling heavily. *How sick is that?* Once the scratch and sniff fest is complete, he begins to wave them in the air over his head, then slips them into his jacket pocket. Now that his panty party is over, the deputy moves onto the back seat. Leaning in through the door, he looks through all of Suzie's gear and spies what's left of her slobber-soaked half-naked baby lying on the floor mat. Because Suzie won't take her eyes off the Sheriff, Reggie has been watching what's happening in the back seat. She sees the deputy fondle Suzie's stuffed battle-scarred baby then discard it back onto the floorboard. What happened next wasn't surprising; in fact, it was inevitable that Deputy Panty Sniffer would find her bat because she always kept it stashed close, in between the driver's seat and the middle console. It's a miracle he didn't see the phones.

"All I found is this bat, Sheriff," the deputy says backing out of the car to hold it up.

Along with my dirty panties, you sick urchin!

"Well, ain't that sweet, you little ladies are under arrest, let's go!"

"WHAT!!!" Both women scream at once, fighting their captors, "what's the charge???"

"I'll come up with something by the time we get to the station. I think I might be in fear for my life or some shit like that, now calm down or we'll have to tie your hands," he says, fighting with Reggie's resistance. When she doesn't comply, she receives a heavy slap across the face, making her head snap sideways, causing her to see stars and receive a split lip. It didn't take him long to realize the consequences of his actions because, within a split second, seventy-five pounds of canine rage had its large front paws landing on his shoulders. Suzie's angry eyes held his in a raging dance; a deep growl emanated from her chest as she emphasized her warning. Thankfully, he was too stunned to react fast enough to deliver on his promise to put her down.

Fearing for Suzie's life because she sees Dempsey fumbling for his sidearm, she lunges forward with stars still dancing around her eyes and pulls her protector into her arms, landing on her knees. "Okay, no more trouble," she says, defeated, holding Suzie even closer, knowing that before this was over, they'd both get their chance at redemption.

"Too late," he says pulling a zip tie from his belt, telling Deputy Tack to do the same with his charge.

Chapter 30

"Hey, I have a carry permit for that!" Pix's voice streams through the speakers in the Club House. All ears listened intently to the conversation rolling into the room, setting their nerves on fire because all they could do is stand immobile like helpless statues.

"What the hell does a little thing like you need a nice piece like this for anyway?" the Club House hears Dempsey ask.

"That's enough Sheriff, I'm tired of this cat and mouse game you're playing, so whatever you got in mind, bring it on!" Reggie's hardened voice travels the frequency tunnel to be spit out at the team's feet miles away, but again all they can do is listen and feel helpless.

John stands stiff with anger at the situation, and his mind reels with the possibilities of what the game could exactly entail, damn he never should have let her go. He's heard this pitch in Reggie's voice so many times it's grown into a constant itch grating under his flesh, burning his nerve endings. He can tell she's trying to stay calm, but her DNA only sees a toxic red film of violence when she's toyed with, or her limits pushed. He silently screams for her to dial her anger back, calling on every molecule stacked within his being. He knows she can't hear his pleas asking her to think before she acts, and it causes his feelings of inadequacy to smother him like a humid afternoon. But he has no choice; all he can do is what the rest of the team is doing, listen from a distance, and picture the scene playing out over the miles that separate them.

173

The speakers portraying the drama couldn't send a visual of the tree line or the forest hiding a canine friend, leaving the team blind. Instead, their ears had to quickly become their eyes, allowing them to watch through a smokey haze. But after the wolf let out its howl of warning, they were able to vividly picture the feral gesture as it threw its head back to put them on notice of the threat. Likewise, the team was able to feel Suzie's response to the warning. They felt connected to the drama and could witness her angry attempts of protection for Reggie through deep guttural growls and snapping teeth. The visual extended through the tunnel and they could feel Reggie's need to protect was just as strong, they felt her do her best to pull Suzie back from her rage.

"What the hell?" Matt screams into the bowels of the Club House, "what was that?"

John was just about to reply and relay his earlier conversation with Reggie concerning the wolves when the unconscionable happened. The Club House became a blind witness to the sound of a heavy SLAP as it connected to Reggie's face.

It was only one, but John heard, SLAP, SLAP, repeatedly as he pictured that uniformed canker sore strike Reggie. He couldn't see straight, he couldn't breathe, he couldn't help imagining himself gutting that piece of shit, but even that wouldn't placate his rage.

"Oh my God," John heard his mother gasp from behind him. He turns and sees her holding her palm to her cheek as if she could feel the slap and residual sting just as Reggie must-have. Her eyes are swimming with liquid concern as she stands just a few feet away, with his father holding her close, his troubled features

174

mirroring hers. It was Reggie; this is their daughter in all ways that matter.

Michael's thoughts recede into the past, thrashing through its darkness and horror before screeching to a halt with the memory of the first time he met her. She was at her most broken but still clung to life as if to say, *I won.* He held her mental and physical health in his hands from the minute the ambulance brought her into his hospital. He set the broken bones he could, removed the glass from her face, and the whole time he prayed, prayed that she could find a way to become whole again. Slowly she began to show some resilience as he helped her accept the new parts of her body, as the originals were destroyed beyond repair. He held her hand in recovery after the plastic surgeon tried three times to mend the severed nerves in her face and then respected her wishes when she said no more. He marveled at her strength to move forward and is so thankful for her part in establishing the team of Mickey. But most of all, he is grateful for the life she is building with his son. But sadly, like now, the life they have chosen puts them in danger. And this time, that life is causing her to take a beating miles away, and all they can do is listen to the act through industrial speakers mounted on the wall, leaving them helpless while visualizing the violence.

Suzie's snarls of rage and need to protect Reggie permeate the walls they are standing within, giving each member of Mickey a murky picture of the unseeable scene. Each one knows Suzie in different ways, but they can all hear her savage torment and feel the ripples of fear for Reggie's safety as it hums through her body. The air in the hanger hangs thin; everyone seems to be having

175

trouble breathing as their minds roam through empty corridors conjuring up dangerous scenarios, all of them dark and blistering. Finally, and sadly, they all had to acknowledge the visions that could lead to the beautiful canine gladly laying down her life to protect Reggie.

"Okay, I'll take Scar Face, the weapons, and the dog. You take blondie and head back to the station; it's been a while since we had an all-night lockup party."

"WAIT, WHAT'S THE CHARGE?" the Club House hears both women scream in unison.

Lockup party,,, SLAP, SLAP,,, lockup party, lockup party,,, SLAP, SLAP, SLAP! The words playing on a loop inside John's head.

John felt as if he'd been kicked in the chest, causing his heart to sputter and fight for life. His mind races with fear as it fights through a heavy fog that insists on choking out all coherent thoughts. "No,,, no,,, no,,," he hisses loudly before picking up the nearest desk chair and throwing it across the room. It scrapes along the concrete floor, crashing into the individual lockers used by the extraction team, causing two to pop open, leaving dents in the strong metal. All John can do is stand with clenched fists full of rage, staring at the damage his actions have caused. His mind begins to scream with the knowledge of Amee's torment, of her broken bones, and the blow Reggie just took. He feels his pores open and begin to leak hot hate that has no boundaries for the monster they are facing. Please, please, please, for Reggie's sake, no more damage to her face; he silently prays to whatever entity may be hovering close.

176

FROM SURVIVING TO SURVIVOR

With his giant fists clenched to the max at his sides, John tries to focus on the room. He can feel the eyes of understanding from the members who witnessed his outburst but has no time for apologies. Finally, he manages to make eye contact with Marco and his team, then screams, "scrub both their phones and activate all three trackers, NOW!" With that being his last thought as a leader, he impulsively strides over to the lockers and kicks the chair he sent sailing just seconds ago out of the way.

"Son, what are you doing?" Michael asks from where he and Abby are standing. "Please take a minute and calm down," he says while watching John pull his go-bag out of his locker, then his Glock.

John doesn't miss a beat once the weapon is in his hand. Years of ingrained military training have him quickly dropping the ammo magazine into his left hand so he can assure himself of the number of rounds, then slams it back into position, checking the safety before slipping it into the holster at his back.

"What does it look like I'm doing Dad, I'm going after her!"

"Not without me!" Matt declares performing the same ritual John had with his own firearm before grabbing his go-bag.

Before John has a chance to angrily slam his locker door shut a large hand comes out of nowhere doing it for him, causing John to go on the defensive. He turns around, lifting his gaze to the mountain with eyes standing next to him, then tries to walk around the solid figure. "Mountain, get the hell out of my way!"

"No can-do Boss," the gentle giant says, "not this time. With all due respect you are way too close to this because it's Miss Reggie out there in trouble. You're not the best man for this mission."

"Same for you Matt," Dominic says walking up to the man and taking his go-bag off his shoulder, relieved when the man doesn't resist.

"Good call Dom," Oscar-D says into the room. "We'll go get Miss Reggie and Pix back for you, Boss, both you guys are way too close to the situation. Well, we're all close to the situation, but not in the same way you two are," Oscar-D says, somehow feeling he needs to explain the obvious. After his little speech he can't help but notice Dominic's nod toward him in agreement, maybe there is such a thing as miracles, maybe there's hope for them yet.

John finds himself taking a few steps sideways to lean around the human obstacle. Mountain stood in front of him with an unwavering resolve to stop his boss, and friend, from being his own worst enemy. Mountain's eyes held understanding as the rage flowed off John's person, but he continued to block his escape. John's brain begins to slide back into common sense mode, back into leader mode, but his anger still simmers on the burner of helplessness. He meets his father's eyes and can only mouth his apology, feeling ashamed of his outburst toward his hero. He receives a nod in return, apology accepted.

"Phones are scrubbed, and all three trackers are up and transmitting Boss," Marco says into the room hoping the information may help to clear their Boss's head.

"Boss," Dominic says, "send the Mountain and I in for retrieval. We know where they're being held because Dempsey said so on the air, and their trackers are online for backup." When there was no immediate response from John, Dominic turned his head to Matt, clearly looking for some input.

"There should be three of you," Matt says, keeping eye contact with Dom, resigning himself to having his hands tied just like the Bosses were.

"I'll go," Oscar-D says striding forward a little slower than he normally would, determined not to let his weakness show, hoping his usual gregariousness would distract.

"Dad," John says not removing his eyes from Oscar-D's, "is he good to go?"

"Oscar-D gives a quick, pathetic glance at Michael willing him to release him.

"I'm afraid not John," Michael says with a look of apology toward the young man, "it's only been two days."

"Well, there ya go Kid, no can do," John says to Oscar-D. "I appreciate you stepping up even though you're not 100%."

"Well, who else ya got man?" Oscar-D says spreading his arms around the room. "I can't believe I'm being side lined because of a damn appendicitis," he says pouting into the room.

"Don't worry Kid, you'll be in the mix again shortly."

"I'll go," a deep voice says from the back of the room. All eyes turn toward the voice to see Doc Xander stepping forward. "I have

179

no patients right now and before this extraction is over the girls may need medical attention."

"I don't think that's a good idea Doc, besides Pix is a nurse," Matt points out to the man.

"And if Pix gets hurt Matt?"

"Doc, you have no field experience is all I'm saying."

"That's enough Matt," John says. "Much appreciated Doc," John says to the man, their eyes sharing an understanding only they are privy to.

"I'll get my bag," Xander says and heads to the med bay.

"Boss, are you sure about this?" Oscar-D asks, reiterating the fact that as far as they all knew the Doc had never been in the field on an extraction detail before. He couldn't help but hope he could still get the green light to go.

"Mountain, Dom, you guys got a problem with the Doc being part of this mission?"

"Nope," Mountain says. It makes sense to me since we all heard that bastard doesn't mind hurting women."

"Dom, your thoughts?"

"I guess I'm good, a little surprised, but what the big guy just said does makes sense."

"Okay, gear up; you roll out in fifteen. You will have plenty of time to discuss the best plan of attack on the road. Keep coms on the entire time and take mobile trackers to place on all the police vehicles. Matt, will you go talk to Bruce in the motor pool, have him give you the spare keys for the car assigned to Reggie just in case the guys can't retrieve the others."

"Mountain," John calls to the walking slab of granite before he leaves the room. "Just for the record, if you ever strong arm me again in front of the team for whatever reason, you can take your little panda jean jacket and hit the road."

"Roger that Boss," the usually quiet giant says lowering his head. "But since we're setting the record straight and all, there's something you should know. Even though I understand where you were coming from, I did what was best for you, Miss Reggie, and the team," he gestures around the room. "And one more thing, since we're laying all our cards on the table now, I was a tick's ass away from throwing you into your locker and slamming the door shut until you came to your senses. For your own good and with the utmost respect, of course," he grins and salutes before turning and walking into the motor pool, leaving his little panda to smile at John upon his retreat.

"What the???"

John was still trying to digest what just went down with Mountain when he saw Xander heading toward the motor pool, his go-bag hanging off one shoulder and his medical bag the other. "Hey Doc," he calls out, motioning him over. Once Doc is close, he leads him out of earshot of any team members and begins to speak low. The conversation seemed intense, but the two men were beyond comfortable with their interaction. Before Xander turns to leave, the two men grasp arms like military brothers would, separating with determined looks on their faces, nodding an understanding. If you watched the interaction, it wouldn't be too difficult to figure out the two men share a past and a secret.

Chapter 31

Reggie's ride to the station was utterly revolting because Dempsey couldn't stop preening over himself and stroking his ego. Why is it that when a man is evil, he constantly needs to build himself up with self-importance? She meets his gaze through the rearview mirror, witnessing his dark eyes dancing with anticipation for the game ahead. She's asked herself so many times why evil needs to be stroked and constantly praised to function, but never found the answer. She's often pictured this building up of self-importance as a deflating balloon needing air to float, or a gas tank needing fuel to set wheels in motion; they both need their elixir to function at total capacity. Maybe if an abuser didn't continue to build himself up, if he didn't continue to feed the evil within, they would have a chance to push back the violence, but who knows. So, years ago, she decided to place that unanswered question in the account with all the others concerning this violence, knowing the bank's unanswered questions would continue to grow, leaving the ledger heavy in the red without a chance of reconciling the debt.

After Dempsey finished pumping up his ego, he picked up the mic to the cruiser's radio and contacted the station. "Station, come in," he said into it, then lifted his finger from the transmit button, but after listening to nothing but silence he tried again. "Deputy Woodard, come in," he said with impatience.

"Deputy Woodard," a shaky voice rang out.

"Deputy, make a call to Carl and Stew, tell them to head for the station right now with their tow truck, and if I'm not there yet, tell them to wait for me."

"Copy that, Sheriff."

Dempsey placed the handheld mic back in its carrier on the dashboard when the radio interaction was complete. Within seconds he met her eyes in the mirror from the back seat: she showed no expression. He looked forward after the stare down, eyes on the road telling himself he didn't care whether the damaged woman was impressed with him or not because he was impressed enough for both. The woman has played the game before and lost, her face being a testament to that fact, making this even more fun. She had to know what was waiting for them at the station house, and he was looking forward to finding out if there was any fight left in this one. The mutt, however, may be a problem; it's protective, aggressive, and dangerous. But maybe he could exploit their connection somehow because she was protective of the dog as well. Yes, that would be a new twist to the game.

Suzie continues to whine incessantly; her anxiety tripped by the confines of the police cruiser and the memories this man has dredged up in her mind. Reggie wishes she could give Suzie her baby, which always seems to calm her, but it wasn't possible because it was covered in saliva decay on the floor in the back of their car.

"When our funs over," Dempsey says continuing eye contact with her, "I'd like to get the name of the man who did that and reach out," he says pointing to his face. "He deserves a stiff handshake and an envious pat on the back for a job well done," he says winking at her through the mirror before turning his attention back to the road.

"Don't worry, you'll be meeting a man, but the last thing you're going to be doing is shaking his hand," she says from the back seat.

"What's that Scar Face?"

"Just picturing something coming your way is all." And right on cue, Suzie delivers an agreement growl barring her prominent teeth, her mouth producing liquid anger to run down the steel barrier dividing the front and back seats. She retreats as far as she can manage within the confines of the back seat, then lunges forward, hitting the divider separating them with all her weight. This man isn't the man of her past, but he's close enough and will eventually feel her wrath, nonetheless.

Reggie frantically tries to calm Suzie, but with her hands tied behind her back, all she can do is lean into her and bury her face into her protector's soft coat. She murmurs the same assurances as before into her ear, promising again that they will all get their chance to exact justice before this operation is over.

Tormented eyes glow up ahead within the denseness of the trees as they seek Suzie's; when they connect, Suzie is comforted by the message that she is not alone. A howl of sadness rings through the trees, following the vehicle as it passes. Suzie turns her head to the back window just in time to catch a glimpse of her distant cousin running along the tree line to follow. As they pull up to the police station and park, no one notices as the wolf stands sentry in

185

the woods, but Suzie can still feel its presence as their connection remains strong.

The Sheriff pushes the gear shift into park, turns the key to kill the engine, and opens his door. Reggie looks on, noticing the tow truck Dempsey had requested, and assumes it's for her car. But no worries, Marco would have triggered its tracker by now; so the team could retrieve it and them simultaneously. It didn't take much to conjure up the vision of the storm coming and the battle that will ensue, and she couldn't wait for its rath.

From the back seat, her eyes travel to the windshield where a comical scene is playing out. Epic is the only word to describe it, as Deputy Panty Sniffer tries to pull Pix out of his cruiser. Even with her hands bound behind her back, Pix is doing everything she can to make her extraction from the vehicle as difficult as possible. And it's too bad the kick she sent to her captor's manhood was off the mark, now that would have been satisfying. Because the driver's side-door was open, Reggie could hear the interaction between the two; Pix's mouth was spitting expletives that even Reggie hadn't heard before. *You go, girlfriend, give him hell!*

"That dipshit," Dempsey says, laughing. He's standing with one foot on the ground and one still in the rig as he watches the antics playing out in front of the station.

"Got yourself a real spitfire there, don't ya, Deputy!"

"Yep, she's a butt load of crazy for sure, Sheriff; this is going to be fun," he yells back. His statement held a dark promise, and the delivery chilled Reggie to the bone. Pix heard the same darkness and had the same reaction, causing her to fight like she never had before. But Pix could only continue to fight until her energy was spent, giving the Deputy control of the situation before dragging her to the station's front doors.

When the show was over, Dempsey planted his other foot on the ground, closing his door. "Your turn," he says, opening the back door for Reggie to climb out. "And don't even think of trying anything like she did, or you'll have more scars added to that face!"

Tramping down her rage, she stays glued to the seat.

"Oh, and don't think about asking for your phone call either; I don't believe in following legal rights and all that!"

"Won't need one!"

"Oh, why's that? Doesn't anyone care about you two?" he asks, sounding perplexed while waiting for her to answer. But at the same time, his mind is racing with possibilities, and he becomes ecstatic about the fact that if there's no one to call, there's no one to come looking. Of course, this means new rules for the game, and a hell of a lot more fun, not to mention more time in which to have it.

"No worries, Sheriff, like I said we won't need a phone call."

"If you say so, now get out of the damn car!"

"Sheriff, I told you no more trouble, but if you don't take these bindings off of my wrists, she's going to give you some; I think you know that!" she delivers, turning her head to look at Suzie.

"I can handle the bitch," he says, placing his hand on his weapon.

"Oh, you think so! Before you could get a shot off, she'd be ripping your throat out, and I imagine that would be a tragedy to someone around here, or I could be wrong, just sayin."

"What is she, your personal guard dog or something?"

"Something like that. Now, are you going to cut me loose so that we won't have any trouble or what?" Reggie says.

"You got a leash for her?" he says, pointing in Suzie's direction.

"Yes, as a matter of fact I do, but it's in the car with all our other stuff."

He thinks about that for a moment, then turns his head toward the station, "Deputy Woodard, get your ass out here," he screams.

Instantly the deputy pushes the door open, visibly trembling from what Reggie could tell. Just like Bud had described, the guy is so thin a small belt could wrap around him twice. "Yyyyess, Sheriff," he stammers.

"Get me something I can use as a dog leash and make it quick!"

Once a piece of rope was delivered to the Sheriff, with Deputy Woodard dropping it twice along the way, Reggie's hands were set free. She took the cord that came flying her way and began securing it around Suzie's neck, whispering that it was only for show because they both knew it wasn't necessary or that it wouldn't make a difference when it came right down to it.

"Move," the Sheriff says happily, feeling confident now that the dog is contained, "you don't want to be late for your own party, now do ya?"

Chapter 32

The Sheriff pushes the station house door open with his right shoulder and pulls Reggie across the threshold with his left. He stands back with the bat in his right hand, still grasping Reggie with his left, all the while giving Suzie a wide berth as she follows Reggie obediently through the door. He's satisfied to some extent to see she's under control and still tethered to Reggie's hand by the rope. But the look those dark canine eyes shot him on her way past caused him some doubt, and his hand tightened around the bat handle. Once the door closed behind them, he roughly pushed Reggie over to the side but didn't let go.

Standing behind the reception counter is the Deputy who brought the rope out, and in the lobby were two men dressed in greasy overalls with matching baseball caps. The contrast between the two men was comical. The one whose name tag says Carl is as wide as he is tall, Reggie guessed about five foot six with a fat round piggy face and small dark piggy eyes to match. Comically, she found herself feeling sorry for the overalls stretched tight across his middle, with the zipper straining to stay closed, every tooth ready to give up the fight. And it didn't take her long to deduce the grease stains down the front mingling with the strained zipper weren't all work-related. Reggie thought she could smell fry sauce over the aroma of oil and grease. *I shall call him... Piggy Face.*

The man next to him was tall and thin, skinny, kind of like the Deputy who was still quivering behind the counter. Reggie guessed he was about six feet four or five inches with a name tag that said,

"Stew". His frame looked like it was made of toothpicks, his skinny legs straining to keep it upright. His long, thin face made his prominent pointy nose stick out like Pinocchio's would be after leaving the Saturday morning confessional. Large eyes sat close together above his protruding nose and large buck teeth, and the image of a Praying Mantis shot through her mind. *I shall call him,,, Praying Mantis Guy.*

Still holding Reggie's arm to show some dominance, Dempsey tells Piggy Eyes and Praying Mantis Guy to head out of town to retrieve her car.

"But we haven't had lunch yet, Sheriff." Yep, you guessed it; Piggy Face whines as he rubs his rotund middle.

Dempsey looks at the clock on the wall, 1:30 pm. "Fine, stop for lunch on the way. I certainly wouldn't want to be responsible for ya wasting away, Carl. Just get that car off the road, bring it back here and unload it around back. I'll figure out what to do with it in the morning."

Right about then, an eruption of the female gender came soaring out from the next room; it was clear where they were holding Pix. Then, adding to the sound of mayhem, the clank of a cell door slamming closed drew Reggie's eye into the room, where she witnessed Deputy Tack frantically trying to remain upright by reaching for the cement wall adjacent to the cell. He seemed to be having trouble catching his breath, and a noticeable sweaty sheen covered his face. His narrow escape from the woman inside the cell was hilarious.

Pix was right on the Deputy's heels, but the cell door slammed shut a second before she could get her hands on him, but she didn't let that stop her; she charged the cell door. A smooth jump onto the cold iron allowed her to plant her feet onto the lowest crossbar about a foot off the cell floor. Then, with her tiny hands, she grasped more iron at shoulder height to hold her position steady; the boys would be so proud. It was like a scene from a zoo documentary; she looked like a cracked-out baby Howler monkey with her screeching and screaming. The only thing missing was the monkey poop flying through the bars at the spectator as she jumped from one position on the bars to another. But we're talking about Pix here and it's early, so anything is possible.

"Come a little closer, Numb Nuts; I'll show ya how I like to party," she yells at the Deputy, who could only stand outside the cell, narrowly avoiding her arms as they stretched through the bars trying to grab him. Yes, the boys would definitely be proud.

"You sure got a wild one in there this time, Sheriff," Piggy Face Carl laughs.

"You alright in there, Deputy?" Dempsey yells over the monkey screeching coming from the cell.

"I think so, Sheriff," she'll settle down in a bit!" He could only hope.

The whole time Reggie stood inside the Station door, her eyes kept connecting with Deputy Woodard's. Yes, he is shocked by her and Suzie's presence, not to mention the Howler monkey in the cell next door, but she could tell he was afraid of the Sheriff. He hadn't moved from the corner behind the reception counter since they walked through the door.

"Carl, Stew, get the hell out-a here and do what I told you to do," Dempsey yells, pointing his head at the door.

"But we can still stop for lunch, right Sheriff?" Piggy Face questions while rubbing his stomach again.

"I said ya could Carl, looks like you lost a few pounds just standing there for the last fifteen minutes," the Sheriff says harshly. And on that note, Piggy Face and Praying Mantis Guy run out the door.

After the door closes behind the two, Dempsey drags his charge and the mutt over to the counter, where he places the bat on top of it before reaching into his pocket for the women's IDs and Reggie's car keys. He tosses them onto the counter in front of Deputy Woodard, then retrieves the bat before telling him that he and Deputy Tack are not to be disturbed. *Oops, too late, they're already disturbed.*

"Yyeess, Sheriff."

Chapter 33

"What's your ETA Dom?" John's exhausted voice permeates the cab of the mission's assigned Land Cruiser. The three men making up the retrieval team sat in silence, listening to the exhaustion their boss was fighting, and could feel the tension riding through the speaker of Dom's phone to surround them.

"I figure we should arrive around 15:00 hours, Boss."

"Copy that," John responds, there will be a couple of hours of daylight left when you get there then; take that into consideration."

"Copy that."

"Any plan yet?"

"At this point, we're only able to speculate, but as soon as we arrive and do some recon, we'll be able to formulate one."

Silence again from John's end... "Boss you copy?"

"Copy that. Dom, Mountain, Doc, I don't care how you do it; stay safe, get them out and come home. We've got work to do guys, keep your eyes open and heads on swivel!"

"Roger that," all three men said in unison before the com was disconnected on John's end.

Not long after they made the turn heading to DuPree they witnessed a tow truck making a U-turn across the road in front of them heading in the same direction.

"Can you make out the plate Mountain?" Dom asks, squinting through the windshield. "Not quite; get closer."

Dom pushed on the gas just enough to lessen the distance between them and the tow truck, but not enough to arouse suspicion.

"Ok, got it. Mountain to Club House, come back, I have a plate on a black Camry four-door; it could be Miss Reggie's. It's hooked up to a tow-truck heading to DuPree," he said before passing on the license plate number.

"Club House to Mountain," Marco says, "yep, it's her assigned car, and the tracker is activated.

"Copy that."

With that information, Dom lifts his foot off the gas a bit, allowing the truck to pull ahead just enough that the driver wouldn't suspect anything. Hopefully, this would help them formulate a plan of attack, but he wasn't exactly sure how. Hell, it might come down to them just storming the fortress and rescuing the damsels in distress. *Shit, now he was thinking like the kid.* The land cruiser continued at a reasonable distance, its occupants sitting in silence with their thoughts. They did not notice the beauty of the landscape, or the clean air as it assaulted their senses. Even the colorful autumn leaves drifting in front of the vehicle doing their dance of fall couldn't be appreciated at this point. Each man was trying in his own way to stay calm, fighting within themselves to formulate the best plan of attack for when they confront the trouble that lay ahead. And all three men knew

194

already that referring to this OP as 'trouble' was unequivocally putting it mildly.

Without warning, Mountain suddenly yells, "STOP!"

And just as suddenly, without questioning the order, Dom does just that.

"Back up until I tell ya to stop Dom," Mountain says without explanation, and none was needed by Dom. They had worked together long enough so that each was confident with the other's abilities when on an OP. "Here," Mountain says pointing to the right where an old overgrown entrance into the woods was visible. "Drive in there, let's see how far in it goes. It could turn out to be a viable recon point or rendezvous location if needed."

The entrance hadn't been used in some time, by the looks of it, the tall weeds growing down the middle of two dirt ruts in the ground made that obvious. There wasn't a no-trespassing sign or chain across the entrance to hinder them. And even if the opening were chained off, it wouldn't have made a difference, because when it came right down to it that would be the least of their worries.

Hoping the unexpected find could help them develop a plan the men carried on. But, of course, it would depend on how far back the old road went before knowing if it could be a viable option. But having a location to hide the rig, if warranted by any scenario, could end up being just what they needed; at least, it was a start.

"Good eye," Doc says from the back seat while Dom turns into the entrance and slowly advances.

It turned out to be secluded, with mother nature taking back what she had lost by heavy equipment and large trucks having their way with her. She was slowly reclaiming the original landscape by adding lush brush and vines as fast as she could. The limbs hanging over the vehicle's top were still young and fragile, leaving them deficient in strength. All they could do at this point was scrape the hood and sides of the cruiser, not hindering their advance in the slightest. The ruts in the road turned muddy from the recent rain, not having the sunlight to dry them out, but Dom continued to follow them to the right, putting the cruiser further into the woods. The men soon realized that mother nature's rebuilding would give them the natural camouflage they needed to sit undetected from every direction.

The three men got out and closed their doors, realizing that stealth wasn't necessary due to the fact they found themselves on the outskirts of the Sawmill. They took advantage of the hiding place to watch the coming and going of machinery transporting logs of every type and length. The noise of the yard would cover any sound they made if this situation played a part in the extraction.

"I say we head into town, find the Sheriff's office, do some recon, and make a plan from there," Dom says to Mountain and the Doc, "agreed?"

"Agreed!"

They backed out of the secluded spot and headed toward town, noting the distance from the hidden location once they arrived within the city limits.

Driving slowly, they found the Sheriff's station, their trained eyes picking up every nuance, including two police cruisers parked in front. Each man noticed the tow truck pull out on the other side of the station, leaving Reggie's car parked where they could see it, at the back of the building. It was apparent that the gravel entrance to the parking lot wrapped around the building to exit on the other side. They continued, past the Sheriff's station, counting the buildings on the main street and judging the distances between them as best they could. They found the bookstore not too far from the Sheriff's office, on the opposite side of the road.

Once they drove past it, they turned around at the gas station, sitting to their right. Mountain and Doc both began to snap pictures of everything they thought valuable. Stopping momentarily at the bookstore, the men took photos of the front and both sides. The foliage on the sides was thick and continued out about fifteen yards from the building. Even though the bushes and ferns caused a dense barrier, a person could still make their way through the natural camouflage by hugging the building as they did so.

Chapter 34

Still reeling from her visitor and the commitment she made for herself and Bud, Amee somehow finds the strength to act normal for the cameras watching from the corners of her proverbial cage. It takes everything in her not to pull the cell phone out of her pocket and call her father. But as usual, the hairs on the back of her neck start to tingle with the reminder that she is not alone, even though she is the only physical being in the store.

Her hand caresses the phone in her pocket, and she thinks, just for a split second, that she could make the call to Bud. But then remembers the promise she made to Reggie concerning her behavior; it would have to stay the same, nothing out of character in the least, and her calling Bud would definitely be out of character. So, to keep her promise, she heads to the back of the store, switches on the bathroom light, and hides the phone in the suggested hiding spot.

Amee begins to re-arrange one of the front window displays when she sees the town tow truck pull into the Police Station driveway and head to the back of the lot. The black four door sedan in tow seemed to cry out to her, and the memory of Reggie's friend leaning on it earlier while she was waiting outside came crashing in on her. She continues to watch the station and a few minutes later sees the tow truck exit on the other side without the car attached. She isn't aware of the slow-moving vehicle passing by because she is too preoccupied watching the tow truck exit to notice.

198

"No... no... no, not again!" Amee cries into the book-filled room, beginning to feel tortured by the knowledge she carries of past situations with women. The shame instantly shrouds her with guilt, and she criticizes herself and the town residents for not speaking up. They knew all along that the Sheriff and his Deputy brought women into that station with no charges filed against them, but no one knew what happened to them after their stay, and no one dared to question it. *"Not this time,"* she whispers with determination.

She had a gut feeling about whose car that was, and she had the means to help before it was too late. Walking casually, for the benefit of the cameras, she turned to the back of the store and entered the bathroom to retrieve the phone she had just hidden inside. She flipped the light switch on, grabbed the phone, then stepped out, closing the door behind her, leaving the light to slip out from under it like she was inside doing her business.

After closing the bathroom door, she took a couple of steps further into the dark corner from the view of the cameras and opened the back door of the store. She took a quick, cautious look in both directions before stepping down and following a hidden path through the overgrowth. She started slipping out the back door a couple of months ago for no other reason than to feel a small snippet of freedom. At the time, she knew she would never be able to get away, but this little show of defiance and fake hope kept her going to make sure her father was safe.

She kept moving, glad that the bushes keeping her hidden hadn't lost all their foliage to the season yet. But, when she approached the end of her trail, she stopped short of stepping out into view. She scolded her boldness as every sensation of doubt began to dance up her spine but was determined to follow through with her single-minded goal of not staying silent this time.

She knelt at the edge of the natural barrier and found both cruisers parked in front of the station, and she was as sure as she was breathing that Reggie, and her friend were inside. That was all the confirmation needed because her gut was leading the way. Turning around slowly to head back, she still had not noticed the vehicle out front and that it had stopped and was taking pictures of her store. Retracing her steps, she nervously pulled the cell phone out of her pocket and pushed the button Reggie had shown her was for emergencies.

"Boss," Marco calls in John's direction, "we got an incoming call from the phone Reggie gave to Amee!"

"On speaker Marco!"

"Hello, hello," Amee says urgently into the phone when it sounds like someone has answered. "Can you hear me? It's Amee; please be there," she says, stepping back into the dark corner of the store and closing the door behind her.

"Amee, this is John; we're here. What's going on? Are you safe?"

"Thank God," Amee says when she hears John's voice. "Yes, I'm fine, but Reggie and her friend are in big trouble. I just saw the town tow truck pull into the parking lot of the Police station with what looked like Reggie's car and exit the other side without it. This will not end well, you need to send help, now!"

"Why do you say that?" John questions through the phone with every muscle in his body fighting his determination to stay calm, especially because he knows that she's right about Reggie and Pix being in trouble.

"Just take my word for it," Amee hisses in response as she paces in the dark corner of the store, wishing she knew how to explain but the guilt was such a burden.

"Okay, I understand. We know Reggie and Pix were stopped on their way out of town and taken to the police station. I have dispatched a team to get them out of there, they should be there any minute."

"You knew this was happening?"

"Yes, and we have it covered. But just so you're aware, you could be leaving that town tonight because of this development, so keep that phone on and close because you may be getting a text. When it comes through with instructions, follow them to the letter. Can you do that?"

"Yes, I can do that. But hear me good, if you don't get them out soon, you'll never see them again!" She waited for a response from the man but only received seconds of silence, leaving her to wonder if their connection had ended. But just in case he could still hear her, she tried again. "Hello, John, did you hear me?"

"Yes, Amee, we hear you and understand, thank you for the information," came a different male voice. "Stay safe now and keep the phone close," Marco says, "I'm going to walk you through the process of putting the phone on vibrate, a precaution for you.

Marco couldn't stand to watch the Boss descend into the tunnel of hell any longer, he was fighting so hard to stay calm and in Boss mode, but it was apparent he was failing and needed help, so he decided to take at least a little pressure off the man.

Noticing the gesture for what it was, John was sincerely grateful. It didn't mean he was losing his military biscuits or his natural ability to lead; it just indicated he needed some help to navigate this nightmare. "Thank you, Brother," John says sincerely. He takes a breath and pulls himself together, "Get me Dom, Marco!"

"Copy that Boss."

Dom's phone lights up, indicating a transmission was coming in from the Club House. All three men sit rigidly in their seats, waiting for the communication. It's the Boss, and they all assume he is getting antsy for a status report, but before Dom can begin to deliver a SITREP, he gets cut off abruptly.

"EXECUTE EXTRACTION NOW!!" The command blares through the phone, "NOW, NOW!!"

"Copy that, Boss," Dominic answers instantly.

With no warning to the other two men, he makes a sharp left turn into the entrance of the Police Station, heading to the back of the parking lot, where he pulls in alongside Reggie's car, cutting the engine. His thoughts are swirling with the realization that they are about to execute what would have been the Kid's plan, and that was to storm the fortress to save the damsels in distress, literally.

Chapter 35

Both men were short of breath when they were finally able to close the cell door behind Reggie and Suzie. Pix kept up her cracked-out frenzy to make the simple task of adding two more occupants to the confines of the cell as difficult as possible; her efforts prolonged their goal, but only for a time.

"Enough," Dempsey shouts into the cell, his determined eyes trained on Pix as if that would make a difference. "Girlie, you got some extreme anger issues," he states darkly with a grin on his face that said; *we'll have to work on that!*

"You have no idea how deep or extreme my anger issues flow!"

That just resulted in Dempsey screaming at Reggie, for what seemed like the hundredth time, to shut that damn dog up, or it wouldn't end well.

Poor Suzie couldn't keep a lid on her ragging anger any longer. So, once she was in the cell and Reggie had removed the makeshift leash from around her neck, she allowed all the emotion she had kept bottled up for appearance's sake, to encompass not only the cell but the room as well. The fur on her back began to stand up straight, and the guttural sounds coming from her maw were unreal as they swam in the saliva draining from her mouth with all-consuming hate. She began to lunge at the cell door, not caring how the impact of the bars shot pain through her body; she needed to get out and get on with the destruction. She could smell the danger flowing off the men just a couple of feet away, protected by cell bars. The barrier held strong but didn't restrain her thoughts of duty and protection for the captives locked inside with her.

"Suzie," Reggie says sharply to protect her protector from harm while moving forward to pull her back from the bars of the cell. Reggie places her hand around the dog's muzzle, their signal for silence. Suzie instantly complies, moving begrudgingly to Reggie's side; she goes through the motions of sitting but shakes stiffly with anger as she holds her haunches inches off the floor, ready to launch herself into action.

"That's more like it, now let's have some fun, ladies." Dempsey laughs toward them while pulling Pix's Glock out of his coat pocket, placing it and Reggie's bat on top of an old filing cabinet near the door to the outer office so he can remove his jacket.

Once his jacket is taken care of, he ever so slowly reclaims the bat and tosses it back and forth between his hands, watching the women's faces in the cell. He had no idea what the results of those two simple actions would ignite within the scar-faced woman. But the woman recognizes the darkness of her past as it comes trudging toward her with determined delight. She immediately tries to push its darkness back, blocking the onslaught of pain she knows will eat at her as it tries to consume every part of her being.

Like a bully on the playground, Dempsey begins to taunt the occupants of the cell by running the aluminum bat across its bars. The ting, ting, ting of aluminum connecting with steel sending out an ear-splitting cry, making Pix scream expletives concerning the absurd action. Suzie sits vibrating, whining, and whimpering from the noise, her sensitive hearing taking a beating, not to mention the fact she was shackled by the command to stay silent.

"Ain't this fun ladies?" Dempsey shouts into the cell, but the only response is the demented laughter of the Deputy.

If Dempsey hadn't been so impressed with himself and excited about the game they were going to play, he would have noticed that one occupant was not making a sound. Reggie had pushed herself back into the far-right corner behind Suzie with her eyes taking on a distant look of horror while her hands covered her ears. All the fight he had hoped to encounter would not be delivered by the woman cowering in the corner, but he was too revved up to notice. His arrogance was being fed by a certain part of his anatomy, and he was getting more excited by the minute.

Pix could see the two men getting all worked up like schoolboys at a frat party, giving herself and Reggie no place to hide from their moronic adolescent taunts and gross antics. But when Pixie looked at Reggie, all the color began to drain from her face as she instantly recognized the battle raging inside the woman in the corner. "No, no, no," Pix screams into the cell, moving toward Reggie in the corner, hoping to pull her back before it's too late, but the eyes looking back at her seemed like dark, vacant tunnels.

The noise and chaos ensued within the cell as Pix and Suzie began to panic within the small area. Suzie didn't wait to be released from her command to stay put once she looked behind her to see her mother cowering in the corner and Pixie screaming at their captors to open the door. The two men seemed to think of all this noise as four play and were happy to keep up the taunting, from the opposite side of the bars, of course.

*****

Reggie finds herself fighting against a tether of emotional darkness; it's pulling her back toward an all too familiar place. "No, I won't go, I won't let you win again!" she hisses into the cell. Reggie closes her eyes tight to fight the darkness off; she shakes her head back and forth with trembling hands clamped to her ears. Sadly, Reggie has traveled this path many times, and she knows what's waiting at the end of it. With every beat of her heart, she knows what comes next. This trigger is just one of many that she continues to fight, and it's the worst one. These circumstances have caught her off guard, she thought she was stronger now, but reality had found a way around that strength once more. She is immediately disgusted with herself, for she can smell the fear she wears.

The strong pull of darkness begins its laugh as it can feel she's still powerless to stand up to it, leaving her to succumb to its will, its cruel calling. She knows she's become stronger, it's harder for the darkness to claim her entirely, but it still seeks and finds her at times. The rope has begun to grow weaker between the darkness and herself, its ends have begun to fray, but it still manages to hold tight at times to win sending her backward.

The all too familiar destination and its occupants sit at the end of a well-traveled path full of ruts and mud, worn down from the many times she's been forced to travel it. In the past, her boots were the only weapon she had to fight the pull of the tether that commanded her presence so many times; she dug the soles in deep, scraping away the grass and weeds. However, now that her physical and emotional health has grown stronger, she can fight more intensely. By digging her boots deeper into the earth and straining with every ounce of self-preservation she can muster, she continues to try and break the connection that controls her.

*****

"Reggie, Reggie, can you hear me?" Pix screams into her face as the bat continues its rhythm against the bars of the cell. Pix grabs her shoulders and begins to shake her friend, feeling helpless as she watches Suzie throw herself at the cell door again. "Reggie, please come back; COME BACK!"

*****

Laden down with painful memories, Reggie acknowledges she's being pulled back into her past. Her strength to fight the horror she will endure when she falls through the familiar rabbit hole into an entirely different Wonderland is waning. She feels her body being dumped unceremoniously into the opening and screams into the space as she begins to spiral downward. As she falls, she sees the faces of the Mad Hatter and the Cheshire Cat that stand sentry to this parallel dimension. Their heads lean into the bottom of the tunnel, waiting for her to join them again for tea.

Getting closer to being dumped out into their demented fairy tale, Reggie begins to panic. With all her might, she kicks out at the walls of the tunnel and suddenly feels small indentations that hadn't been there before and are just big enough for the toes of her boots. Acknowledging the change of the tunnel walls, she begins to claw the air, curling her fingers of flesh and bone into hooks to find the same purchase her boots have.

Quickly she realizes that her descent has not only slowed but has stopped as she finds herself hanging on with a death grip to the sides of the tunnel. But the strength in her legs is waning already, and they begin to tremble. Her fingers start to cramp, causing toxic thoughts of what is waiting for her below if she can't hold on.

"Come on down, Deary," the Cheshire Cat mews seductively from the bottom; we have been waiting and waiting for you, I'll just go freshen up the tea," he says gleefully, stepping out of view with his enormous tail swishing behind him, always the accommodating host.

Her hold is beginning to slip as her fingers are cramping with pain, and her palms have become sweaty with adrenaline and fear, but she digs into a reserve of strength she has recently acquired and continues to fight the descent. The Mad Hatter continues to stand sentry at the bottom of the opening, smiling with rotten black teeth and playing with a newly acquired mustache, which looked so out of place in a children's story. But this is the Devil's fairy tale, it doesn't exist for children, it exists only for the many unlucky that have found themselves as victims.

*****

The barking seems far away and out of place but familiar at the same time. It's an angry, agitated sound she's heard before; she's sure of it. Then she hears a woman's voice, it's panicking and calling her name. "Reggie!" the woman's voice permeates the tunnel.

*****

The Cheshire Cat returns to the opening and sticks his head back in, "it's almost done My Dear," he purrs.

"Why do we always have to wait for her?" a voice yells from the table behind the two characters.

"Alice, mind your manners," the cat reprimands, not turning his face from Reggie's. "You know we will always wait for Reggie because she needs reminding so often! It's a shame really, that she doesn't just join us permanently instead of fighting against us all the time."

"Maybe you could put something in her tea," the Mad Hatter giggles, while playing with his gross mustache.

"Well, I, for one, am tired of treating her special, and I'm certainly tired of waiting for her all the time," the girl declares as she pushes her chair back from the table loudly, then comes to stand at the bottom of the tunnel, peering upward. Reggie almost lost her footing when she noticed the girl who was supposed to be Alice looking up at her with a petulant scowl on her face. She just assumed this Alice would look like the one in the storybook, but wow, this gothic wonderland sure has done a job on her. Where there should have been long blonde hair with a blue silk ribbon holding it out of her eyes, this Alice has stiff black spikes standing straight up on the top of her head. In addition, she isn't wearing the frilly blue dress with the white apron. No, she is wearing a plaid mini skirt with black combat boots that lace up to just below the knee. She wears a black tank top and has dark tattoos of bloody artwork running down both arms and across her neck. Black seems to be the color of choice, it adorns her stubby fingernails and coats her petulant lips, the lips that continue to loudly voice her opinions.

Reggie suddenly realizes that the tea party she has always attended before has changed considerably. Is it possible she's hanging out, literally hanging out, in the wrong rabbit hole? No, she won't let her thoughts entertain that possibility. It has got to be the same hole; it's the same players, just darker. This parallel universe has always played out the

209

Devil's fairy tale. But now, because they are tired of this assignment, they have decided to show the dark side of their characters by revealing themselves in their true light. She's pushed them too far and is delighted with the outcome because it means she's finding personal power. They're tired of her growing strength and are afraid she is slipping out of their grasp. They no longer have the luxury of waiting because 'HIS' rath will be severe if they fail. Just the thought of the punishment they will endure has them changing physically, hoping it will intimidate her into compliance. The characters become frantic because they have failed to keep her in line. Her strength is their weakness, in 'HIS' eyes.

Their assignment has always been to bring her back into the pain, by delivering a refresher course of what she endured. 'HE' craves the chance to reminisce the past with her, to watch her fall back at his feet where she belongs, begging to be allowed back into his darkness.

As her body trembles and almost betrays her will, she screams at the three characters at the bottom of the tunnel. "NO, NOT THIS TIME!"

*****

Her head pokes out of the entrance to the rabbit hole, and as she pulls the rest of her body through the opening, her eyes begin to clear, and the feelings of pain in her legs and fingers start to dissipate. She stands tall, peering back down into the darkness, expelling the toxic air that had filled her lungs, replacing it with the crisp, clean air of strength and freedom. Reggie knows she will be summoned again for tea, but that doesn't mean she must attend. She's encouraged by the knowledge that she can beat the pull at times and *'him.'* She can hear the characters below as they scream and scurry around the table, the noise of porcelain teacups and matching saucers breaking against the walls as they blame each other for their failure. They will receive a punishment for her escape, and on some level, she can sympathize because they're still victims with nothing to look forward to, unlike her.

Chapter 36

Still curled up in the corner of the cell, Reggie is slowly pulling herself back from one nightmare to be dropped right into another. She can hear Pix shouting into her face and feel her hands gripping her arms tightly as she is shaken awake. "Reggie, come back!" The barking, Suzie's barking, is penetrating her thoughts, and she can feel every ounce of anger and fear her protector is feeling.

Even though Reggie's head is completely cleared now; she sees the here and now being played out like a slow-motion video.

"I told you what would happen if that mutt didn't shut the hell up!" Dempsey bellows angrily. He drops the bat at his feet and pulls his handgun from his side, pointing it through the bars of the cell at Suzie. Reggie instinctively rushes forward without thinking of her safety, grabbing Suzie in her arms. She places herself between Suzie and the monster, hugging Suzie tightly to her chest, with her back to Dempsey. What happened next consisted of flashes of pain and noise. The bullet Dempsey shot into the cell hit Reggie's right shoulder, passing straight through to exit in front, piercing Suzie's left cheek leaving a bloody path of destruction before embedding itself into the wall at the back of the cell.

The back of Reggie's coat begins to change color as the stickiness of her blood spreads across the fabric. Her groan of pain fills the cell as she slumps over to the wall dragging Suzie with her. Suzie's muzzle is pressed into Reggie's chest, leaving her T-shirt stained with a trail of blood from her wound.

With a lack of concern for herself, Suzie begins to whimper, trying to draw all Reggie's hurt into herself. Finally, she lifts her nose to Reggie's shoulder, sniffing the copper scent oozing from the bullet hole, and only manages to issue a few painful barks, bringing everyone back from their shock.

"Holy shit, Sheriff, what happened?"

Chapter 37

With no time to formulate a concrete plan, the three men can only look at each other, nod, and, as silently as possible, climb out of the SUV. Mountain notices a back entrance into the station and points, walking with determined strides towards it. He reaches out to the door handle with his beefy hand and tries to turn it. "Damn, I thought maybe we'd get lucky, and it wouldn't be locked."

"Now what?" Xander asks as he takes in their surroundings.

Mountain looks around the parking lot, noting the cars in the lot and witnessing the few that drive by on the main street. He makes a split-second decision, "wait here; I'll be right back."

Dominic and the Doc nod in response as Mountain takes off around the building.

The minute Mountain steps through the door to the Sheriff's Station, the onslaught of yelling from Pix, the tormented barking from Suzie, and all the other noises travel through the walls of the adjacent room, into the reception area.

Mountain's heart beats with indescribable rage, hearing the voices screaming in the other room. He knows his girls, his sisters, his friends aren't going to make it much longer, so he will have to deal with the piss ant behind the counter quickly.

Deputy Woodard takes in the giant that just marched through the front door and almost lost his bowels. He wants to scream a warning to the Sheriff because, at this point, he would welcome his abuse instead of a beat-down from the specimen of hugeness full of anger standing in the doorway.

Mountain's eyes drill into the extremely agitated Deputy standing behind the counter. He quickly takes three deliberate strides in his direction to shut down any thoughts the little man may have had of delivering a warning. "You know why I'm here?" he says with anger, leaving the Deputy to try and figure out if it was a question or a statement.

The Deputy can't take his eyes off the fists poised to deliver a punch if he doesn't answer truthfully. But it doesn't matter; the answer is the same in both scenarios. All the Deputy can manage is to nod his head in the direction of the other room and all the commotion.

"Splendid!" Mountain says, lifting his fists angrily, slamming them down on the counter for emphasis, "so far, so good. You got the key to the back door?"

"Whaaaat?"

"The back door, you got the key?"

"Yeess," the Deputy squeaks as he fumbles behind the counter, eventually finding the office keyring holding it out for Mountain.

"Good, now place your side arm on the desk there, very carefully, and come on around the counter, you're coming with me."

"No, I can't, the Sheriff will have my hide if I help you."

"You won't have any hide to worry about if you don't," Mountain delivers as he reaches his beefy arm over the counter to grasp the Deputy in a controlled rage, then harshly nudges him around the desk, successfully holding back the urge to just drag him over the top of it.

Holding the Deputy's arm, Mountain stops at the door and looks at the ring of keys in his hand. "One of these for this front door?" Mountain growls.

"Yes, the square one," the deputy points.

Mountain glances through the glass door to see that it is clear before reaching up and turning the sign on the door to closed. Then he pushes the deputy out the door in front of him, holding onto his arm while locking the door. Finally, satisfied that the lock was in place, he drags the scrawny man toward the station's back door, never taking his eyes off his surroundings.

"Now, what have we got here?" Dom asks, smiling at the terrified eyes of the little man.

Deputy Woodard looks from one set of eyes to the other before trying to pull away from Mountain's grasp.

"The Deputy has graciously offered to help us; he's going to open the door," Mountain says while pointing in its direction with his head. "Ain't that right, Hoss?" He confirms for the men, slapping the Deputy hard on the back, sending his face to connect with the cold steel door.

"Please, don't make me do this," the little man pleads to the small crowd, while wiping blood from his nose. If he finds out I helped you I'm going to wish I was dead."

"Don't worry about that; we'll make it look like you were a poor victim in all this, you little shit," Dom snarls. "I bet your momma is so proud!"

"Not really!"

"Open the damn door, NOW!"

With trembling hands, the Deputy manages to insert the key and turn the knob. Dominic enters first, knees bent and weapon up, scanning the surroundings of what turned out to be a small maintenance room and supply closet. The Doc hangs back, holding the door open for Mountain to enter with his new buddy. Daylight was waning but there was enough to peep through the open door, giving Mountain a chance to peruse the area.

He notices a large bundle of heavy-duty zip ties hanging on a nail affixed to the wall behind a workbench. He grabs one, then pushes the Deputy to the floor next to the bench and tightly secures his hands around one of the legs. After that, he leans down and whispers close to the Deputy's face, "are ya going to be quiet?" he asks while picking up a grease rag from the corner of the workbench, "or do ya want to chew on this for a bit?"

"Quiet."

"Thought so."

Before the Doc closed the door behind himself, which would shroud the men in darkness, they could see the space was probably about 8x8 with another door up ahead. At this point, Dom and the Doc could hear what Mountain had already, the screaming and barking, and the Sheriff was yelling to shut the dog up. Standing behind Mountain, the Doc still held the door open and was able to see the light bulb hanging from the ceiling with a pull chain attached, so he taps Mountain on the shoulder and points; after Mountain pulls the chain, he lets the door close behind them. They knew there was a fifty, fifty chance the glow of the light could be seen in the next room as it seeped through the small space between the floor and the door but assumed that no one would notice with all the commotion going on.

Mountain looks around the area, noting all the tools and spare parts for radios on one wall and what looked like carpenter tools on the other. There were also assorted power tools, gas cans, ladders etc. A full-service entity by the looks of it.

"Reggie, Reggie come back," the men hear Pix scream from the next room. Suzie's barking has taken on a protective panic the listeners have heard before, urging them forward.

"That's it, I'm done with the mutt!" the voice rages, and the men assume it's the Sheriff.

"No, no," Reggie's voice screams just before the blast of a handgun permeates into their room.

"Holy shit, Sheriff, what just happened?"

Chapter 38

Dominic is the first man through the connecting door, his weapon up, catching the Sheriff and his Deputy with stunned and belligerent looks on their faces. The Sheriff still holds his gun in his hand as he listens to his ego; it pushes and builds the inner man's imaginary importance, rendering him stupid enough to bring it up and attempt to point it at Dominic.

"I wouldn't!" Dom screams in the Sheriff's direction, his Glock up and poised to shoot. "You'll lose. Drop it!" Dom says, then watches as the gun hits the floor along with its owner's ego and self-importance.

"Who the hell do you think you are, breaking into my station?" the Sheriff bellows, still trying to sound in control and hoping to intimidate a bit.

As Mountain advances on the man, there is no verbal response to the Sheriff's demand, just actions of rage the gentle giant seldom let escape. He places his big hands around the Sheriff's neck, dancing him around to put his back against the cement wall across from the cell bars. The Sheriff begins to claw at his throat in a panic because he can't breathe. His eyes are bulging out of his red face, they're close to popping out onto the floor, but the pressure doesn't subside.

"Stop, you pile of waste!" Mountain screams into the Sheriff's face. But the man keeps struggling until he realizes his feet have left the floor. Then, he finds himself swinging like the favorite toy of an Orangutang, putting on a show for the visitors at his zoo.

Doc enters on Mountain's heels and zeros in on the cell and its occupants. "I got to get in that cell," the Doc yells in Dom's direction.

"Keys!" Dominic screams at the Deputy, who is still standing immobile from shock. Asking again didn't register, but it took only a few punches strategically placed on the Deputy's anatomy to get him to focus and pull them out of his pants pocket. Once in his hand, Dominic turns and finds the correct key to slip into the lock of the cell door.

"Gun!" the Doc yells from behind Dominic; the Deputy had retrieved Pix's Glock from the file cabinet and was fumbling to pull the trigger. But just as quickly as the Deputy had brought the weapon up to fire, the Doc leaned back on his left foot while bringing up his right foot to come down onto the outside of the Deputy's knee, causing an ear-splitting crunch. The dismantling of the man's knee was just as satisfying as his scream. It pulled a smile from Mountain and caused Dom to berate himself for not securing any weapons within reach of the two men. On the other hand, he wasn't aware that surgeons were trained like that but felt lucky this one was.

Everything played out simultaneously. The clanking of the keys as the cell door was opened, the swinging of the Sheriff a foot off the floor, the screaming of the Deputy, and the sad sounds emanating from Suzie and Reggie. Pixie's adrenaline took a dump, and her screaming died out as she swiftly went from prisoner mode to RN mode. She reached Reggie and Suzie in two strides,

220

positioning herself to cushion their fall as they slid down the cement wall, waiting for the Doc to break through the cell entry.

Doc opened the bag he had slung over his shoulder when they left the SUV and started to work. He gently pulled Reggie from Pix's arms so he could see the entry wound as well as the exit. She was losing blood but still conscious, and from his quick assessment it didn't look like there would be any serious damage.

"I told him we didn't need a phone call, and I was right, the calvary is here," Reggie says through the pain with a slight giggle to Pix. "And that deputy has my favorite panties in his jacket pocket, the pervert," she slurs through painful gasps.

Laughing, the Doc places gauze pads on the entrance and exit wounds wrapping her uptight to keep them in place while they get her back to the Club House. He looks at Pix, who even after all the terror she faced today, was smiling at what Reggie had said.

"The pink silk ones with the little black bows?" Pix asks.

"Yes!" Reggie exclaims through the pain, Oh Doc, this hurts like a mother!"

"I know, I'm sorry, here's something for the pain," he says, pulling out a syringe and administering it into her upper arm. "I'm going to check on Suzie now," he says softly. He then asks Pix to let Reggie lean into her so he can get a good look at Suzie, instructing her to keep pressure on Reggie's wounds. The ex-military sniper, now registered nurse and full-blown member of Mickey followed the Doc's orders with a slight shake to her hands.

The bloody gash to Suzie's beautiful face was deep, and he began to apply antibiotic ointment while receiving kisses and whines. It would need stitching, but that isn't what was worrying him. When he examined her body, she would let out painful whimpers, especially when he poked and prodded his surgical fingers around her chest. Pix watched as he did his examination, telling him she wouldn't stop trying to get to the Sheriff.

"She flung herself into those bars repeatedly, trying to get to him. It was the saddest and bravest thing I have ever seen," Pix whispers brushing tears away from her cheeks.

"I'm going to give her something for the pain as well, hopefully they will sleep all the way to the Club House. Now, it's your turn Pix, how are you?"

"Doc, I'm fine, but can I tell you something?" she whispers.

"Of course," he says with concern, hoping he will be able to help if she needs it.

"I've never been so scared, not even over there in the sand box."

And his fear of not being able to help reared its ugly head, he couldn't find the words she needed to hear, all he could do is reach out and grasp her hand lightly, giving her an understanding nod. "I can only imagine," he says softly, knowing it wasn't enough.

"Are they good to go?" Dom asks from outside the cell bars while retrieving the Sheriff's gun from the floor and placing it in the waistband of his cargo pants. Then, still waiting for Doc's response, he enters the cell and heads to the back wall where he kneels and, with his knife, digs the bullet out of the wall that tore through Reggie and Suzie. It and the gun may or may not come in handy, but he knew the Boss would want them.

"Yes," the Doc finally responds.

"What should we do with these two?" Mountain asks, his grip still snuggly placed around the Sheriff's neck.

"I got that covered," the Doc says while rummaging through his bag wearing a wicked smile and coming out with three additional syringes. He walks over to the whimpering Deputy, leans down, and plunges one of the syringes into his neck, instant silence.

"What was that?" Dom asks.

"Magic."

He then stands and does the same to the Sheriff and Mountain instantly let's go to watch him slide down the wall and hit the floor with a satisfying thud. "One more," the Doc says and points to the back room.

Mountain heads back to retrieve the skinny dude.

"Wait, I helped you, so you don't have to do this. I won't tell anyone," I promise.

"Think about it, if they wake up and see nothing has happened to you, they're sure as hell going to wonder why. They're going to know you helped us," Mountain explains. "You should be thanking us."

"Thank you."

Chapter 39

While Mountain gingerly carries a sedated Reggie out through the back door to their assigned cruiser, Dominic does the same with Suzie, holding her close and accepting her slight kisses. "You'll be okay, Suz; we'll get ya fixed up in no time; you did so good," he says, silently wishing he could give her one of her babies for comfort.

Mountain gently places Reggie in the back seat of the SUV and secures the seat belt in such a way; it won't rest across her injured shoulder. Then, floating on pain meds, she slumps her injured body into the padded seat, whimpering softly and asking about Suzie through the sedation. "She's okay; the Doc says she's pretty beat up, but he's taking good care of her, Miss Reggie," he whispers into her ear as his heart breaks for her. Then, pulling his sorrow inward, he stands and does a 360 turn of his surroundings, looking for trouble; he can't believe it's been this easy and hopes their luck will continue for this unexpected extraction.

The Doc is on the other side of the vehicle opening the door; he slides into the middle dragging his bags behind him, quickly making room for Dominic to place Suzie next to him. Once Suzie is secure, Dominic opens the driver's side door and promptly searches for any threats, just like Mountain had. He's also surprised by their luck but satisfied their surroundings are clear. Dominic sits behind the wheel, feeling the rage he's been carrying since hearing the gunshot from the jail cell. He wills himself not to look in the back seat at Reggie and Suzie, for that would reignite the anger.

Instead, he closes his eyes and tries to calm himself as he waits for Mountain to come around to his side of the vehicle so they can talk.

"You and Pix secure that mess inside, then grab Reggie's car and head back.

I don't want you on the road too far behind us just in case an alarm goes up, understand?" Dom says while handing Mountain a small canvas bag with spare keys to Reggie's car, just in case, and the vehicle trackers. "Make sure the trackers get planted on the police cruiser's before you head out; see ya back at the Club House, Brother."

Mountain hesitates at the car door. Taking one more look around the area, he leans down to peer into the back seat of the vehicle, "Doc how long will that shot of magic last on those guys?"

"A couple hours, give or take, why?"

"Well, I've been thinking," he says to both men. "If I can make sure they won't be going anywhere when they wake up, say to give us at least another hour or two, maybe Pix and I should pull Amee out when we leave. It's getting dark and we could make it quick; all we'd need to do is drive over there," he says, pointing at the bookstore, "and pull her out."

"Makes sense," Dominic says after visualizing the easy plan, at least what seems like an easy plan, "I'll run it by the Boss. After you've finished up in there, he says pointing to the station, wait for a transmission from the Club House."

"Copy that," the big man acknowledges stepping back from the vehicle, shouldering the canvas bag, "drive safe. We'll wait to hear from the Boss about pulling Amee now," he says with one last look into the back seat. Then, making eye contact with Xander, he says, "take care of them, Doc," and receives an affirmative nod.

Pix can see Mountain heading back to the station; his head turns from side to side as his eyes take in his surroundings. His body language portrays an angry bull, and she instantly knows it's almost time to go. She turns slowly, taking in the carnage around her, the lovely, magnificent massacre laying at her feet, and it warms her heart.

Again, no judging because you weren't there locked in a cell waiting to be a pawn in their sick game. The horror of the men's intended game repeatedly plays in her mind, and the act of violence bestowed on Reggie and Suzie fuels a fit of dangerous anger.

She retrieves her Glock, placing it in the waistband of her jeans at the middle of her back. She picks up Reggie's bat and heads to the outer office area to grab their IDs and the car keys off the reception desk, but along the way, she can't help but inflict some of her own carnage. Standing over the now unconscious Deputy, she lifts her right foot high, bringing it down heavily to smash it, one more time, on his destroyed knee. She realizes she's feeling elated and satisfied with her actions when she hears what's left of bone as it cracks one more time. The sound is sick as it escapes from beneath her boot, and she wishes he was awake to hear its destruction and endure the pain.

Was her action childish?

Yes!

Was it justified?

Absolutely!

Was it satisfying?

HELL YES, NO WORDS TO DESCRIBE!

As she comes through the outer office door, she sees Mountain in the small maintenance area, searching for something. "I'm ready to go," Pix says to the big man, holding up the items she had retrieved while stepping over the immovable bodies. On the way, she takes one more look at the deputy, and for a split second, she deliberates with herself but doesn't follow through.

"Hold on, we're not done here!"

"Okay," she says and places the objects she's holding in her hands back on the old filing cabinet. "What's your plan?"

"This," Mountain says beaming at her, holding up a huge roll of duct tape. "I love this stuff."

"You love duct tape? You need a girlfriend big guy, or at least a hobby."

"Help me move these specimens of crap up next to the bars," Mountain says as he drags the Sheriff over and places him in a sitting position with the bars behind him, then does the same with Deputy Tack while Pix begins to move Deputy Woodard into the same position.

"Now what?"

Pix watches with fascination as Mountain peels back the end of the tape from the roll. He then holds the end of the tape to the Sheriff's forehead with his left hand, and with his right, sends the roll through the bars and back out front to his forehead. He repeats the action again, just for good measure, making sure the Sheriff's

227

head is secured tightly before roughly ripping the tape from the roll. He then repeats the action with the other two men, before affixing their wrists to the bars at their sides. Standing back, he grunts his approval, looking pleased with his work.

"Normally, I'd say that was overkill, but they deserve much worse," she says with anger, trying to keep her emotions from taking charge, again. Mountain stands next to her, watching her fight the urge for violence rear its ugly head within herself. He waits for more, looking for the indication that he would have to save her from herself and her actions. He knows first-hand it feels good delivering deadly vengeance, but the consequences are harsh, and he will do everything he can too spare her from that.

He watches her shut down right before his eyes, feels her fear of what almost happened as it crawls out of her pores, landing on his chest begging for help, which he is more than ready to give.

Finally, she looks up with resignation in her eyes and says, "every time, and I mean every damn time I'm sure I've seen the worst, the universe just flips me the preverbal bird and laughs at me." She moves close, looking up at the big man, "Mountain, I watched Reggie be pulled down into her past abyss and fight so hard against its demands. I stood helpless as her eyes went dark and vacant just before she mentally left that cell, and it terrified me. But then I watched her fight her way back from the darkness, using every ounce of strength she keeps hidden. It was amazing to watch; one minute, she's full of darkness, and the next, her eyes clear, and she's back. That woman is the strongest human being I know."

"I've seen it too Pix," he says, "and I wish this could be the last time she has to fight that demon from her past like that!"

Chapter 40

When Dominic turned out of the Sheriff's station parking lot to head out of town, dusk was beginning to shut down the day. The beautiful sunshine that showed Reggie and Pixie the way into town this morning couldn't do anything to stop the day from turning into a nightmare. Secured in the back seat being tended to by the Doc was the evidence. The coppery smell of blood lingered among the physical damage, rendering Reggie and Suzie to wounded warrior status.

Unfortunately, wounded warrior status is one he is all too familiar with, for he had participated in inflicting that status on many and lived it himself numerous times. He can still feel the sticky blood on his hands and the strong scent it released as he tried to help his brothers on the battlefield, and it saddens him that no matter the war, there will always be casualties to the good guys.

The howl of their wild escort keeping pace with them through the tree line landed on deaf ears; even Suzie's due to the sedative she'd been given. The solitary wolf kept up with them, running through the trees as long as she could, but eventually had to give up and slink back into the cover of the tree line where her sad reality of loss waited to encompass her. Her mate of many years had been ripped from her side, leaving her full of hate toward man.

"Club House, Club House this is Dom," he speaks into the com link of his phone, knowing everyone there will be anxious for his SITREP.

"QUIET... quiet," John says to the team on his end, "Dom, what's the situation, how are they? Give me some good news, brother!" He had to hear some good news; he was wound so tight from not knowing what was happening on their end all afternoon, he thought he would implode.

"I've got Reggie, Suzie, and the Doc; Pix is fine and coming back with Mountain."

"Thank God," Dominic hears Matt say."

"Boss, Reggie and Suzie will be fine, but they're injured, I'll put the Doc on to fill you in," he says with a sigh, handing his phone over his right shoulder to Xander. He suddenly feels very tired as his adrenaline rush, from the past hour, takes a dump onto the seat next to him.

"Xander, what's wrong with Reggie?" John screams into the coms, not caring what his outburst revealed to the others.

"Hold on, Boss, just for a second," Xander says, "Michael, are you there?" his voice rattling through the com line, determined and precise.

Michael steps closer to the communication device and rests his hand on his son's shoulder, hoping to lend some comfort. "Right here, Xander, go ahead."

Just as earlier in the day, when the Club House sat spellbound listening to the interaction between the girls and the Sheriff, every person sat ridged waiting for Xander to explain Reggie's and Suzie's injuries. A respectful silence filled the area as they braced themselves to hear how two of their own were physically maimed and hurt.

Michael stood with his hand still on his son's shoulder, ready to lend comfort, while Abby stood beside Matt, rubbing his back as a mother would do.

"She's okay, Matt," Abby whispers, hoping that now that he knows Pix is fine, he will be able to exhale the breath he's been holding for hours.

"Thank you, Abby," is all Matt can say now but takes her hand in his and squeezes softly.

"John, the most important thing for you to focus on is that Reggie is going to be okay. She suffered a GSW to the right shoulder fired at close range which caused a through and through injury. It entered through her back shoulder blade and exited through the front. But because she was holding Suzie close to her chest the bullet tore through Suzie's cheek on its way out the front of her shoulder."

"Oh, my God," John says softly, finding it hard to stand on his feet; his thoughts swirled as he grabbed the closest desk for balance. He manages to tune out the gasps and whispers of concern from behind him, his mind blocking all the compassion coming his way from the team. All John could manage to focus on was the GSW, through and through. He knows how that wound feels; he can still feel the hot lead as it tore through his own shoulder, leaving the scar to remind him every time he looks in the mirror. He feels helpless where he stands; all he wants to do is take Reggie's pain away. It's like he's treading water and losing the battle, sinking deeper into the cold clutches pulling him down, suddenly realizing you can't breathe water.

Sensing his son is going to lose it any minute Michael asks, "how are her vitals Xander?"

"Good, vitals are good, and I've controlled her blood flow. She's sedated now and not feeling any pain. Have the Med Bay ready with plenty of suture kits and fluids for our arrival; we shouldn't have to dip into her blood supply because, as I said, I've stopped the bleeding."

He looks over at Suzie with her head leaning on his left shoulder, "also, the damage Suzie took to her cheek when the bullet exited out the front of Reggie's shoulder is severe and will need stitching. And her chest is bruised and tender, I don't know exactly what's going on, but when I examined her, she was in tremendous pain. According to Pix, she kept throwing herself against the cell bars to protect them. Call old Doc Shoemaker and tell him to haul his sorry ass off the bar stool; his favorite lady needs his help. Hopefully, he hasn't been sitting there all day!"

"I'll call him right now," Abby says standing behind John. She pulls her phone out of her pocket and heads away from all the commotion in search of a quieter spot to make the call.

"Boss," Dominic says as Xander hands the phone back to the front seat, "Mountain brought up a good idea. Those three pieces of crap will be out for about two more hours thanks to the Doc and his magic cocktail, and Mountain thinks he can keep them waylaid for an additional hour give or take. That's a huge chunk of time to work with, this could be the perfect opportunity to extract Amee. They could grab her on their way out of town, what do you think?"

Still trying to come to grips with the fact Reggie was shot, John was having trouble making an instant decision, he needed time to think. Silence held heavy over the com link on both ends, the Club House and especially the cruiser.

"Boss, did you hear me?"

Eventually John responds, "sounds like that should work, I'll begin coordinating all moving parts from here." His mind kicked back into Boss mode after making his decision. "I'll talk to Zee and see who his closest guardian is to Bud's assisted living facility. We need to place a guardian there for the safety of Deloris and her staff in case Dempsey comes calling. After Mountain and Pix retrieve Amee, the three of them can head back to Leavenworth to get Bud." There was a lot to take care of in a short amount of time, but his head was already making a mental list. What's your ETA Dom?" John asks with a sudden hit of energy.

"We should be rolling in about 19:30 hours, that's if we don't run into too much traffic."

"Roger that, 19:30 hours."

Chapter 41

Mountain was just about to suggest they finish their clean up when his phone pinged with a text message from the Boss.

'Setting extraction details in motion for Amee and Bud. Finish cleanup and wait for my go ahead. Be safe!

'Copy that Boss!'

"That was the Boss," Mountain says to Pix, he's on board with pulling Amee now on our way out of town."

"Well, that's the first positive scenario I've heard all day, good thinking Big Guy!"

"I have my moments, Little One."

"Let's finish up here," Mountain says, pointing to the top of the filing cabinet, indicating for her to grab the items and follow him. But before he steps through the door to the maintenance room, he pulls his phone out of his pocket and snaps a few pictures of the carnage they will be leaving.

"You should send those to the Club House, they've been blind through all this, maybe a visual like that will give them a boost! Especially the Boss!"

Once Mountain shoots the pictures over to the Club House, they pass through the door into the maintenance room and Mountain lifts a drill off the bench on the way. Stopping, he presses the trigger, and the drill bit begins its high squeal, spinning into nothing. That's all the test he needed to make sure the battery was good and headed to the outer door.

"What are you going to do with that?" Pix asks from behind him.

"Have some juvenile fun," he says, hitting the trigger repeatedly, watching the bit spin, while smiling like a teenager. "Head to the car, I'll be right behind ya," he tells her.

Pix gives him one last look, then heads to the car leaving him to it, you're just as bad as the kid sometimes," she laughs over her shoulder.

Mountain knows they've been lucky so far; no one has noticed them or tried to come into the station, even after the Sheriff's gun went off. Timewise, he figured from the minute he stepped into the station asking the scrawny Deputy for help, which we know he offered willingly, until now, their presence has been about forty-five minutes. Knowing their luck could run out at any time, he had to make his acts of vandalism quick.

For Mountain the art of performing stealth moves has always been hindered due to his size, but he stayed as close to the building as he could, making his way toward the two police cruisers parked outside the entrance to the station. He feels exposed as he continues to watch his surroundings, not able to believe their luck, still all clear. Finally, chuckling to himself, he crouches down at the front of the closest vehicle and drills a hole in both front tires, then plants the tracker up under the front grill, out of sight. Remaining crouched as best he could, he then moves quickly to the other cruiser and repeats the act. The satisfying hiss of the tires deflating is music to the big man's ears. He continues to crouch between the building and the vehicles, waiting for a human encounter that never comes.

Mountain shakes his head in disbelief as he scans the parking lot again, his mind registering still all clear. Then, finally, he makes his way to Reggie's car, where Pix visibly vibrates behind the wheel, her fingers tapping out an adrenaline beat. He opens the passenger door dropping the drill on the floorboard but has trouble folding himself into the compact seat. It looks like he's the clown, and this is the clown car.

Pix watches the big man fight the space and asks, "did ya have fun?"

"Yep!"

"What's with the drill Mountain?"

"I've been meaning to get one, so I got one."

"So, you committed an armed robbery of a police station for a drill?" she says, laughing.

"It's not armed robbery because I wasn't armed," he laughs while stating the obvious."

"That's true enough, now what?" Pix asks before she places the car in gear.

"We're supposed to wait for the go ahead from the Boss," Mountain says, "I'll send him another text and let him know we're good to go."

Mountain: Good to go on our end.

John: She's on her way. Sorry about this but once you have her, you'll have to head to Leavenworth to retrieve Bud. Everything will be taken care of for his extraction by the time you get there. Stay safe!

Chapter 42

After breaking communication with Dominic, John knew they couldn't waste time, so he pushed his exhaustion into a memory to move forward. He could think clearly now that he knew Reggie was on her way home. Yes, bruised and battered, but safe.

"Listen up, Club House," John says, raising his voice. "We have to organize many moving parts in a short window of time, so let's get to it!"

John was about to detail their roles moving forward when his cell phone came alive with a bugle sounding reveille, indicating an incoming text. Stopping in his tracks, he pulls his phone out of one of his many cargo pockets and watches his screen; the picture from Mountain begins to download, bringing a slight smile to his face. He couldn't wait to share the photo with the team; they needed to see this after the turmoil they've faced today. Lack of sleep is feeding the exhaustion they feel, each one of them wearing it as a piece of heavy clothing which they are continually trying to shed before it has the chance to bring them down.

"Marco," he says with a laugh, "pull this picture from Mountain off my phone and send it around to all the monitors. This is good, Brother!"

The picture was just what the team needed to remind them what their dedication was all about. It reminded them once again that they were still human, and they made a conscious choice to go to war with the inhuman. He could hear Laughs and high fives from as far back as the motor pool and the other sections of the hangar, the picture seemed to be the jolt of adrenaline everyone needed.

"Damn, I miss out on all the fun," Oscar-D laughs sadly into the room, "Mountain is an artist, and the sculptures look so life like!" He continues to stare at the monitor, asking himself again why people are born with an organ they don't need. "Damn appendix," he mutters, knowing it will be a long time before he lets this one go, because sitting on the sidelines doesn't work for him.

After letting everyone bask in the glory of the picture, John proceeds with his first order of business, which is to connect with the team's Head of Surveillance, Zee. The man is responsible for logistics and all technical aspects of the guardianship role. He knows where all the guardians are at any given time and which ones are available. He will know who to send to Deloris's facility in Leavenworth with that up-to-the-minute information. Deloris and her staff need to have eyes on them because it's a sure bet Dempsey will show up to cause hell with Bud when he realizes Amee is gone. And, sadly, as they have learned, it wouldn't make any difference to Dempsey who he had to lean on or what method he had to use to extract the information he needed. John's main concern is that the guardian won't be able to get there in time, but the silver lining is they have about a three-hour window. Hopefully, one of the guardians is close.

"Who ya got Zee?" John asks as soon as he sees the man coming in his direction with an iPad in hand.

"I just dispatched Ax; he's been visiting his mother in Monroe after winding up a guardianship role in Louisiana."

"Monroe is only about seventy miles, give or take a couple of miles, from Leavenworth. He's already on the road and will use the ruse of installing new computer software if anyone asks. It will be a good cover because he can stay close to Deloris and keep his eyes on everything from her office and the reception area. "I'll reach out to Deloris and explain what's happening and that we're sending protection her way? I'm also going to send Ax's photo, thought it would be a good idea to send his picture, so she knows who's coming. We wouldn't want all those tattoos to scare the crap out of her."

"You think Ax can make himself look like a computer nerd?" John asks.

"Hey, I think I'm offended Boss," Marco says from his perch in front of three monitors.

"Don't be Brother, you are definitely an exception."

"Good thinking Zee," John says turning his attention back to the man. "Yes, reach out but use her cell phone," John replies. "Let her know that three people will be coming to get Bud, and one is Amee."

"Remind her again that she and Bud need to act as if nothing is happening because we don't know how many pairs of eyes Dempsey has lurking around that place."

"Roger that, Boss," Zee says heading back to his desk.

Now it was time to reach out to Amee.

He makes his way over to Marco, "Hey Brother, can you give me the number of the phone Amee was given." Within seconds he had the information in his hand; it looked like chicken scratch, but John could still make out the numbers. Technical people like Marco didn't spend very much time writing in long hand, they preferred keyboards to communicate. "Thanks, Marco; I'm sure you already have but make sure the trackers Mountain planted are registering in your system."

"Way ahead of ya, Boss!"

"I had no doubt."

With that taken care of, John retreats to the glass-walled conference room to have some quiet while he calls Amee. Hopefully, she could follow Marco's instructions for placing the phone on vibrate, and she has kept it close. He begins to plug in the digits but is suddenly overwhelmed with the day's events. He can't seem to get the vision of Reggie protecting Suzie with her body out of his mind, and he can almost hear the shot as the bullet screams from the gun.

It sends him reeling back in time to relive an identical encounter with hot lead as it entered and exited his body, the memory causing him to touch his own shoulder automatically. This situation leaves him feeling inadequate in the worst way, all he can do is imagine the scene as it must have played out in that locked cell. He can physically feel Reggie's pain and knows how much she's hurting and wishes he had the power to take the pain away.

"Shit, shit, shit!" he spits into the empty room, bringing down bunched-up fists to connect with the table. He thought he might feel better from this action, but all he feels is helplessness and the

241

pain of bruised knuckles. "Okay, moving on," he says into the room, "that didn't help any!"

He picks up his phone with shaking hands, steadying them enough to send Amee a text. Finally, after what seems like exceptionally long seconds he gets a response.

Chapter 43

Amee stands behind the counter of her bookstore inwardly falling apart, every breath feeling like torture heightening her anxiety to unfathomable levels, even for her. It was to the point where she thought it would suddenly eat through her chest-wall as it screamed for an explanation of her actions. Ever since her phone call to Reggie's team to warn them of the danger to the two women, she has been in a panic.

Hang in there a bit longer, the man said.

Keep the phone close, the man said.

Act as normal as possible, the man said.

Nothing hard about those instructions unless your life is on the line.

She sensed the man knew the depth of his requests, she could tell he felt inadequate as to his ability to help over the phone, but words can be a powerful tool when delivered sincerely.

Reaching into her pocket and placing her hand around the cell phone she had been given seemed to be the only way she could feel the possibility of freedom. It is solid proof that she and Bud have a chance; her fingers brush its promise within her pocket, causing her world to continue to spin with hope for their future. One minute she sees the innumerable options waiting for them once they are set free, but the next minute the curtain of captivity drops at her feet with its silent warning, no second act for Amee and Bud. But as terrified as she is, her hand finds the courage to reach out and pull the curtain back slightly, searching for a glimpse of what a second act would look like. Did she dare to dream?

Amee continues to stand behind the counter doing what looks like busy work for the cameras, hoping her performance is a stellar one. But unfortunately, her mind is on a continuous loop that runs one minute with the certainty that Reggie's team will be successful, and the next that they will fail miserably.

Every few minutes, she turns to the side, pretending to look for something behind the counter. She doesn't know how many times she has secretly reached into her pocket to grasp the cell phone, constantly needing reassurance that the small tangible symbol was still there to give her hope. But, unfortunately, her hand trembles as she clutches the lifeline to her future, and her mind can't shake the nagging feeling she didn't follow the man's instructions correctly for placing it on what he called vibrate.

She was never allowed to have a phone, so the unfamiliar was daunting. She reasons if given enough time, she probably could have figured it out on her own but now was not the time to take a chance, so all she could do was wait and see. She needs to find the strength to endure the unknown and wait for the text the man told her would come with instructions. Again, wait and see. Sure, no problem.

Suddenly her attention is drawn to the window behind the counter, and she witnesses an SUV pulling out of the Police Station parking lot. She watches as it heads out of town, knowing who the occupants inside must be, and sends up a prayer of thanks. She knows the vehicle is connected to her escape and suddenly feels an enormous onslaught of panic that she missed her instructions.

Anxiety has been a normal sensation for her for as long as she can remember. It has always stood next to the fear, pain, and hopelessness of her existence. But today, that feeling is taking on a new twist, and she wants to use it for self-preservation; she wants to feed it with every morsel of lost hope and strength she can dig up. She thinks she can remember where they were sent so many years ago to lay dormant in the darkness. Just thinking of finding those two emotions again begins to turn the anxiety into a hidden rage. She feels the buildup as it pumps through her soul and watches as it raises its head to dance before her eyes. But she can't allow it to come out and play just yet, there will be time for that. Yes, once she and Bud are safe, a plan can be made for Dempsey, his father, and this town.

Amee allows herself one satisfying vision, and that's this entire town burning to the ground. Like the scene from the movie, 'The Burning Bed starring Farah Faucet,' when she had enough and set her bed on fire with her abusive husband passed out in it. But she knows, even as the satisfying vision flashes behind her eyes, that she will never follow through with it entirely, because there are too many good people in this town. People like her, stuck within a dark community, run by an even darker family.

So her rage is placed on simmer for now, on the back burner with the heat on low, and when the time is right, Big Daddy, Dempsey, and the two deputies will feel the scorch; she will send them to hell to wallow amongst the inferno of that existence.

She turns back to the counter, cursing the waiting as she flounders among a sea of emotions, wondering how long it will be before she hears something. It's almost closing time, and Deputy Tack will be coming to get her soon because of his daily orders to do so. She wishes she knew what was happening in the station now, or on second thought, maybe she doesn't want to know, she just wants to be gone.

Amee realizes she's been fighting a raging headache and brings her fingers up on both sides of her head to massage her temples. It's weird, because of the circumstances and all, that she finds herself wondering why people do this; it certainly doesn't help any.

It's just like her tooth; she is constantly massaging her cheek to no avail. Finally, she drops her hands to her sides and looks out the window again, seeing nothing except night approaching, wondering if she's ever set free if the night will still be as dark as it is now. She imagines the level of darkness will be the same, but her freedom will allow her to see more clearly.

Suddenly, she feels the vibration coming from her pocket and manages to keep her head down, so she doesn't look up at the nearest camera. First, she feels relief that she has finally been contacted, then excited about what she will see when she can look at the phone. She tries to stay calm for the cameras as she makes her way to the bathroom; once inside, she sees the text that will change her whole life.

John: Amee I know you're scared but you need to follow my instructions immediately. Understand?

Not sure how to text a response she begins to panic, she never thought of this problem. She wills herself to take a deep breath and think. Finally, she realizes she has no choice and decides to go for it and begins pushing buttons. It must have been luck watching over her because eventually she figured out the process, but not before she was having a full-blown anxiety attack.

John: Amee???

Amee: Yes, can you get me out of here now?

John: Yes! Don't bring anything with you, no purse or ID. Step out the back door and walk across the street to the back of the police station. Two members of my team are waiting in Reggie's car to get you out of there. Go Now!

Amee: What about Bud???

John: That's your next stop! Now go!!

Chapter 44

The minute Amee stepped out the back door of the bookstore leaving her prison behind, the air smelled immediately different, the night not so smothering and dangerous. Without even realizing it, she was experiencing the effects of freedom and noticed her perception of darkness wasn't so daunting anymore. She wanted so badly to take off running to the people waiting for her but thought it better not to draw attention, besides the brace she wears is too stiff for running.

"Here she comes," Pix says into the confines of the vehicle, but before she reaches for the door handle, she turns to Mountain and gives a suggestion.

"I think you should hang back, for now, Mountain; she's already scared, and one look at you might send her screaming for the hills. No disrespect Big Guy, but you can be very intimidating until people realize you're just a big marsh mellow."

"I am not a marsh-mellow, but I get what you're saying. I'll hang by the car while you greet her."

"Okay then."

Pix and Mountain exit the car at the same time, and true to his word, Mountain hangs back by the car, leaning on the hood.

Pix walks ahead to greet Amee, when she stops there is a few feet of distance between them. "Amee, I'm Pix, a friend of Reggie's and part of the team that will get you out of here."

Amee manages to acknowledge what the woman said by a sharp nod in her direction but then her questioning eyes travel over to the car and the intimidating man standing next to it. Pix follows Amee's eyes and turns pointing at Mountain, "and that huge specimen is Mountain, don't let his size scare you, his heart and compassion are just as big as he is."

"I remember you from this morning," Amee says nervously looking around the parking lot before her eyes fall on the police station. Turning back to Pix she asks sadly, "are you alright? And Reggie?"

"I'm fine and Reggie is in good hands." Pix didn't want to go into the details of Reggie's condition, it would just add to this woman's torment, besides she would find out soon enough. It was so important at this point to help Amee move forward as easily as possible, she didn't need anything else to stress about.

"What about Dempsey and the Deputies, are they still inside the station?" Her instinct to retreat begins to rip through her body, she can't stand still, her feet have a mind of their own and are programmed to preserve her safety.

"I need to know what is going on; where are they and when do we go get Bud?"

"It's okay Amee," Pix steps closer trying to reassure her, "you're safe now I promise. And Bud is already being protected, we'll be heading to Leavenworth to get him shortly. As for the first question concerning Dempsey," she says with a wave of her hand toward the Police station and a wicked smile on her tiny face, "I'll let Mountain answer that one."

"Mountain," she says, "let's show Amee how we left the DuPree Police Force."

Speaking softly, so he didn't scare her, he says, "be glad too, but let's get in the car first and head out. We don't need to hang around any longer."

They pile into the car, Pix behind the wheel, Mountain riding shotgun, and Amee in the back. Mountain brings up the picture of the three sorry excuses for men they left hogtied to the cell bars and hands it to Amee.

"HOLY SHIT," Amee exclaims. "I mean really, HOLY SHIT," she says again before handing the phone back to Mountain. Suddenly, she's having trouble wrapping herself in the safety she's been promised, it keeps slipping through her trembling fingers when she's brave enough to reach out. She knows Dempsey's rage will be boiling over within him, it doesn't matter that he's unconscious and tied, it will only grow stronger waiting for its release. No one messes with him like that, and it will be even worse when he finds out she's gone.

She begins to massage her cheek, lost in the truth of what is coming next and feeling like she should have done more to explain to Reggie how dangerous this will be for all involved. That picture depicts the beginning of the rampage he will wield down on everyone, and she finds herself trembling from head to toe in the back seat.

"How long will they be out like that?" she asks Mountain.

"Because of the sedative about another hour or so and depending on how long it takes them to be discovered, longer than that. Don't worry, they won't be able to cause any trouble for a while." Mountain looks at the picture one more time and exclaims, "I think this is my best work so far!"

"I think you're right. Can't wait to hear what the kid thinks of it, he's your biggest fan you know.

"The text I got said we are heading to get Bud now, is that still the plan?" Amee asks.

"Yep," Pix says as she navigates the parking lot, taking a left at the exit and heading out of town toward Leavenworth.

"I can't believe this is really happening or find the words to express what you have done for us. I don't have to imagine what you went through Pixie, at Dempsey's hands, I know his habits all too well. How do I begin to thank you for enduring what that man and his boot lickers did to you? There are no words," she hiccups through tears from the back seat, "there just aren't, and a simple thank you doesn't cover it. I will always be in your debt," Amee says exhausted as she wipes her wet eyes in the back seat. She can only hope that someday she can repay what she is desperately accepting, and not just to Pix, but also to Reggie and the team as well.

Pix continues to drive through the darkness, doing her best to stay calm after what Amee said. Unfortunately, Amee has a hard-earned notion of what happened today from the time Reggie, and she left the bookstore, and it eats at her heart that Amee has lived it for so long. The all too familiar cancer some men carry spreads its way through their women with no cure in sight. But this woman in the back seat is proof that, in some cases, no matter what stage the cancer has attained or how long it has been growing, it can be fought and beaten. But at the same time, it leaves the sad reality that the disease is still spreading among others, and they will never be able to stop it.

She suddenly finds herself agitated and having a hard time getting comfortable behind the wheel, her body crumbling as the adrenaline of the day's fight begins to fade. The terror they swam through today comes washing over her like angry ocean waves, pulling her under so she can't breathe or fight her way back. As she sits there with obvious turmoil embracing her whole being, she feels a large hand on her arm, it is a warm comfort she didn't know she was longing for, but one she needed very much.

Amee continues talking from the back seat, but it's only background noise at this point. Pix turns to Mountain, sees the understanding in his compassionate eyes, and takes a calming breath. Today is just one more in a long line of more to come, and she will count it as a win at this point, even though it didn't start out that way. She plays Amee's thank you through her mind and reiterates to herself again, yes today was a good day.

"Does Bud know we're coming?"

"He should by now," Mountain says still looking at Pix. "Don't worry we've already got eyes on him and the facility, he's safe."

"I don't know how to thank you," she cries from the back seat again, "really, you have literally saved our lives."

Mountain: Package secure

John: Roger that, good work

252

Mountain: On our way to get Bud

John: Deloris is ready, and Ax is on site. Good luck Brother!

Chapter 45

"Hey, how they doin back there, Doc?" Dominic asks from the driver's seat.

The silence in the SUV was over-powering in between the whimpers of pain from the injured. Both were uncomfortable; the medication could only do so much to alleviate the pain as it kept fighting to torment their bodies. Reggie would whisper Suzie's name through her painful fog, and Suzie, through whimpers, would ask for Reggie, and you didn't need to speak dog to know that. Doc sat in between them, doing what he could medically while trying to assure them they were each going to be okay. The darkness had settled in all around them, making their situation seem dire, leaving him to deliver platitudes of reassurance softly. He kept telling them both that they would be home soon, and everything would be alright.

"They're doing fine, as well as they can anyway. Will you turn on some light back here? I'm going to push more pain meds to help them through the rest of the journey. How much longer do you think until we're home?"

Dom looks at his phone, "just under an hour or so."

"Copy that," Doc says while administering the meds.

"Hey Doc," Dom says, looking into the back seat via the rearview mirror, "I never thanked you for saving my ass back there, so, thank you."

"No problem."

Well, that was short and sweet, Dom says to himself, wanting more. "I had no idea those kinds of moves were taught in medical school," he says, laughing, hoping it would open some communication between them.

"I wasn't always a Doctor, Dom!"

Dom watches the Doc through the mirror, hoping, waiting for more, but when the Doc's eyes locked with his, it was apparent there would be no more discussion.

Dom had never seen this side of the man before but knew enough to back off and follow the code of the team, they all had a past, a story, and he wouldn't push.

"Well, anyway, thanks again, I owe you one."

Silence, once again.

Today had been a very long strange day, not just because of the events that played out at the jail but because of the unexpected extraction they performed with no planning and the danger they faced because of it. But there was more to it than that. This morning gave the team a glimpse of Oscar-D that no one imagined was there, and now, he has witnessed a part of the Doc's past as well. And seeing the Doc's actions at the jail, he understood why the Boss was on board with the idea of him coming along.

Chapter 46

As many times as Amee had made the trip to Leavenworth, she found herself having trouble dealing with the ride. But in all actuality, it was a short distance, but minutes drug on like hours, and the few miles they had to travel seemed like an endless road trip. All she could think about was Bud and getting to him as soon as possible.

The picture she saw of Dempsey should have reassured her, it should have made her feel safe, but it didn't. Bud was still out there, and she wouldn't believe he was safe until she saw him with her own eyes and wheeled him out of the facility herself; there was too much at stake. The horror film that rolled behind her eyes was daunting; it warned her of what could happen, it kept tormenting her with the many gruesome possibilities for an ending that would not be in their favor.

She watched, transfixed on the road as the car's headlights danced through the darkness showing the way, bouncing off one reflector at a time as if showing the path to freedom. All she wanted to do was follow that path once Bud was safe; she depended on those lights in the middle of the road to show her the way. They symbolized so many things, like the promise of internal peace and a sign of newfound courage to grasp a new life. Those little beacons would help her and Bud to run as fast and as far as they could into the arms of an actual future devoid of pain. And this very minute, sitting in the back seat driving away from all that she'd endured, she believed they could run, but the hard part would be to find a place to hide from the DuPree's. Reggie had promised protection, and she was placing their lives in her team's hands.

But Dempsey wasn't the only obstacle; Big Daddy would play a part in the many horrible possibilities that could play havoc with ending this madness.

He will not like the embarrassment confronting him when the town finds out what happened to Dempsey at the station and, of course, the fact that she was finally able to get away from his son. He will not tolerate the laughs or disrespect of the townspeople behind his back. He is an evil man hiding behind a giant smile and tons of money.

Big Daddy believes there is nothing he can't buy his way out of, and if by chance money didn't work one day, he would simply remove the obstacle by any means necessary. And unfortunately, any obstacle would be human.

The silence inside the car grew to proportions that suffocated the travelers as they sat nestled between the car doors. Amee felt its weight begin to smother her dark thoughts, making it worse than the waiting at this point. But finally, the road sign she'd been looking for came into view; thank God, she says to herself, only ten more miles to go. Only ten more excruciating miles to sit in panic and wonder what's to come, of what will become of her and Bud. At least they will be able to face it together, which brought her a tad bit of comfort.

"How long has it been since you've seen your father?" Mountain's deep voice crawls through the silence into the back seat.

"The last time I saw him was right after Dempsey rearranged my jaw. With my mouth wired shut and sporting fresh bruises, he took me to see Bud and show off his handy work. That is one of Dempsey's greatest pleasures. He loves to torment Bud by showing him how in control he is of both of us." Her fingers begin to softly apply pressure to her cheek as she tries to remember what it was, she had done the day he decided she needed a tune-up.

It really didn't matter because he constantly introduced what he called 'New House Rule!' And as much as she tried to remember them, there was no way because he would announce more or change the existing ones. When the urge hit him to beat her, his first comment before the act began was; now Amee, did you forget the rules again?

The broken jaw had been the worst she'd received in a couple of months, a lesson for breaking one of the House Rules. But since then, the beatings he delivered hadn't left any broken bones. She smiled to herself as she thought about how hard the man tried to leave her broken physically and emotionally; yes, repeatedly, he tried. But he was never able to destroy the Amee she kept protected, the one that saved a small piece of her soul to regenerate if a day like this one ever came along.

Sitting in the dark confines of the back seat, she reflects on the beginning and how the bruises to her face became an everyday occurrence. Dempsey would tell her to cover that shit up before leaving the house; he didn't want anyone to see her like that. Once, she thought to defy him, thinking, praying, that if she made him look at his handy work, he would feel some remorse, or shame, at least give a half-hearted apology as most wife beaters do. Maybe he would promise it won't happen again, but Dempsey just proved to be the worst case of evil; he didn't feel anything but the need to dominate and cause pain.

Over the years, she not only endured the actions of his rage but could do nothing to stop the grief she felt as her soul continued to be cut away a tiny piece at a time. Small increments torn and ravaged to be discarded and added to her emotional garbage heap with all the others. These past actions leave her to wonder if she will ever be a semblance of her old self, or is she too damaged at this point?

The ting, ting of the bright green blinker brings her out of her questionable thoughts as she finds herself delivered to the man that gave her life. But sadly, the future the man had wanted for her turned out to be only a dream, replaced with a nightmare of physical pain and smashed hopes. The bright future was a distant memory, completely obliterate by evil.

But now, she's being told that could and would change. So, she just needed to fight back and cling to a different future, a bright new future she can envision for herself and Bud, and she will fight like hell to make sure Dempsey doesn't take it away.

"Here we are," Pix says as she slips into the first handy cap parking spot.

Chapter 47

"I'll be right behind ya," Mountain says to Pix, "just need to send the Boss an update."

"Copy that."

> **Mountain:** **Just arrived in Leavenworth heading into facility now.**

> **John: Roger that, they're ready for you. Stay safe!**

> **Mountain: Miss Reggie?"**

> **John: Still enroute, should arrive shortly.**

As Mountain finishes his text with John, Amee and Pix are already halfway to the facility's front entrance. He can see Amee is in the lead with Pix's short legs trying to keep up. Fortunately, it didn't take him long to find himself right on their heels.

Amee pushes through the glass door looking like a wild animal that just escaped its cage and doesn't know what to do or where to go from here. The two people standing behind the reception counter meet her with concerned eyes: it's obvious she's anxious and scared. And they have no idea that Amee feels like letting loose a blood-curdling scream for Bud that would cause ears to bleed for anyone unlucky enough to be standing too close.

Even though Deloris can only imagine what is running through the poor girl's brain, she is at her side instantly. And by doing so, she unknowingly shut down Amee's impulse to scream in terror, waking the dead as if that was even possible. Pix silently moves in on Amee's other side to lend physical and emotional support.

"Where's Bud!?" Amee asks heatedly, not even trying to pull herself together.

"He's in his room waiting for you Honey, he's been briefed by Ax, the gentleman at the front counter. Bud can't wait to see you; he's been so anxious about your safety."

"Take us to his room," Pix says, giving a nod to Mountain letting him know where they were going.

As the three women head down the hall to Bud's room, Mountain hangs back to keep an eye on everything, and it would give him a chance to get a SITREP from Ax. The man is sitting behind the reception desk fiddling with something connected to the computer, and Mountain had to admit he looked like he knew what he was doing.

"Any problems so far?" Mountain asks in a deep whisper, leaning over the counter.

"Just picking up a mild threat so far but can't quite put my finger on it, my Spidey-senses are tingling," he says with a soft laugh, "but don't worry, I'll find it. Marco sent me an audio transcript of Bud's and Reggie's meeting; I listened to it on my drive here. And after discussing the situation with Deloris and Bud, I agree this is the perfect time to pull him. That Sheriff sounds like a chained dog getting close to breaking its tether, or should I say duct tape. Beautiful Mountain, beautiful, I'm like so impressed," Ax says laughing.

"Why, thank you," Mountain says smiling, "it's a gift. And you're right about going forward with the extraction now because I saw that piece of waste in action in the DuPree Police Station; he has no soul. We got there just in time, even though it was after he was able to get a shot off through the cell bars trying to put Suzie down. But as you probably know already, Miss Reggie took the bullet for her. It makes me sick when I picture what could have happened to them. And in my heart, I know we wouldn't have heard from Miss Reggie, Pix, or Suzie again if we hadn't been there!"

"Yes, I heard! Any word on how Reggie is doing now?" he asks as his eyes follow a woman pushing a coffee cart down the hall.

Mountain was just about to respond when he noticed he had lost Ax's attention. Having his large frame turned away from the hall he couldn't see what Ax could. Slowly, Mountain pushes himself off the reception counter to adjust his frame to its full height, because he could feel his own inner alert system start to react.

"Man, what is it?"

"I've seen that woman many times since I got here. She has pushed that coffee cart up and down this hall several times, glancing my way as she passes, but I've never seen her hand out a cup of coffee. My trusted Spidey-senses tell me she's a little too interested in what's going on."

"Roger that," Mountain says, turning, seeing the woman is now on her way back toward them. "Boy, a cup of coffee sounds

262

really good right about now; I hope it's hot," Mountain says loud enough to be heard as he turns and begins walking toward the woman, his look more menacing than usual. The woman stops abruptly, frozen in place, her hands visibly shaking as she watches the big man get closer.

Looking like a deer caught in the headlights of a car, she manages to say, "I'm sorry, Sir, I just ran out," then quickly tries to make a dash for the door, which she learned immediately was just a futile attempt.

Ax moves quickly, coming around the receptionist desk to head her off, getting there just in time to position himself between her and the door.

"Let me pass," the woman says clearly agitated, "I was only doing what he told me to do!"

"And getting paid pretty good to do it I'm guessing!" Mountain says with anger.

"You don't know shit!" she spits out the words in his direction.

"You're coming with us, so you can explain it, how's that sound?" Ax says dragging her by the arm into Deloris's office. Once inside he roughly pushes her into a chair in front of the desk, while Mountain closes the door behind them.

"What's your name?" Mountain demands, standing close, causing her to scoot as far back in her chair as possible. She takes in the man's height and girth, which seems hugely menacing because of her disadvantage of sitting in a chair. But the intimidation the man was trying to portray wasn't working; she had to protect herself, so she didn't respond.

"You're NAME?"

"Listen man, I don't care how big and tough you are, I WILL NOT TELL YOU SHIT!" She's glaring at both men now, her vision beginning to blur as tears of fright escape with a quick blink to run down her face, but these two men are not the ones she's frightened of. Her legs begin to giggle up and down as she sits in the chair wiping her cheeks dry with her sleeve, "you have no idea what he will do to me or my family if I tell you anything."

"Are you the only one passing on Bud's movements to the Sheriff?" Ax asks, getting her attention.

"Probably not, but I don't know," she says with a sad laugh. "All I know is Big Daddy sent me here and told me to report everything about Bud Ainslee to the Sheriff. Now please leave me alone."

A growl from above asks, "Are you saying it isn't the Sheriff who is paying you?"

"Back off Big Guy!" she screams.

"Why?"

"Why what?"

"Why do it?"

"Why," she yells back as if the two men are morons and can't figure out the obvious. "To protect my family, now do what you're going to do because I'm done talking!"

With frustration, Mountain pulls out his cell phone and calls the Boss.

"Go Mountain," John says as he picks up the call.

"Hey Boss, you got that list handy of employees you guys were goin to check out?"

Mountain hears John yell to Marco, "How we doin with that employee list? Any financials looking funny?"

"Two that I have found so far could be possibilities," Marco says and points up at one of the many monitors adorning the walls of the hangar, where he had displayed the information.

"We got a Marcy Picket and a Yvonne Baker," John tells Mountain.

Mountain growls at the woman, "you, Marcy, or Yvonne?"

"I told you," She screams into the room, DONE TALKING!"

Looking up at Mountain, Ax tells him he's got it covered there and waves his hand at the office door. Mountain gives an understanding nod and leaves Ax to follow up with Marcy/Yvonne, the spy.

As Mountain steps out of the office Ax hears him say, "Boss, got some interesting info."

Chapter 48

Mountain feels anxious as he watches Amee come down the hall pushing a wheelchair with an occupant, he can only guess is Bud. Deloris and Pix are bringing up the rear and chatting quietly amongst themselves.

Watching Bud and Amee as she pushes the wheelchair his way, he sees and feels their story as it gets closer. It sits in the man's lap alongside the self-imposed guilt he carries, guarded and exhausted. It screams for hope to come calling, his daughter's nightmare needs to end because she deserves a happy ending.

Standing in the hallway, Mountain acknowledges his anxiety as it settles into his core; he allows its presence and feels it spread like a putrid disease. Yet, his heart wrestles and fights against the disease, pushing it back, allowing only the truth from today's events to scream into his mind relieving most of his unease.

He shakes inwardly as the truth rages, solidifying that what Reggie and Suzie, not to mention Pix, had gone through today was the beginning of a fight for their lives. He imagines what would have happened if they hadn't arrived in time.

He has no doubt their bodies would be lying in a hole beside other unfortunate individuals that didn't figure out in time that they had walked into hell, to eventually vanish like smoke from a campfire into the darkness of the night, never to be seen again. The realization is sad, and he quietly sends up a thank you to the silent guardian they've all had at their backs numerous times. There's no other way to explain their many favorable outcomes, so they accept the shadow of protection. And now that they are privy to the fact Big Daddy is just as involved and dangerous as Dempsey, he has no doubt their silent guardian will have to be more diligent.

He sighs slightly, remembering that both women have sustained injuries in the past while extracting victims. But this one seemed to slap him in the face with its cruel and twisted intentions, and he finally realizes it's because he witnessed it firsthand. Listening to encounters through the coms is gut wrenching, but nothing like watching it play out in front of your eyes. He tries to soothe himself by acknowledging everyone on his team made it out safely, even though they were shot, battered, and bruised. Yeah, that might work.

His only instinct now is to get everyone the hell out of this town and back to the safety of the Club House. Damn he's tired.

Once the group stops in front of Mountain, Pix steps around the wheelchair and begins introductions. "Mountain," she says, "this is Bud." And to Bud she says, "Bud this slab of granite is Mountain." The two men size each other up with interest, which ends with an earnest handshake. "Damn, girlie," Bud says to Pix, "couldn't you find a bigger one?"

"Haven't found one yet!"

Deloris makes her way over to Mountain, saying, "I've followed all of John's instructions to the letter. "I bought the clothes Bud has on just this morning and removed all the tags.

We have switched out wheelchairs as instructed, and he left everything in his room except that picture," she says, pointing at Bud's lap, "I hope that's okay?"

Mountain moves closer to Bud and stretches out his hand, his meaning clear. Bud hands the big man the framed photo of him and Amee and, in no uncertain terms, makes it clear he's taking it with him.

Mountain runs his fingers around the frame; it's nothing special, just your run-of-the-mill frame you could pick up at Ross or a Target store. He flips the picture frame over, looking for anything out of the norm. Next, his fingers brush the back cover, trying to feel a small lump hiding between the picture and back covering. Then his fingers run along the outside of the frame itself, feeling for any niches or splits. He didn't find anything, but they couldn't take a chance that this innocent item could be their downfall; after all, he was taking them back to the Club House; their safety depended on it.

"How attached are you to this frame, Bud?"

"I don't give a shit about the frame, son; it's the picture I won't leave behind!"

With that, Mountain removes the picture from the frame and hands it to Bud, we'll get you a new frame Bud, thank you for understanding.

"What now?" Deloris asks.

Mountain waves in the direction of her office, "Ax will stay as long as needed. He'll be getting updates on any of your employees connected to the Sheriff and Bud, leaving it up to you to deal with them as you see fit. It's more than likely that you will get a dangerous visit from either the Sheriff or Darwin DuPree, but don't worry, Ax is a one-man show; he's got it covered. Thanks again, Deloris, for being there for us," Mountain says, shaking her hand.

"Yes, thank you Deloris," Pix adds.

"Of course, and please give Reggie and Suzie my love and hopes for a speedy recovery."

"I absolutely will."

Mountain turns and waves to Ax while Deloris Takes a few steps away to embrace Bud and give him a good luck goodbye. Then she leans closer to Amee, shakes her hand, and whispers a heartfelt message of, 'be safe.'

"I will; thank you so much for the care you have given Bud; I'm so appreciative."

Pix waves goodbye while opening the door for Amee to push Bud's wheelchair through. Mountain comes up on Pix's side, and each gives their surroundings a thorough inspection. Then, without a word to each other, they know it's safe and carry on.

"I'll get the trunk for Bud's chair," Pix says, "and you find out how he is to transition from the chair to the car? I'm sure there's a method or something."

Mountain heads to Bud and Amee while Pix pops the trunk and begins to shift backpacks, boots, and Reggie's bat out of the way to make room for Bud's chair.

With Pix behind the wheel, Mountain riding shotgun and Amee and Bud in the back seat they begin their journey back to the safety of the Club House. It's time to send the Boss an update.

Mountain: Extraction complete, heading home.

John: Roger that.

Mountain: Reggie and the gang?

John: Pulling in now.

Mountain glances into the back seat, where he sees Amee asleep on Bud's shoulder. It's an exhausting sleep stemming from years of fear, stress, pain, and love. So, sleep Amee, he says to himself, you are safe now.

Chapter 49

"They're at the back gate," Brent, the motor pool manager's baritone voice, booms through the Club House speakers. Its pitch mingles with the whispered concerns of the team members standing vigil, waiting for a chance to see their sisters emerge through the door.

The lights in the Club House had begun their dimmer dance as soon as Dominic informed the team, they were about five minutes out. The lighting sequence slowly went from bright to dim, bright to dim, indicating an incoming trauma. If the injuries had been life-threatening, the light dance would have glared on and off accompanied by a red strobe light followed by an ear-splitting siren. So, there was that to be thankful for, at least.

The medical situation with Reggie and Suzie is emergent but not life-threatening, a blessing for sure. But sadly, the team has seen at times that dedication can ask the ultimate price, and they are about to get a first-hand look, AGAIN, of that price.

John and Matt disregard the gurneys rolling out to the motor pool; they ignore all the warnings Michael and Doc Shoemaker voiced, choosing instead to push forward as if they were back on the battlefield. And in a way, they are. It's a constant reality, an endless hurt that continues to plague them; the proof is in the vehicle that just entered the motor pool.

John's heart, broken and vulnerable, is pounding through his muscled chest as every heavy booted step takes him closer to the

SUV that just stopped abruptly a few feet away. Dominic is out of the vehicle practically before he throws it into park. He runs around to Reggie's side of the car as John reaches for the door handle.

"Doc says she's going to be fine, Boss, through and through."

"I know!" John says and roughly pulls open the car door. There she sits, strapped in tightly, small and battered, her face pale as cream. He gazes down at the reason his life makes sense and begins to tremble with, *what if*. He watches her eyes flutter, ever so slightly, as she reacts to the movement around her.

"Reggie, Baby," John whispers, "I got you; you're home now, you're safe."

Carefully, he reaches over and unlatches the seat belt as he continues to reassure her. She moans as the pressure that was holding her still drops away, and her body shifts in the seat, sending pain through the drug-induced sleep.

"Oh John, it hurts," she manages to say.

"I know, Baby, it's going to for a while, but Dad and the Doc will fix you up." He knows she's no stranger to pain; time and time again, she's endured it on unimaginable levels. She's weathered the storms of rage and violence multiple times, and sadly, he knows, she's not the only one; all victims have lived through some semblance of it.

"How's Suzie? Did she get hit?"

"She's in good hands," he says, looking across the back seat at Xander, receiving an affirmative nod.

The other passenger door opens a second later, and Matt takes charge of Suzie. John reaches in and lifts Reggie from the seat; staying mindful of her shoulder, he carries her into the Club House and heads toward the Med Bay. Matt follows with a whimpering Suzie cradled tenderly to his chest, whispering assurances that she and her Momma would be ok.

Xander grabs his Med bag and slides out of the back seat; he takes off at a run, passing John and Matt with their battered cargo to find Michael and Doc Shoemaker waiting in the Med Bay for the wounded to arrive.

"We're all set, Xander," Michael assures him as he rushes through the door.

"Good, both of them are still stable; I assessed their injuries again right before we came through the outer gate," he reports through halted breaths. His attention shifts to John; he watches the man through the glass walls of the Med Bay carrying Reggie gingerly to deposit her in their care. Then he sees Matt following not far behind, and he turns to the other end of the room to deliver the latest assessment to Doc Shoemaker. "Hey, Shoe," he yells across the brightly lit sterile space, "Suzie is going to need x-rays of her chest and forelimbs. She's very tender, whimpered like crazy when I examined her."

"I'll take care of my patient you take care of yours!" the grizzled vet snaps across the room.

Before Xander can snap back a retort, he feels Michael grab his elbow and turn him around to face him. "Let it go," Michael whispers to the man, feeling Xander's anger as it rumbles through his body. "That old vet loves Suzie, and he's the only one Reggie trusts with her care; we just need to deal with it, for Suzie's sake and Reggie's piece of mind."

"Michael, Pix said that dog threw herself into the cell bars, again and again, trying to get to the Sheriff, she beat herself up beyond the call to protect them."

"Where do you want her?" John says urgently as he makes his way through the door. Michael is by his side in seconds, indicating the empty gurney a few yards to his right at the back of the Bay. The sterile surroundings are daunting to John's eyes, and he's overwhelmed with what the sight indicates, leaving him once again to ask himself; how much is too much?

"Okay, Baby, Dad's here and ready to patch you up." Before being told to leave so they can do their work, John leans down to Reggie's ear and whispers a very heartfelt promise. But, of course, we didn't need to hear that promise, and it wouldn't tax our imaginations in the least to figure out judging by John's ridged stance. "Dad, please,,," John begins to say but is cut off with a hug.

"I know, go now, Reggie and I have been here before," he says and points to the door where he notices for the first time Abby is leaning on the glass wall watching the commotion as it unfolds inside. The people she loves are hurting and all she's got to offer in way of comfort is to be there when, and if they need her. It's been known from the dawn of time, a constant reality, that a mother's job can be the hardest, especially when all she can do is stand back and watch. And Abby has watched in horror as this team has run into danger time after time, and she has prayed for these men and women as they fight every day to make a difference. The nuances of a mother's job are just as important and often harder, especially when all she can do is stand on the sidelines.

Abby watches the medical dance Michael, Xander and the nurses perform flawlessly but it doesn't help her deal with the horror she is seeing. She steps away from the glass and hurries the few steps to the door, catching John in a motherly hug as he emerges, it's all she's got, and she hopes it helps in a small way.

The lighting in the Club House returns to normal and the team members take that as a good sign, feeling confident their team-mates will be patched up to fight another day. Every one of them has no doubt they will see Reggie and Suzie battle back to fight another day when healed. But work must carry on, diligence is still important for the others out in the field and normalcy is what is called for, they need to carry on while they wait for news from the Med Bay.

John hugs his mother holding back the tears that threaten to emerge down his cheeks. He feels comforted by her actions and tells her so. "She'll be okay, Mom," he whispers into her ear and feels the affirmative nod of her head as she agrees in motherly silence. Who was comforting whom at this point?

Abby notices Dominic heading their way and steps back from her son, reluctant to break the physical connection, so she keeps her hand on his arm.

"Boss," Dom says as he comes to a stop a few feet from them, "sorry for the interruption, he says, nodding at Abby." Then, without hesitation, he holds out the mutilated blood-soaked piece of brass and the gun that fired it. He watches John's eyes take on a red rage he hadn't seen since they were overseas.

"Oh, my God," Abby whispers.

John takes the bullet from Dominic's hand and holding it between forefinger and thumb, rolls its sharp, blood-soaked jagged edges back and forth between his fingers while holding the gun with a white-knuckled grip in his other hand.

"I grabbed the gun once the Sheriff dropped it to the ground, with a little help from Mountain, then dug the bullet out of the far wall of the cell once the Doc assessed Reggie and Suzie's injuries. I thought, you know, maybe they will come in handy."

"Thanks, Brother."

Chapter 50

Darwin 'Big Daddy' DuPree stands outside the jail cell as three pathetic specimens begin to stir. His attention, however, isn't focused on them; instead, it's on the back wall where he knows, without a doubt, could indicate trouble for him on so many levels.

He seizes with a fit of familiar anger, one that consumes him when he realizes that once again, he must clean up a result of his son's actions to protect everything previous generations of DuPree's had worked so hard to build. Whoever dug the embedded piece of brass out of the wall also has the weapon that fired it. And that weapon is registered to him.

He doesn't like feeling vulnerable, he needs to wield control over every situation, but right now, he's backed into a corner, blind to the identity of his enemy. But he isn't one to concede to anything; he finds himself working the problem, he will not wait for trouble to come knocking. Instead, he will find it and shut it down, like always. And all he can do is hope he has passed enough money around over the years to make any consequences from his actions, or those of his dumb shit son, go away.

He hears a pitiful whimper from the floor at his feet and looks down at his son. He tries to figure out for the hundredth time how he could have produced this witless pile of waste and comes to the same conclusion as always, the boy's mother is to blame. For generations, DuPree's had produced strong, intelligent specimens, that is, until this one.

He never forgave his late wife for her failure, the son that carries his name is insulting and embarrassing, and he reprimands himself for choosing weak stock when he married. And by the time he realized he couldn't beat the DuPree genes into his boy, no matter how often and imaginative the trying, there was no fixing the damage she had caused; that's when he decided the boy's momma had to go.

Dempsey begins to wake somewhat and tries to release himself from the duct tape bindings holding his wrists to the bars of the cell. He screams behind the barrier taped across his mouth and fights even more when he can't move his head. His eyes continue to grow to the point of popping out of his head as he sits shackled and immobile, enduring the disappointing hatred of Big Daddy, standing there like his judge, the whole damn jury, and worst of all, his executioner.

"Boy!" Big Daddy booms into the room, "you are like a boil on my ass needing lancing. You carry cancer bent on destroying this family and its name!"

"You hear me, Boy?" Darwin yells to the heavens; his chest is heavy with contempt for what lays at his feet and the woman that produced it; she had no right to fail him like this. What she left for him to deal with is pathetic and embarrassing to him personally. Looking back on the generations of fathers before him, he can't help but feel their judgment, for none of them produced sons with demented proclivities such as these.

Big Daddy's hatred for being saddled with this boy continues to bounce off the walls of the jail. It grows with contempt, filling every square inch of space, even burrowing its way into the cracks

278

in the concrete floor after mingling with the blood evidence that could take them down.

Deputy Woodard stirs, slowly coming around to the booming of Big Daddy's rantings. Then, as the reality of the situation sets in, he immediately soils himself right there, trussed up like a thanksgiving turkey replacing the aroma of stuffing with the smell of a putrid side dish.

Deputy Tack remains still; too bad he's missing the, what did they call it? a lockup party?

Big Daddy leans down and, with one big hand, roughly removes the tape from his son's mouth. "Who was it, Boy!?"

Struggling against his bindings, Dempsey looks up at his father with the expectation that he will be cut loose, but Big Daddy only towers over him, waiting for some answers.

"Cut me loose, BD," he demands with all the humiliating courage he could muster. He continues straining against the tape, growing angrier with every second his father doesn't make a move.

"Now!" Dempsey screams.

"You're gunna want to check that mouth, Boy. Did you forget who you're talkin to?"

Dempsey can only sit immobile while his father's eyes roam the room, and then the other two worthless maggots taped up next to him. But with Dempsey's head secured tightly to the bars of the cell; he can only follow the man's gaze so far.

Instead of cutting his son loose, Big Daddy heads to the door of the adjoining front office, making his way to the reception area where he grabs one of the hard plastic chairs used for visitors. He mutters obscenities into the room and slams the chair into the counter with frustration hard enough to send a tingling sensation up his arm.

But he does not allow himself to falter in his madness as he performs the same act of violence with the chair on the door frame before throwing it into the room, following like a panther after its prey. The rage is building; it's feeding on years of disappointment and disgust, leaving him to wonder why the years of punishment. His mind is swimming with resentment, pushing him to ask how much longer am I expected to carry this burden?

Big Daddy retrieves the chair and deliberately places its legs over Dempsey's taped ankles.

"What the hell, BD?"

"Boy, every time I think you have tripped the dumbass meter to the top, you manage to start all over again at the bottom!"

"But,,," Dempsey tries.

"SHUT THE HELL UP BOY!"

Big Daddy is so angry the veins in his temples are bulging and throbbing to the beat of his high blood pressure. His bulbous and veined alcoholic nose and cheeks red from the drink are only inches from Dempsey's face.

"I'm going to ask you one more time you Dip Shit, WHO WAS IT?"

Dempsey does the best he can against the fear slamming into his chest, "I don't know who they were; I've never seen them before," he says, squirming under the scrutiny of his father. "One guy was huge, built like a cement truck, and the other two were definitely ex-military or something."

At this point, Dempsey's forehead is dripping sweat profusely, the reaction stemming from the look on his father's face. His eyelids blink rapidly as they try to dispel the salt dripping off his lashes into his eyes, and his legs are cramping from the cold cement floor as it hungrily leaches the heat out his body.

"And tell me exactly why the cement truck and ex-military ascended on my Police Station?" Big Daddy knew the answer of course but wanted to see his burden squirm.

"I DON'T KNOW!" Dempsey cries weakly, trying to sound confused.

"Don't you lie to me; you DEMENTED SHIT HEAD!"

"When you didn't make it to the diner for dinner, I went ahead and ordered without you. Then those two tow truck clowns came in and couldn't wait to tell anyone who would listen that the Sheriff was at it again. They said you had two women in there and planning on having some fun, and they all knew what that meant. Now how do you think I felt sitting there with my Tuesday night meatloaf special in front of me with all the diner's eyes on my back?"

"Those two idiots," Dempsey chokes on his bad luck.

"News flash, Boy, those aren't the only idiots. Are ya feelin me? Because of you, once again, I'm a laughingstock. But mark my words Boy; everyone who lives in this town will be reminded of who owns it, and them, even if I have to use you as an example!"

Big Daddy continues to glare at his son as he assesses the tape confining him, and weirdly the predicament gives him some twisted pleasure. He lifts his considerable bulk from the chair and pulls it from Dempsey's legs before heading to the door.

"BD, God damn it, cut us lose!"

He laughs at his son and looks at the other two idiots, "maybe between the three of ya there's enough brain matter to formulate a plan to free yourselves, if not, sleep well. That is if you can with the stink and all," he says looking at Deputy Woodard. At the door, he pauses for effect before delivering one last message. "By the way, while you were busy here," Darwin says sarcastically pointing at the mayhem around him, "your wife ran off with some new friends to collect her daddy from Leavenworth."

"She did what?" Dempsey screams at his father as the door slams shut.

Chapter 51

The glass barrier surrounding the Med Center teases the uninjured as it gives them a glimpse of what is happening on the other side. Michael and Xander, along with two trusted nurses, work diligently on Reggie, their hands moving and flowing, no words necessary as they have worked together many times. Across the room, Suzie lays immobile as the vet shaves hair from a hind leg to insert an IV; they won't know the extent of her injuries until x-rays are taken and scrutinized.

As he watches through the glass walls, John internally vows that his team will continue a slow and precise culling of the evil they chase, fueled by the knowledge that they will never be able to dismiss the hatred scratching on their souls. The itch pushes them forward, making them stronger so they can endure nights like this one.

He knows without turning from the scene he is witnessing through the glass that his mother, Matt, and anyone else not immediately on duty will stand vigil alongside him for as long as he needs. So, he allows his mind to wander, running amuck with hatred, seeking some explanation for this violence. But like all the other times he has reached for any reason for the madness, he finds himself right back where he started, his hands tied and feeling helpless.

His mother's touch is warm on his back; she runs her delicate hand up and down, whispering encouragement, reminding him

Reggie is strong and stable. He looks down into her angelic face, doing his best to acknowledge the motivation behind her words. His head nods in agreement on the outside, but he finds himself ashamed of his dark thoughts. They seem to gather like moths to a flame where their constant presence is allowed to burrow into his resolve. He knows that he's become damaged in so many ways over the years. He can only assume they all have from their choice of vocation.

He fears that if his mother could read his thoughts, he would witness unbelievable horror crack her porcelain features, leaving him to die a little inside as she shrank from his presence, pulling her love from his world.

After all, how could she love him when he relishes thoughts of Dempsey, still alive, laid out on a cold steel table to be dissected in hopes of finding the evil to confront it and hopefully destroy it? He longs to hear the screams of agony as the evil fights the slow, agonizingly painful process of extraction.

He envisions the methodical act, wishing it were his hands plunged into the body savagely searching for evil, and the more vicious and painful he could make it suited him just fine. Then after numerous amounts of splicing and dicing, specimen jars would be filled and sent for screening in hopes of finding some answers. But he knew the answers would never come, and the team would have to continue its fight blinded by evil.

His thoughts are exhausting, and his body is ready to fall, but his determination to be there for Reggie wins out. He can't take his eyes off the room; this is their life now when she cries, he cries; when she bleeds, he bleeds. They share a painful connection at times, but one that holds the other up; he believes she's his better half. He was lost before she came into his life, riding on his military career and the recognition he earned because of it. He was floundering in a sea of unknowns, looking for something just out of his reach, and praying he'd recognize it when he found it. And once she came into his life, it all began to make sense, and he began to breathe, to live.

John catches his father's eye through the glass, just for a second, but long enough to relay encouragement and put his worries at ease, somewhat.

He feels a tap on his shoulder, acknowledges it, but doesn't pull his attention from the scene behind the glass. "Boss," Marco whispers, "Mountain and Pix are about 5 miles out, thought you'd want to meet them."

"I've got it Boss," Matt says.

"Appreciated, thank you," he says as Matt heads to the back gate through the motor pool.

Relief.

Finally, he feels a semblance of relief flooding his chest when he sees his father and Xander step away from the table and remove their surgical gloves.

Each one gives final instructions to the nurses for the care needed moving forward.

She looks so tiny lying in the middle of the table, surrounded by bloody gauze and sheets draped across her torso painted with crimson artwork. How much more is she expected to take, he asks himself.

His father comes through the door first and his mother is instantly by his side, waiting for details. "She's stable, and the loss of blood was minimal, thanks to Xander," Michael indicates with a nod of his head toward the man. "She's going to be fine, I promise Son," he says moving closer to lay a comforting hand on his son's shoulder.

"Thank God," John says, bending at the waist, placing his hands on his knees with relief.

"Did Doc Shoemaker tell you anything about Suzie's condition?" Abby asks, peering through the glass wall at the other table where the lady in question is still lying motionless. "She'll be Reggie's main concern when she wakes."

"That old goat isn't going to tell us anything," Xander says hotly.

"He's sure as hell going to tell me!" John says as he heads to the door, consumed with determination to get some answers. He's fueled with anger at the fact both his girls were damaged on the front lines, *again*, and knowing himself so well, he won't be able to deal with it until he knows Suzie's condition.

"No, John," his mother says, pulling on his arm to stop him, "I'll go talk to him; you need to calm down."

"Fine," John relents, can I go in and see my girl?"

"Good idea, it will give you a chance to pull it together, but all you can do is sit with her because she'll be out for a while yet," Xander says.

Michael and Xander watch Abby enter the room ahead of her son. She makes her way to the far corner where Suzie and Doc Shoemaker are, and John heads toward Reggie's bed.

"I hope she can get something out of him," Xander says harshly, turning to Michael. "She has her ways; watch and learn."

Abby makes her way to the table Suzie is lying on; she watches her fury chest continue to rise and fall, the multi-colors of her coat rippling with each breath. She suddenly realizes it's become hard for her to breathe; the day's events have begun to weigh heavy on her shoulders, just like the rest of the team. She reaches out tentatively to pet the top of Suzie's head, whispering so softly only she can hear the words. This beautiful canine stands at the heart of Mickey; she's gone over the top with her selfless actions in the field and the Club House. And Abby finds herself wiping a stray tear from her cheek as she waits for Doc Shoemaker to say something.

"Jesus Carl," she says to the Vet's back when he doesn't acknowledge her, "can't you find some compassion for the humans that love this team member? Give us something at least!"

"Not now!" his voice, gravely from years of smoking, is projected to his patient because he still has his back to her.

"YES, NOW! Abby spits to his back; you will tell me something on her condition, right God Damn now!"

When Matt opens the door of the Med Bay to get John's attention, he's surprised to hear Abby so worked up over in the corner, and even more so when he sees her grab onto Doc Shoemaker's arm and roughly spin him around to face her. Abby's voice is stern and leaves no misunderstanding of what she expects. "Listen, Suzie is not only a member of this team, but she's also my family, so pull your head out of your ass and give me something!"

Nice, he thinks to himself before he whispers, "Boss, they're here, pulling into the motor pool now."

"Take care of it, Matt," John instructs, "I'll be out in a few."

"Copy that."

After Matt leaves, John finds he's lacking in energy, and now, all he can manage to do is lay his head on the bed next to Reggie's still body. He takes her hand in his and feels his relief pulling him down to a place where the only thing that matters is this short amount of time where he can be thankful that her injuries weren't any worse. He lifts his head slightly, peering over Reggie's body, and is comforted by the strength he sees in his mother as she delivers her rath onto the Vet.

"Holy crap," Xander says when he witnesses the interaction between Abby and the Vet, "I had no idea."

"Welcome to my world Buddy" Michael says with admiration as he looks at his wife with her finger poking into Doc Shoemaker's chest once, twice, thrice.

"Suzie has a severely bruised breastbone and chest muscles, two cracked ribs, not to mention the deep laceration to her cheek that I would be stitching up now if I wasn't being interrupted."

"Poor baby," Abby softly says as she strokes Suzie's head.

"Yes, poor baby.

If that's all, can I get back to work now?"

"Of course! And thank you for your stellar bedside manner," she says sarcastically while turning to leave, suddenly realizing she agrees with Xander; the Doc is an ass.

Chapter 52

Matt is the first to greet the members of the second extraction of the day, team members, and victims. He heads to the driver's side door and pulls it open with relief and so many other emotions that seem to be flooding him physically and emotionally. Pix climbs from behind the wheel, falling into him with deep feelings of her own, stemming from memories of a past extraction.

About two years ago, when Pix had just joined the team, the extraction they were performing ended with Matt carrying Pix's bloody body, from stab wounds, into the Med Bay. Covered in her blood, Matt found himself reeling and debilitated with self-imposed failure. He was just a couple of minutes too late to protect her from the abuser they were trailing, and even after all this time, the guilt still stings. Nevertheless, he remained by her side through every minute of her recovery, and they became close and have been inseparable ever since.

"I'm fine," she whispers, trying her best not to fall apart in front of him, but knowing if she did, he would calm her down in a way she wouldn't feel weak. "I won't lie though it was some heavy shit those maniacs had planned for us. Thank God the cavalry arrived when it did."

"Are you sure you're, okay?" he asks, holding her close.

"I am now, so how was *'your'* day Dear?"

Matt only laughs saying, "oh you know, same old, same old."

Mountain is at the back of the car with the trunk open, pulling Bud's wheelchair out from among the go bags, Reggie's bat, and the hiking gear. Lifting it effortlessly, he unfolds the chair and pushes it around to the passenger door, where Bud is waiting for the big man to lift him out and place him in it easily.

Pix breaks away from Matt and makes her way over to Amee. She towers over Bud in his chair and looks tiny next to Mountain, at her side. "It's almost over, Amee," she says, "you and Bud are safe here."

Matt steps forward slowly and introduces himself. He and the other men on the team have learned that victims when finally rescued from an abusive man, are very cautious of men in general, at least at this point. And because of this, Matt finds himself working hard to show them there are still good men out there and hopes they can eventually believe it.

Amee stands behind her father's chair and looks like a doe caught in a car's headlights. She's battered and broken, with her hands clutching the handles on Bud's chair for support. She's shacky, that's obvious, and Matt doesn't think she's even blinked; the only sign that she's not frozen in place is when she lifts a hand to touch her cheek and begins moving her jaw back and forth. Her husband had broken it months ago, just another warning to stay in line or her father would pay. He watches her jaw move and her fingers massage her cheek, then lets his eyes wander down to her ankle, where she sports a hideous plastic brace encompassing the results of another cruel act. But there's something else to this woman, it's obvious she's had enough, and the look she gives her father is one of love, the pain just an afterthought because she could and would endure much more for his safety.

Matt reaches out his hand, and she takes it in a confident grip, "nice to meet you, Matt, and thank you so much; my father and I are beyond grateful."

"How's it goin, Brother?" Mountain asks Matt as he steps forward and grasps him in a man hug, which looks hysterical because Matt is only 5'10" compared to Mountain's towering presence.

Mountain turns with a huge grin, "Father Bud, this is Matt."

"Are you the Boss Man Mountain keeps talking about?"

"Not even close, Bud; it's nice to meet you," Matt says as they shake hands.

Bud whistles from his chair, "this is some operation you guys got going here."

"Well, let's get inside so you can see the rest. Then, after a quick look around, we'll get you settled in," Matt says.

As they move toward the Club House, Amee asks, "how are Reggie and her dog? Please tell me they're alright!"

The atmosphere stills around them, but Matt keeps pushing forward as if he can run away from the question.

"Matt," Mountain says, "the lady asked you a question," and we'd all like to know the answer, Brother."

Matt stops at the entrance to the Club House and turns around to face them, "I don't know for sure; let's find the Doc for an update." After making eye contact with each of them and holding onto Pix's hand, they enter what looks like, to Amee and Bud, a bridge to one of the fleets attached to Star Trek command. And if you asked the team members their thoughts, they would say it's their Enterprise, and they wouldn't be surprised if Captain Kirk asked to take the helm and go for a joy ride. Numerous workstations sat in a circle sporting multiple high-tech monitors varying in size, with personnel sitting in front of each. The stations consist of different categories and responsibilities, each buzzing with background noise and conversation. Still, there was a semblance of order if one looked close enough, they all had a specific job, and it looked like they did it well.

"This is incredible, just incredible!" Amee whispers to Pix.

"Yes, it is. We can do so much good from this place. We're very proud of what we've built and how many people, like yourselves, we've helped."

As they make their way through the heart of Mickey, faces turn and smile, nodding a welcome, trying to give the newcomers a sense of safety. There are large wall-mounted monitors spaced around the heart of the Club House, each one displaying the outside chain link fencing with entrances and exits. There are no guards on the gates, well, none that can be seen anyway, because that would draw unwanted and dangerous attention. The looks of disbelief on Amee's and Bud's faces matched the initial reaction of all the victims that came before them, the unfortunate ones who sadly needed a place like this.

Amee and Bud are still riding on a high of disbelief, but for Matt, the atmosphere seems to still as he looks across the room. He can see the small huddle of people standing outside the door to the Med Bay, so he makes a correction and heads for it. Then, as if one, all his followers trail behind with Bud and Amee bringing up the rear, still in awe of their surroundings.

John steps out the door reluctantly to join the others.

"What did Doc Shoemaker tell you Mom?"

Sighing and still royally agitated from her exchange with the Vet, Abby relays what he told her. "He says she has bruising to her chest muscles and breastbone; two cracked ribs and he's stitching up her cheek now! I'm sorry I couldn't get more, and I agree with you, Xander, that man is such an ass, and I could smell liquor on his breath. Oh, and he mumbled something about not being able to work in these conditions. As if."

Listening to his mother, John becomes aware of how connected he, Reggie, and Suzie are. He and Reggie share bullet holes to the shoulder, and she and Suzie share scars on their faces. To him, the very definition of a family unit means the three of them share a soul. When one of them is wounded, they're all wounded; each of them feels the pain as if it were their own. And when one of them bleeds, the other two wish they could replenish it with the elixir pumping through their hearts. Their family dynamic is definitely unusual, but it's one neither of them would pass on.

He's brought out of his thoughts when Matt and the others approach; Matt looks past all the concerned faces and focuses the Med Bay, "everyone wants, no, everyone needs to know how they're doing,"

Xander and Michael relay Reggie's condition, leaving Suzie's status up to Abby to deliver since she was the one who talked to the Vet. After the update eased everyone's immediate fears and questions were asked and answered, Mountain takes it upon himself to introduce Amee and Bud.

Amee steps forward and extends her hand to everyone in the group as Mountain introduces them. Their gestures of welcome and promises of safety are written all over their faces. She immediately recognizes John's voice as the man she conversed with over the phone, and she can't help herself; she grabs his hand again.

"I can't, we can't," the words won't come; she's suddenly numb and confused as she tries to speak, her mind engulfed in a dense fog, and her voice has suddenly taken an emotional vacation. Then, taking a deep breath, she tries again, "I can't thank you enough for what you've done for us, and the sacrifices made to get us out," she says, looking past the small crowd to peer into the Med Bay as Matt had done. "I'm so, so sorry for what happened!"

"You're welcome, Amee, and it's good to meet you both."

"So, you're the Boss Man," Bud states, "I can see that; you wear it well, young man."

"Thank you, Sir."

John instantly likes the man and has no doubt, even after just meeting him, that the chair won't slow him down a bit now that he can make his own decisions.

Abby steps forward and begins welcoming them to the Club House; she touches Amee's arm and asks her if they are ready to be settled in. "Tonight, you both will try and relax if you can.

We've got comfortable and safe accommodations in the Bunk House," she says, pointing to the other side of the hangar. "You can shower if you want, and we have a supply of clothing in every size and style you can imagine; just take what you need."

Once Abby leads them into the Bunk House, she gives them the tour. "This is John and Reggie's quarters," she says, pointing to the room as they pass it. There is another room on the other end with a shower, but only one bed. I'll let the two of you decide on that, and for the one who draws the short straw, he, or she, can pick one of these bunks. There are additional showers just over there and stocked with everything you may need. But if there's something else you need, all you need to do is ask.

"What is it, Honey?" Abby asks when she realizes Amee has stopped following her through the Bunk House.

"He'll find us, I know it! Please promise me that no matter what happens to me, you will keep Bud safe!"

"Amellia, stop talking like that, we are safe here. These people know their stuff and we'll be just fine!" Bud says harshly, hoping he can get his daughter to start thinking about a future of happiness, not a future of more pain. They just need to do exactly what this team tells them to and wait for Dempsey and Big Daddy to be dealt with. Over the years, he has envisioned deadly scenarios in which he has taken out the two men with his own hands, but looking at this operation, he's sure his ideas are mild in comparison.

"Seriously, look at us Bud, we couldn't be more broken," she says with her fingers on her cheek, massaging it intently with small circles. "How am I supposed to believe we will ever be safe?"

"Amee," Abby says softly, touching her shoulder, "we've done our homework on your husband, his father, and the town. We know how dangerous your husband is and who Darwin has in his pocket. I admit there is still some info to glean, but I'm confident this will be over soon. So now come with me and get some rest, we will talk in the morning. And after we talk, there's a friend, a team member; I would like you to speak with, if you agree.

Her name is Harley; she's a women's advocate and psychologist. She counsels victims of every degree of Domestic Violence, and she does it very well because she's stood in your shoes. We helped her escape a dangerous situation, and when the extraction was complete, she joined our team. You can speak to her, or not, your choice. But you'll find she's a straight talker and a great listener. Sometimes, that's all a person needs, a good listener."

The tears begin to fall, and they won't stop. They flow down Amee's cheeks in thick rapids as if rushing on an endless river, being pushed over the obstacles of her life like boulders beneath the flow. And just like the river flows toward its ocean, Amee's tears travel their own way, bypassing the cuts and curves of the flow, cleansing their way toward a different destination. Not realizing it yet, because she's still too raw, the destination will be safe, and she'll eventually be strong enough to move forward. But the emotional fear and physical pain she's lived with for so long continues to fight against the current of tears. It begins forming a protective barrier to keep her guarded and unsure of what's to come. He's done this to her, and she feels dead inside.

"I can't let myself believe we're safe; there's too much at stake. I want to believe you can stop Dempsey and Darwin," she says, hiccupping and wiping her nose. "But I've lived in their darkness for so long my head tells me this will only end badly. Dempsey won't stop because his father will see my leaving as his son's weakness, and he will not be humiliated. It won't be over until Dempsey drags me out of here by my hair with all of you watching just to save face in his father's eyes."

"Amellia girl let's get some rest now; you are so strong; you've been so strong to keep me taken care of and safe; now it's your turn to let someone keep you safe. Please try to believe we will get out, please for me because I have sat back long enough watching you be battered and bruised for my safety. I can't; I won't do it anymore!"

Chapter 53

She knows where she is; her shoulder reminds her with biting pain every time she moves. Her eyelids feel heavy with grit, and she contemplates the action of sitting up and planting her feet firmly on the floor, but a hazy thought is as far as she gets, there will be no feet planting. Then, glancing at the bedside table, she sees a bottle of water and a vile of pain pills; she hates the damn things but has learned it's like asking for help. You may not always need it, but it's nice to know it's there if you do.

"Miss Reggie, can I get you anything?" Oscar-D asks from the doorway of hers and John's quarters.

"Nope, got everything I need in this little bottle right here," she says, rattling the pills inside the container for effect. She's propped up on three pillows, trying to get comfortable from the pain in her shoulder and the awkward position the sling is causing her to hold her arm.

She lifts the water bottle and tries to twist the cap off but finds it more challenging than it should be. "Let me get that for you," Oscar-D says. He walks to the bed, takes the bottle from her hand, twists the cap, then takes the pain meds from her other hand and does the same thing. He begins to dump a few pills into his hand but decides to read the label first. Two, okay.

He watches her put the medication into her mouth and take a drink from the bottle. She hands him the bottle so he can replace the cap and sighs; she must admit that as much as she dislikes taking medication, she knows all will be right in her world in a few. Just a little help.

"You can sit for a bit," she says to Oscar-D patting the bed beside her, "I don't bite."

"Ah, I know but I don't think the Boss would like me sitting on his bed next to his girl."

"Holy crap, I think the meds just kicked in, did you say *his girl?*"

"Well both his girls," he says pointing at Suzie who is bandaged up just like Reggie, laying with her head in Reggie's lap, cradling a fresh baby. Sensing she's being talked about Suzie slowly lifts her head and gives a pitiful whine. The young man tries to explain his reluctance but finds himself stammering from embarrassment and can feel his face turning all kinds of red. "Damn, I wish there was a chair in here or something to sit on besides the bed. I just got released by the Doc and Michael to full duty and would like to keep that status if you don't mind. Broken bones, not to mention all that blood would no doubt cause me a setback, JEEZ."

"You're so cute."

"It's the meds, right?"

"Yep."

"I'll take the compliment anyway, get some rest you two," he says turning to the door, feeling confident he has skirted around any acts of dismemberment from the Boss, and smiles.

300

Time marched on after Oscar-D's visit, the pain medication doing its trick, allowing Reggie to get some rest. She finds herself slowly crawling out of a sleepy fog, and as her mind becomes clear, she immediately reaches out to Suzie to snuggle her close. "How's my Suz doin? Did you get some rest?" The soft snort from Suzie's cold nose brings tears to Reggie's eyes, and she feels her heart swell with love. She couldn't remember much of what happened because she had mentally checked out for a bit, but she does remember the fear-driven instinct to protect Suzie that threw her in front of the bullet. When Pix tried to lead her down the path of events, she was so high on meds that every piece of information felt like pieces from a million different puzzles, none interlocking correctly. The picture just wouldn't come together.

Reggie looks at Suzie's face full of stitches and sympathizes with her as she struggles in discomfort to lift her head and plant a soft lick across Reggie's cheek. She knew the length of the sacrifice Suzie would have given to protect her, she would have given her life in a selfless act of protection and love, which is exactly what Reggie almost accomplished in return.

"Will we ever see an end, Suz?"

"Does she ever answer you?" the voice asks from the doorway.

"In her own way, yes."

Reggie sees Amee standing in the doorway with an empty wheelchair. She looks tired and worn to the bone, and it hurts that she has seen it so many times she recognizes the signs. There's been hundreds before her and will unfortunately be just as many behind. It will take time for her to regain her inner strength and stand tall once again. This woman took care of business for a long time, she wears the scars to prove it and can't mask the look of mistrust she carries, the barriers she has been forced to build are too strong. She can't instantly knock them down just because a group of people tell her she's safe, how could she? Amee has suddenly been thrown into a world so far-fetched, in her eyes, she's afraid to allow the possibility to be believable, her top priority is, and will always be, Bud.

Reggie has seen victims fight the possibility of a safe life multiple times; the idea washes over them in heavy waves as they wait for the darkness on two legs to rear its rage and eventually find them. They can feel the holder of their old life as he searches and tracks, as he slithers in and out, seeking what he lost as if it's a dog that became unchained and broke through the backyard fence. Each victim knows that if the inevitable comes knocking and she is reclaimed like a piece of property, there will be more pain, demoralizing acts, and threats will be delivered with intense cruelty. There's no room for trust after that.

Fear is their constant companion, but it's why they're still alive. It won't be able to stop the procession back to the yard and chain from which they escaped, but they will still exist. And they know that now, because of their escape, the chain will be bigger and heavier, and the threats more promising. They can only hope that their constant companion will still be by their side, encompassing their body and soul with its protection.

Without living it or understanding how it can happen, no one can comprehend what it feels like to have someone in complete control of your life. He uses the fear he's instilled in you, feeding it by promising physical harm to you or a loved one; threats are the weapons of choice, and he relishes the idea of turning them into reality. So often a victim finds herself inundated with constant threats against loved ones and begins to push her family and friends out of her life, giving him the control he's worked so hard to achieve. It doesn't happen all at once; no, it's a slow, sneaky process, one that, by the time it's realized, any connection there was with anyone other than him is destroyed.

But Amee is consumed by something else and will explore it further once she can believe that the team can deliver on their promises for Bud's safety. Once that fear no longer rules her actions, she doesn't care if Dempsey finds her; in fact, she wants him to find her so she will be free to seek *revenge.* But the girl doesn't realize that no matter how sweet the revenge would feel when executed, the thrill of the act is short-lived; it won't heal the broken pieces of her soul. She won't suddenly be able to smile and laugh, go day to day as if the life she had been living will fade and the darkness encompassing her battered self will release her. Sadly, real revenge doesn't work that way. The team's job is to save her from acting on her need for revenge, and they'll do that by taking it on for her. They will deliver a devastating message to Dempsey that will allow her to look ahead with promise, and not be hindered by acts of vengeance. Because if Amee takes matters into her own hands, most likely she'll become too emotionally damaged to move forward and chase the promise of a future, because it will always be out of reach. She'll feel the pain from her broken soul, and the fear that she has become a monster will block any chance of a normal life. Reggie knows how it goes, she's been on both sides, and she'll do everything she can to spare Amee the endless miles of that dark road.

Reggie gives Suzie a loving squeeze as her thoughts of Amee's future drift off with some of her already depleted energy. "So, where'd you dump Bud?" she asks with a sleepy laugh pointing at the wheelchair.

Chapter 54

Amee pushes the empty chair into the room and parks it next to Reggie's bed. Forcing a laugh, she obviously doesn't feel, she says, "this isn't Bud's, it's yours. Doctor's orders, it's time to get out of that bed for a bit."

"I can walk you know!"

"He told me you'd say that, but you can't while on the pain meds, they're pretty strong," knowledge they share because they've both been here before.

"But I can't leave Suzie alone, look at the poor thing," Reggie says above Suzie's head where it's cradled in her lap.

"He said you'd say that also, so I brought a sitter, Bud." And right on cue Bud's chair wheels through the door.

"Suzie and I will be just fine, I borrowed this book from the kid out there and am looking forward to it, I haven't been able to concentrate on a good book for a long time." Bud holds up the book so Reggie can read the title.

"Laughing Reggie says, "You better be prepared to be quizzed on that Bud, Oscar-D will be all kinds of disappointed if you don't really get into it, he loves all the Clive Cussler books."

"He pretty much said as much, now off with you two."

"Wait, is that a Dirk Pitt or an Oregon Files adventure?"

"Dirk Pitt."

"Those are good," Reggie says looking up at Amee and letting out a resigned breath. With one last look at Bud, she gently repositions Suzie's head on John's pillow, then lifts the covers off her legs and swings them over the side of the bed. "And by he I'm guessing you mean John!"

He was one of them, but I was given instructions, no I guess you'd call them warnings, by everyone out there on what to expect from you. You know, I don't see it. I mean you don't look that scary to me."

"That's because I'm on meds, I'm not always this docile."

"Duly noted."

As Amee pushes the chair out the door Reggie looks back at the bed, and she is comforted by what she sees. Bud had wheeled his chair next to the bed and held one of Suzie's outstretched paws with one hand and his book in the other. I wonder if he'll read to her, she thinks to herself wearing a dreamy smile.

Amee wheels Reggie through the Club House with every team member acknowledging her presence and wishing her well; they're thankful for the reassurance that one of their leaders is on the mend.

"Do you mind if we go into the kitchen for a few minutes to talk? Then, we can finish the rounds after if you're still feeling up to it."

"Sure, but remember I'm on drugs, so if you're going to ask for any advice, you might want to take it as possible crap."

Amee parks Reggie's chair next to the small kitchen table and pulls out one of the chairs for herself.

306

"Abby wants me to talk to a woman named Harley; what do you think, should I?"

"Absolutely! And as soon as my head clears a little more, I'll also be talking to her."

"What am I supposed to say to her? I mean, is she going to expect me to tell her all the dark, gory details of my life with that man. What he did to Bud and me, how cruel he was?"

"Amee, this woman has been there; all she's going to do is start a conversation and let you take it where you want. The last thing she's going to do is push you, I encourage you to think about it.

"Well, that's the thing; all I want to do is voice all the gory details of hurt I want to do to that man."

"I want him to disappear in the darkest, cruelest way possible. What will she think of me when she hears shit like that?" Amee's fist hits the table in front of her, and she is immediately appalled at herself for acting out, causing heads to turn in their direction from the Club House.

Thinking she should be ashamed of her thoughts and actions she realizes she can't, it's like she's still trapped under his thumb with him telling her what to think and feel. She can't sit still any longer and quickly stands, the action sending her chair reluctantly across the tile floor, making a sharp scraping sound. Then, with her fists clenched tight at her sides, she begins to pace, back and forth, back, and forth. Then suddenly she stops in front of Reggie's chair and whispers into the space between them, "I want him to bleed!!! I want him to bleed until the evil he carries inside seeps into the ground!" Then, with her eyes locked with Reggie's, she lowers her head to within inches of her face to relay the rest of her wish for her husband, "I want him dead, Reggie!"

Reggie's sorrow for this woman is indescribable; her heart screams with memories of her own past, her emotional pain of wanting revenge was this epic, and all she can wish for at this moment is to save Amee from her self-imposed destruction. Can they do it? They sure as hell will try.

The commotion in the kitchen doesn't surprise or catch the team members in the Club House off guard. They've come to expect and accept these outbursts because, unfortunately, they've seen them so many times. And, like so many before her, Amee is dancing on the edge of raw emotion. She's trying to find her rhythm, and until she finds it, her future is still out of reach.

Reggie begins to speak softly, placing her fingers gingerly around Amee's upper arm, "go pick up the chair and have a seat." When Amee is seated once again at the table, Reggie begins.

"Believe me, I've been there; I was this close," she says, holding her thumb and forefinger so close together it was hard for air to pass through the opening. "I've got a story to share about revenge and the emotional and physical consequences one can endure because of it."

Reggie zeros in on Mountain, pointing out to the Club House, "you've met that gentle giant, right?"

"Yes, he helped me and Bud escape. He seems like a nice guy."

"You have no idea," Reggie says. She had no qualms about sharing Mountain's story because he insisted everyone knew it before he agreed to join the team. "Mountain and I were on our way to send a message to an abuser; we had just completed a risky extraction of his wife Clarissa from the hospital. Michael believed, and the team concurred, after acquiring her medical history from multiple hospitals around the area, that each incident was getting worse; it meant her husband was escalating. Because of what we had seen and dealt with in the past, we believed that she was running out of time.

During my initial contact and the other interactions with her, I slowly began to see multiple correlations between my abuser and hers. Don't get me wrong, there are always similar likenesses between the cases we take on, but this one kept scratching on the fact that I didn't get the chance to wield my hatred to end him myself. Ironically, the piece of crap did it himself, subsequently robbing me of my justice. Long story short, the universe took care of my problem when it saw he was driving drunk and decided to help him park his truck around a telephone pole. For the longest time, I felt cheated and believed that was one of the reasons I couldn't move on."

"Anyway," Reggie says, turning her head back in Mountain's direction, "Mountain was a merchant marine, and as you know, they are out to sea for long periods of time. His only family was his sister, and he began to notice less and less communication between them, but that wasn't unusual because they were often too far offshore for cell or internet service. But when he did connect with her, he could tell she was off somehow, and he was worried."

"So, when he finally got off the ship, he immediately headed to his sister's house, which he found out had been put into

309

foreclosure. He was lucky enough to see her next-door neighbor, who told him she was staying at some hotel in town with her low-life boyfriend. He didn't even know she had a boyfriend.

When he pounded on the door to the hotel room, an angry guy with bloody knuckles answered. Mountain pushed himself into the room and saw his sister lying in a pool of blood, her face almost unrecognizable. He ran to her side, followed by the boyfriend, who kept screaming for him to mind his own business. When Mountain realized his sister had no pulse, a deadly rage filled him, and he delivered revenge with fists fueled like two jackhammers. The police report said the victim, the boyfriend, didn't stand a chance."

"Mountain ended up in a cell for seven years, but it would have been longer if not for the circumstances surrounding his sister's death."

Amee sat still at the table, a single tear running down her face, but she didn't break eye contact with Reggie as the story continued.

"On our way to deliver our message that night, my mind kept telling me this was my chance to exact the revenge I didn't get to wield. We drove for about twenty minutes in silence; it was about 2:00 in the morning, and the darkness was comforting, giving me the courage to ask Mountain if his revenge was worth it. He didn't answer right away, but when he did, he told me it felt right and justified on so many levels. But once he found himself living the consequences of his actions, he realized the only one hurt was him."

He couldn't even bury his sister, and he had to sit in a cage for exacting revenge, and the worst part was it didn't bring her back, and it wasn't what she would have wanted anyway. So, then he told me there are always consequences for our actions. He said he could read it all over my face, that I was planning to deliver this message as my personal revenge. I didn't try to defend myself or deny it; I couldn't have if I tried. But then he told me that because he loved me, he would stop me before I went too far, and he did."

"He stopped you?"

"Yes, and I'm grateful, because I was already carrying around a butt load of guilt."

Reggie sits up as straight as she can and looks out at Mountain again, "Amee, I won't let you go too far, I promise. Talk to Harley; it's a good start on moving forward; I've seen it. She wasn't here when I could have used her, and I struggled for a long time. You guys will be here for some time while Abby helps you and Bud make plans for your immediate future; take the time to talk to her, please.

Amee listened and absorbed every word extended to her; she had a lot to think about.

"Let me ask you a question Amee, what do you want for your life now?"

"Let me ask you a question, will I be a survivor like you?"

"I can't answer that because it will be up to you, but we'll be here all the way."

"Tell me all the years of brutality will fade!"

"Fade yes, disappear, no!"

"Can I have the life I was meant to?"

"Only if you can go back in time and change things will you have that life. What I can tell you, is if you work hard, you will find one just as meaningful."

"Please tell me he won't find us," Amee pleads.

"I can't, but if he does you and Bud won't be alone, we'll deal with him."

"So, I ask again, what do you want for your new life Amee?"

Amee sat across the table from Reggie and slowly became shy but hopeful. "I want a song with a good and gentle man. I want to share every note and lyric as we begin to know each other. I want to be comforted and held tight by the rhythm of love and trust. That's what I want. Can you help me with that?" she asks choking out a soft laugh.

Returning the laugh Reggie looks at the woman, "well, we're not a dating service but you never know. Let's get rid of Dempsey and then check out suitable prospects. Now, can you take me back to my room? This outing has zapped me, and I need to check on Suzie."

Chapter 55

It's been four days since the extraction, and an anxiety-funded silence is the only thing they're receiving from the town of DuPree. Every team member is walking a different path as they wait on the edge for the reprisal of their actions; they know they're involved in a small war against an unhinged enemy. Amee and Bud have repeatedly assured them that they haven't come close to ending this against Dempsey and Big Daddy. Amee especially can feel the storm coming, and she can't accept the solace from reassuring words as they have begun to fade. The reassurances of, we've got this covered, and you're safe now, have become hopeful promises replaced by the itch of fear as the waiting continues.

John has called for a meeting of the minds. He stands by the door to the conference room, watching as the team members slowly make their way toward him. Looking at each one as they enter, he can tell they've been able to rest some, but the burden of the unknown weighs on them because, in this instance, no news is definitely *not* good news.

His girls are the last to arrive, having done another eight laps around the inner perimeter track on the second floor. The stairs leading up to the track and the track itself are made of a heavy metal grating as you'd find on any ocean-going vessel. The grating is functional for a human who wears shoes, but it's not for Suzie's paws. So, while Reggie and Suzie were on bed rest, the team laid Astroturf on top of the grating so she could walk off her bruises and gain her strength back. Reggie and Suzie had never used the track because of the discomfort it caused to her right leg, but she knew Suzie needed the exercise and would heal faster if she walked with her.

They come through the door, and Reggie claims her seat next to John and is happy to show everyone she's no longer wearing the sling. Suzie follows her usual routine of trotting around the conference table, stopping at each team member to receive her royal praise, and they don't disappoint. With her loop completed, she plants herself between John and Reggie. She scans the table-top for a tray of sandwiches or bagels, and when she sees the table is devoid of both and anything else she may have hoped for, her sad face shows colossal disappointment. *Boy, things are rough around here.*

"Ok, everyone," John says to the room, "I'd like to start this off with medical updates, starting with her," he says, pointing at Reggie, who suddenly feels the need to protest. "Nope," he says, holding his palm in front of her face before she can even open her mouth, "zip it!"

"Dad, Xander," he says, smiling a wicked smile in Reggie's direction, "what's her status?"

"Damn it, John, I'm sitting right here!"

"Exactly, you're sitting right here among my witnesses. Dad, Xander?" He enquires again without taking his eyes off her.

Xander speaks first, "the x-ray's we took yesterday look good, the wound is healing nicely. The muscles in her shoulder took a beating but they will strengthen with physical therapy which she is going to start today."

314

"Dad?"

"I agree with Xander but am going to add a timeline, at least another four or five days on the bench. The sports reference of riding the bench wasn't missed by anyone at the table, especially her.

"Michael..." she begins but realizes it's a lost cause because she's shut down before the first syllable could be pulled from the back of her mind and formed, not to mention voiced.

"And,,, at least two months before she steps into the batting cage."

"WHAT!"

"Don't worry Miss Reggie, the time will fly by," Oscar-D laughs with a sad understanding of how she feels.

"And Suzie's condition?" John asks, looking to the far corner where Doc Shoemaker has exiled himself, not wanting to become part of the team.

"She's mending, she's strong and determined to get back to work, and she's cleared to do so if that's what's required."

Reggie places her hand on Suzie's back, runs her fingers through the soft coat, then looks up at the Vet, "what do you mean, *if that's what's required?*"

"I mean, she's getting older and has sustained many injuries, not to mention that arthritis is setting in; I recommend she be retired from active duty!"

Reggie stands and stares at the Vet as his recommendation takes a chunk out of her heart; disbelief and denial flood her veins as she stares into the corner where her new enemy is standing, challenging the team. "How can you say that? You've cared for her since she came into my life, and you know she would regress if she couldn't join me in the field. Tears of fear started to swell behind her eyelids, causing her body to tremble; what would she do without her best friend? How could she do her job? There's always been the fact that she had avoided, that Suzie would need to slow down, but not now; she knew Suzie still had good years left to help the team. But thinking back to the visit with Deloris; she'd watched Suzie favor her right leg as she entered the first resident's room and had made a mental note to contact Doc Shoemaker when this case was over.

John reaches out to take Reggie's hand, but she pulls away and heads to the door with Suzie giving a soft whimper as she follows. "What the hell, Shoe?" John says to the Vet, "are you serious?"

"Yes, I'm damn serious, but I admit I could have handled that better; I'll go talk to her."

"Good luck with that," Michael says.

The room's occupants sit in silence after their initial gasps of disbelief went unheard by Reggie, they couldn't fathom the extraction team without Suzie, and the fact that might become the case left them spinning.

After the awkward silence lifted, John cleared his throat to get things rolling again but found himself looking through the glass walls of the conference room, following Reggie as she made her way through the Club House, with the vet closing the gap.

"Marco," John says to the room, "any movement on the trackers Mountain planted?"

"Vehicles still haven't moved, Boss."

"Okay, everyone let's meet back here in an hour to proceed."

"Copy that Boss," the team responds in unison, they knew what he needed to do and supported him in doing it.

Chapter 56

John finds Doc Shoemaker sitting on the floor in front of Reggie with Suzie at her side. The Vet speaks softly, but John picks up on the words the closer he gets.

"We can put her on a low dose of Rimadyl for now. It's a medication that will help with her inflammation and joint pain caused by arthritis."

John doesn't interrupt as he takes a seat next to Reggie, placing his arm around her shoulder. She leans into him feeling helpless; the inevitable for Suzie sits in limbo between her head and her heart, leaving Reggie to pray she will be strong enough to make the right call when the time comes.

The Vet nods in his direction and continues. "We'll monitor her closely for the usual side effects and do regular blood draws to look for liver or kidney damage signs. Those are serious conditions but are usually caused by long-term usage of the drug."

Crying openly now, Reggie tries to speak clearly and finds herself comforted by Suzie, who has moved closer. Suzie leans into Reggie's legs, trying to draw out her pain and carry it herself because she believes that it's her job, to absorb the pain for others. "Thank you, Shoe; my biggest fear is that I will make decisions for her health that will be good for me and not her."

"I think that's a normal reaction Babe," John says, still holding her close.

318

"Yes, it is," the Vet says, agreeing with John while acknowledging Reggie's fear at the same time.

Reggie slowly shifts her body weight from John, trusting herself to sit straight without any help, and places her hand on Suzie's back to run her fingers through the soft coat. She searches the beautiful eyes that connect with hers, she probes, asks for guidance, and implores the canine for help with all the love she has. And she gets it, all of it, and nods.

"Suzie will tell me when she's done, and I promise to listen and do what's best for her. But in my heart, I know she's not there yet. So let's start the pain medication and assess regularly," she says while wiping away the tears from her cheeks. "John and I will instruct the team to look for any signs of concern and immediately bring them to us. She interacts with all the extraction team members differently so they may pick up on something we miss."

"Take a few minutes to calm down and get some love from our girl," John says, pointing at Suzie, "I told the team to reconvene in about," he looks at his watch, "fifteen minutes."

"We'll be there," came the sad reply. But before John can turn to walk away, she asks him, "what am I going to do John?"

"What's right, Babe, you'll do what's right, no matter how hard it is or how much it hurts, but you won't do it alone because I love her too, we all do!"

Chapter 57

Reggie makes her way back to the conference room with dry, gritty eyes, and she feels the weight of exhaustion as it takes up space on her tiny shoulders. Her life has never been easy, but this will be the darkest test she'll ever take on.

Her boots feel heavy as if sorrow has added weight to their soles; their tread carrying the emotional cement that encases her feet tightly, making each step incredibly daunting. Yet, the conference room's glass walls provide a clear picture of the faces that follow her procession, and she finds herself comforted by what she sees in their eyes as she moves closer to the door. She knows that once she enters, they will be able to see right through her outer layer, just like the glass walls, and immediately share every bit of sadness that plagues her. Because in this family, if one is hurting, they're all hurting.

She is greeted at the door by John's parents with a kiss on the forehead from Michael and a motherly hug from Abby.

"I'm okay," she whispers to them both.

They voiced only three words, "whatever you need."

Reggie nods a thank you and makes her way to the chair next to John, and he bends down and plants a soft kiss on her lips. Then, Suzie makes her customary rounds again to the seated members at the table. When done, she heads back to the door, where she drops her butt to the floor, waiting for the rest to join them and receive more love as they enter. In Suzie's world, you can never get enough love. After she's satisfied with the lavish praise she receives from the stragglers of the team, she takes her seat between Reggie and John.

John looks around the table with hopeful eyes and stops at Marco, who is sitting at the other end, "anything yet?"

"Nada, Boss, and this is trippin me the hell out!" Everyone sitting around the table had to agree with that.

"Copy that! Harley," John says, and all eyes turn to the newest member of the Mickey team, "can you give us an assessment on Bud and Amee?"

The woman sits uncomfortably in her chair because of the back brace she needs to wear for hours each day — another testament to the cruelty they face. "Well, as you all know, the sessions are confidential, but I can say I've met with both twice. Bud is doing well and is so grateful to be here, but Amee is struggling with the future and the unknown of what comes next. And there's more, I can feel it and see it in her eyes, but she's not ready to talk yet."

"What comes next," Reggie says to herself knowing exactly what the, *what comes next means,* after Amee's declaration in the kitchen about wanting Dempsey to bleed.

"Okay, please continue to meet with her if she's willing."

"Of course."

"And Mom, how are you're doing with the new identifications and possible relocation sites?"

"I've created the new identities, and they're solid. Both Bud and Amee have given me choices for where they would like to settle. Whether they will need to separate from each other is a wait-and-see scenario. Amee would like to keep working in the book field; I explained why that's not the usual protocol and why, I think she understands. She has time to figure something else out, and I'm coming up with some ideas myself, but it will depend on how this all ends. I'm also working on Bud's Social Security disability claim as well as an in-house pension, amounting to an impressive monthly stipend.

I've done what I can now since we haven't concluded the case and are in the dark about what comes next."

Everyone around the table knew what she meant and nodded in agreement.

"Okay, Matt."

"Yo, Boss," Matt says, sitting up straighter as if in a Saturday morning high school detention class being called on by the teacher who drew the short straw.

"Fill us in on the two kids, Candis Levine and Chad Pomeroy."

"I've been thinking," he says, looking around the table," that there's no reason to bring them and their families into this. At first, we thought they could give us some insight into Dempsey because of what he did to them, but Dempsey gave us that insight himself by his actions against Reggie and Pix. Candis Levine, at this point, still hasn't left her parents' house, and it's been years now. I mean, she literally never steps out the front door, a heavy case of Agoraphobia. Abby has found another one of those black files showing the girl receiving a generous payoff every month from Darwin for the despicable act of multiple rapes performed by his son. And poor Chad Pomeroy will never leave the long-term care facility he's in, and all those expenses are being covered by Darwin as well. So, I recommend not reaching out to either family because of what we know already. If Darwin were to find out someone is asking questions, it could jeopardize the financial contributions; excuse me, I mean payoffs. The hush money doesn't make up for what destroyed their lives, and it's lacking by millions. But it's all they have. Just sayin."

"Everyone?" John asks the room, watching all hands raise in immediate agreement.

"Dom, what about the Sheriff in Leavenworth?" any inclination on just how wrapped up he is with the DuPree's?"

"Abby's file shows him receiving large amounts from Darwin but not regularly. So, I started comparing dates, the first big payoff was the same week as the incident with the two kids, Candis, and Chad. I'm guessing he delivered a threat to be silent from Darwin; hence the large sum of cash deposited into his bank account. It also lends credence to why the two families withdrew their statements and didn't pursue pressing charges, Darwin sent the Sheriff to have a chat with them. Since then, there are multiple deposits, but I couldn't find a connection to Dempsey. I am assuming he has been called on to take care of situations concerning everything Darwin is into."

"Sum bitch," Oscar-D growls, "whatever happened to law enforcement integrity? Not to mention honor and pride!"

"I can't speak for out there, kid, but I know it exists in here!"

"Zee," John says, moving forward," do you have guardians on the line for Bud and Amee?"

"I've started a list, put a few guys on notice, but until we have a location, it really is, just names on a list."

"Copy that, Zee; I know it's hard to work with your hands tied."

"And that goes for everyone," he says to the team, "we can only work and plan with the information at our fingertips, and right now, we are treading water."

Like the Whiley Coyote, the team knows the Road Runner will drop the anvil; they just don't know when. They've been on high alert before, waiting for the door to open, and when it does, they battle the evil as it crashes over the threshold. And no matter how many times they face the unknown, they always try to scratch the itch to move forward, they feel the need to make a concrete plan, but the door needs to open first. And once it does, they will use one of their many satisfying scenarios to push themselves into action.

"We know the tracker's Mountain planted on the Sheriff's SUVs haven't indicated any movement, but Dempsey could easily use another vehicle, leaving us blind. And with that scenario, Zee, have there been any issues for Deloris and Ax?"

"Ax checks in regularly, and all seems quiet."

Chapter 58

As Reggie and Suzie stand and begin to follow the team to the conference room door, Harley reaches out and touches her hand, "I could use a cup of coffee; how about you?"

Reggie's first instinct is to fall back on old habits and retreat, especially with all that happened earlier concerning Suzie. But she finds the strength to pull herself back from that ledge, a testament to how far she's come. "I think that's a good idea; let's head to the kitchen."

Exiting the kitchen after retrieving their coffee, both women head out to the small front office that John uses for his private security business. They navigate through the short hallway, directly off the Club House floor, and step through the doorless entrance. Even though there isn't a door to shut out the usual buzzing coming off the Club House floor, the dividing hallway wall renders some privacy for the two women to talk.

Taking the chair behind John's small desk, Harley tries to get comfortable, no small feat as always. "Reggie, I know that what the Vet said had to be upsetting, well honestly gut wrenching is probably a better description. How can I help?"

Reggie places her coffee cup on the small desk and sits in one of the visitor chairs arranged in front of it. She sighs and instinctively reaches out her hand and finds Suzie exactly where she knew she'd be, right by her side with her baby cradled softly in her maw.

Watching her fingers travel down Suzie's back as they swim through the soft layers of fur has always had a calming effect; it was a true constant, and the idea of Suzie not being by her side is emotionally debilitating.

"Harley, I knew Suzie would slow down someday; I even got a glimpse of it while we were in Leavenworth. I saw her limping, favoring her right foreleg, and made a mental note to call Shoe when we got back. But, oh God, Harley, I'm so afraid I'll make a wrong decision, one driven by selfishness that will make *me* feel better and won't be in *her* best interests," Reggie confesses while looking at Suzie. The furry princess recognizes Reggie's turmoil, that's always been part of their bond, and places her large head over Reggie's lap dropping her baby into it.

"Very understandable in these circumstances," Harley says softly. "Is there a plan moving forward? I mean, it can't be all or nothing. But what do I know, I'm not a veterinarian?"

"We're going to start a medication to fight the inflammation of her joints caused by arthritis, but I know it's just a band-aid; meant to manage her pain, not cure it."

Reggie's voice quivers with emotion through trembling lips as she continues, "Suzie is the only real family I've ever had, until the formation of Mickey, that is. From the minute we met, she has been my protector, my mother, and the child I will never have; she's, my world."

With that confession voiced, she leans down to encase Suzie with her arms knowing the sadness, when it comes, will be a storm of emotional proportions.

326

"Sadly, Reggie, there's no cure for old age."

"Well, there should be!" Reggie demands loudly but accepts that old age will eventually be another painful place to exist; no one will escape it. And it hurts to realize that we have just as much chance of curing it as we do of eradicating Domestic Violence. And we all know how that's been working out.

"It's not over yet, Reggie; at present she can continue doing her job of protecting you while in the field. And Reggie, I need you to hear me because I'm confident you will think only of her and what's best when it's time for Suzie to retire. And there's no doubt in my mind that you will step up and address the next phase of Suzie's life by using the strength that makes you who you are."

"It might help if you thought about it like this. How would you deal with the guilt if you were to selfishly keep Suzie in the field when she shouldn't be there, and she became seriously injured? I know you've dissected and dealt with the guilt of your past by traveling down an emotional path, one that showed you there was nothing for you to feel guilty for. But the guilt you would feel if Suzie became injured because of that selfishness is one you would never be able to get past because you would have to own it." Harley lets that insightful question and spot-on reality hang within the room.

"So, when it's time to decide, think of that consequence and go from there. And remember, when Suzie retires from the field, she doesn't vanish; she will still be here with us, with you and for you, keeping the home fires burning."

"That word consequence and what it means," Reggie says, looking at the woman, "dictates every decision for action that we make. Sometimes we listen to the warnings of what our actions could cause to each of us personally, and sometimes the injustice we face makes us deaf and blind to them. Especially within the world we live in, have you noticed that?"

"Unfortunately, yes."

"Now, I'd like to pick up where we left off the last time we talked," Harley continues. "We touched briefly on what happened in that jail cell. I believe you labeled it as, checking out and falling down the rabbit hole, again. Care to elaborate?"

Reggie roles her shoulder as it has become stiff since sitting; her arm has been immobile for too long. "It was the bat that started pulling me into the hole; I let myself remember the pain it delivered in the past, not the strength I draw from it in the present. Dempsey kept hitting the cell bars; Pix kept yelling at him to stop, and Suzie, well, Suzie, couldn't be tamed. It's the same demented trip I've taken many times before; I fall down the rabbit hole, like the Alice in Wonderland story, and end up at the table having tea with the Mad Hatter and Cheshire cat. I know it sounds outrageous, but they pull me down when they see me becoming weak from one trigger or another from my past. They try to exploit and push the fear I lived with for so long so they can deliver me back to the evil."

"Shouldn't you be writing this down or something? It would be an excellent article for a psychology magazine. You could title it; *Is she crazy or isn't she.* Or; *Be careful with whom you have tea.*

"Reggie, please continue."

"Right. But this time, I was able to slow my descent down the hole; I found small grooves in the walls where there hadn't been any before. I was able to grab them with my fingers and find purchase with the toes of my boots; at one point, I stopped falling altogether. Those grooves were never there before, so I wondered what was different and suddenly realized it was me. I was stronger emotionally and ready to fight. I knew what waited for me at the bottom and I wasn't going to give them a chance to pull me in again."

"The Cat and the Hatter kept sticking their heads into the bottom of the familiar tunnel I was traveling, saying they wished I would hurry because the tea was getting cold. That's code for welcome back to hell," Reggie says hurriedly to save time. She knew Harley well enough by now and knew the question would come. "And what do you think the statement, *the tea is getting cold,* means Reggie?"

Reggie takes a deep breath and continues, "and then a dark Alice stuck her head into the opening at the bottom of the tunnel. She wore gothic attire with high black boots and a short skirt barely covering her booty. Her face reminded me of death with black makeup on her eyes and lips, her hair was short and spiky, and yes, it was black also. She yells; I don't understand why we always end up waiting for her. Everything is always about her!"

"Not exactly the fairy tale you remember, is it?"

"So, what brought you back, Reggie? What helped you pull yourself out of the hole?"

"Well," Reggie says as she carefully runs her fingers across the fresh pink scar on Suzie's muzzle, "she did."

Reggie was about to elaborate when Marco's deep voice slithered its way around the wall partition and down the short hallway, eventually finding its way into the office.

"Boss, one tracker is on the move!"

"Sorry, Harley gotta go, thank you."

Chapter 59

Finally, the waiting was over. The team endured two hours with their eyes glued to a screen as a little red car, portraying the tracker signal, traveled the highways in their direction. Every monitor that hung from the walls of the Club House had dozens of eyes glued to the screens. The more time passed and the closer the tracker came toward them, the unspoken consensus was, yes, they would have a visitor. But the question remained, how did Dempsey know where Amee and Bud were?

"How much time we got, Marco?" Dominic asks not taking his eyes off the screen in front of him.

"Taking in his current location and factoring in the speed he's traveling; I'd say about thirty minutes."

"But how the hell does he know?" John says to the team, "I thought we had everything locked down."

"We did, we do," Mountain and Dominic answer simultaneously.

"Then what the hell is happening?" John asks sternly, more to himself than any individual. Seconds later, John sees movement out of the corner of his eye and turns to see Amee and Bud as they make their way to the center of the Club House where the extraction team has congregated.

"What's happening?" Amee asks Mountain as she slows Bud's chair, to stop next to him.

331

"Trouble," is all Mountain has time to say, before---

"Mountain, Pix," could you have missed something when you retrieved Bud?"

"Doubtful," Mountain says. "Deloris told me she followed your instructions to the letter. She changed out Bud's ride," the big man says touching one of the handles of the wheelchair. He was wearing all new clothes right down to his skivvies. She had purchased all of it herself and removed all the tags."

"Bud," John says, "did you bring anything with you from your room?"

"Only this picture," he says pulling it from his shirt pocket, "it was in a frame, but the big guy said I would have to leave it and only bring the picture." John turns to Mountain and receives an affirmative nod.

Shifting gears now, John looks at Amee, "how about you Amee?"

"I did exactly as you said, walked out of my store with nothing but the clothes on my back. Not even my purse like you said."

"Any jewelry or keys?"

"Nothing, except the phone Reggie gave me," Amee says massaging her cheek again.

"Where are the clothes you were wearing at the time?"

"In the room you assigned us."

"Go get them please and meet us in the conference room."

"Right away."

"I'll go with you," Reggie says.

"Marco, keep an eye on the tracker, everyone else follow me."

"Copy that, Boss."

Once Amee and Reggie had retrieved the clothing in question, they joined the team as were instructed. Amee's hands were trembling as she placed everything, she had been wearing the night of the extraction, right down to her bra and panties. Reggie then adds Amee's boots from that night.

John and Dominic started to scrutinize each piece of clothing and came up with nothing. "Where the hell is it?" John hisses, "there has to be a transmitter embedded somewhere!"

"Matt, did you instruct the motor pool to scan the car Pix and Reggie were using?"

"Didn't have to, Boss; Pete was already on it; he knows his stuff. He followed protocol and said all was clear."

"What about the ankle brace? Amee needs to wear that all the time," Bud says pleased with himself for being able to contribute.

Amee immediately sits down in the closest chair and pulls up her pant leg to show the heavy-duty brace. Mountain kneels in front of her like Cinderella's prince and carefully removes her boot so he can retrieve the brace, but before he turns to place it on the table, he gently massages her ankle. Sadness etches his face, but there's a rage dancing behind his eyes like an uncontrolled burn. The intensity of the situation causing his fingers to turn white as they grip the apparatus. Finally, he puts the item on the table where Dominic picks it up and heads to the door asking Xander to follow.

Dominic couldn't see anything strange about the brace, and the quick scan performed in the Med Bay didn't detect anything either.

Once Amee has replaced the ankle brace, she leans back in her chair, "now what?" she asks bringing her hand to her face making small circles with her fingers on her cheek.

"Do you have a bad tooth, Amee?" Reggie asks, "I notice you are always massaging your cheek like you're in pain."

"Well, yes, and it's constant. I've lived with it ever since my jaw was wired shut. I hoped it would stop when the wires were removed, but it didn't. So I thought I would ask one of you doctors to have a look or ask about a dentist once this was all over."

It was like an industrial sized light bulb coming to life within the room, "son-of-a-bitch," Dominic growls, "he planted a tracker in her tooth!"

"WHAT? Wait a minute," Amee says as Mountain and Dominic gently pull her from her chair and head out the door with Michael and Xander following.

"Amellia," Bud calls to his daughter, but she couldn't hear him because she was being double timed to the Med Bay.

"Bud," Reggie says as she sits next to him in the chair that was just moments ago occupied by Amee. "She'll be okay, they need to Xray her mouth to make sure what they suspect is true. And if it is, we will call in one of our trusted dental affiliates to proceed."

"How much more will she have to endure because of me?" Bud asks, looking into Reggie's eyes, reaching for comfort.

Chapter 60

Just minutes after Amee is hustled out of the conference room, she finds herself in a make-shift dental chair in the Med Bay with Michael and Mountain hovering over her.

"When we say so, just keep as still as you can," Michael says, laying the heavy protective bib across Amee's chest and pelvis. Once she was protected, Xander appeared, pushing a portable dental X-ray machine with Dominic hot on his heels.

"Okay, Amee, just don't move."

"I still can't believe this, I knew he was controlling even before he installed the cameras in the Book Store, he said it was for security, but I knew better. But this,,, this is,,," she says gesturing with quivering hands, "is beyond demented and so evil!"

Mountain squeezes her hand for assurance before backing a safe distance away. He wanted to be out of range before Michael took the Xray of her jaw, he wasn't going to take a chance that his little swimmers would be zapped and begin to glow.

"There it is," Dominic says pointing to the image coming to life on the desk monitor. "That must be some high-tech shit to transmit a signal through the porcelain filling."

"Can you take it out?" Amee asks in anguish, "I want it out, now," she pleads to the men in the room. Fear and disgust clung to her chest in a thick sweat, clogging every pore in her skin before being absorbed into her lungs. It felt like she was trying to breathe through a plastic bag Dempsey had slipped over her head, it was that restricting. The sudden need for air ascends upon her as she struggles for her next breath, causing panic like she's never felt before as it begins to scream for survival. "Well,,, can you?" she finally manages to ask through gulps of air.

"I know this is a shock Amee," Mountain says, trying to sound as calm as possible while helping Michael remove the lead protection bib.

"Do you Mountain? Do you really know?" she says in anger to the gentle giant, then is suddenly filled with remorse for her words.

"I think I do, yes," the big man says standing at her side, his eyes filled with sadness. "You can't chase the evil of man like we do and not know."

"I'm sorry, Mountain, you didn't deserve that," Amee says shamefully. "It's just that I honestly didn't think there was anything else that Bastard could think to do to me that he hasn't done already. Whether it's physical or mental, Dempsey plays the game well," she says in a harsh whisper, "because when it comes to torture, he's a master."

"We'll get rid of it, Amee, but we'll need to consult our dentist on the best way to do it," Xander says, "but for now I can you give you something for the pain!"

As Xander is handing Amee a low dose pain killer, John is making his way to the Med Bay to join them but is stopped in his tracks by Marco before he's halfway there.

"DuPree Police cruiser at the back gate Boss!"

"Shit, I thought we had more time," John says, "who's on the gate today?" John's voice booms through the Club House.

"Marvin."

"Radio him with instructions to stall for as long as he can before opening the gate."

"Copy that, Boss."

John motions for everyone in the Med Bay, along with the rest of the extraction team, to follow him to the core of the Club House. When everyone is within earshot, he asks for a report on the X-ray, finding himself just as disgusted as the rest with the findings. But at least now he knows how Dempsey found them and is looking forward to a face-to-face with the monster. Then he felt it, just a pinch really, at the back of his neck where all his ideas originate.

"Marco, can you jam the signal of the tracker somehow?"

"I can probably figure out how to disrupt the feed for a small amount of time, but it would only be temporary."

"That's all we need. Dad, will you get ahold of our Dentist and get him here as soon as possible."

"Consider it done!"

Seconds later Marco says over the crowd, "Boss, Marvin just informed me there are two men in the vehicle."

"Copy that!"

"The other person is either his bootlicking deputy, Tack, or Big Daddy," Bud says as Pix wheels him close to join the crowd.

337

"My bet is on Big Daddy," Pix laughs, giving Xander a sideways glance, "Deputy Tack won't be comfortable riding around in a vehicle any time soon.

"Amee, Bud," John says, looking at each one earnestly, "no matter what you hear from that office," he says pointing in its direction, "you are not to make a sound! Understood?"

"Yes, absolutely," they both state.

"I hope you do because he will push all the right buttons. You can expect he will try anything and everything he can think of to get to you just like he always has, so you need to be ready for it and not react."

"We're good John," Bud says while reaching out for his daughter's hand.

"And the same goes for you two," he says taking Reggie's hand with one of his own while reaching out with the other to comfort Suzie, who's picking up on the tension surrounding him.

"I'll do my best," Reggie says squeezing his hand, "be careful."

"Marco, let Marvin know he can open the gate now, and do what you can with jamming that tracker signal."

"Copy that."

"Matt, on my six."

The crowd watched the two men head to their lockers to retrieve their guns. They exchanged no words; eye contact was the only communication needed after years of training; brothers be brothers no matter where they stand and on what soil. Finally, each

338

man secured his weapon at the small of his back and headed to the security office.

Once inside the small office, John takes position behind the desk, choosing to stand instead of sitting in the desk chair. His stance is firm, feet placed firmly on the floor about a foot apart, with his face forming an unreadable picture. His heartbeat is visible as it dances through the vein at his temple, and his muscled arms are crossed tightly at his chest, twitching with the anticipation of what's to come. Matt takes up his position a few feet behind him, mirroring his façade, he's seen the Boss deliver this picture to the enemy many times, and he's ready.

Chapter 61

John and Matt watched as the cruiser came into view and parked directly in front of the Security Office door.

"Well, here we go," John says, looking back at Matt.

"Yep! Here we go."

The two men took their time stepping out of the cruiser and once their boots hit the ground they began to surveil their surroundings. The man who stepped out of the passenger side of the rig was tall and barrel chested, he wore a dark arrogance like a second skin which he used to dominate all he encountered. He was a man who demanded and expected respect, and if he didn't receive it blindly, he'd acquire it with his fists, or he'd throw money at it. But he was in for a rude awakening today. Surprise!

All John could think of by watching the man was: you can pay for all the respect you want, and you can dominate by actions causing fear, but I respect no man, or woman, who hasn't earned it. You're on my turf now Big Daddy, you've allowed my family to be hurt, and I promise those actions will not go unpunished, by either of you.

Dempsey was a smaller version of the other man, and even at this first glance, John could tell who was in charge. After all, Dempsey was only playing at being Sheriff. But to John, it didn't matter who called the shots in DuPree, Dempsey went after his people, one of which lived in his heart, and he was not going to let that go.

340

The big man entered the office first, making a show of his entrance by walking through the glass door like a bull, and not caring that it hit his son in the face when he didn't hold it open for him.

"Afternoon," John says curtly, "what can I do for you?"

The big man gave no acknowledgment or response to John's inquiry. "Are these two of the men that made a laughingstock out of you Boy?"

"No, Sir."

"What's your business?" John asks again, losing what little patience he had.

Taken back by the harshness in John's voice and total lack of respect, Darwin found himself becoming enraged. His eyes traveled the room, landing on Matt, and he saw the same lack of fear and respect as the man standing behind the desk. So, he adjusted his stance to try and look more intimidating to the two men, but somehow they just looked bored, which infuriated him even more.

After a few incredibly tense seconds Darwin began to realize he wasn't going to get these men to fold at his feet, leaving him no choice but to stop the; Cock-of-the-walk show and get to the point.

"My dip-shit son here," Darwin says pointing at Dempsey, "has lost some property and he wants it back!"

"We're not private investigators, so if you don't mind, we have a busy day, you know where the door is," John says and begins to turn from the man.

Not able to swallow another minute of this lack of respect for his self-proclaimed importance, Darwin explodes into the room. "Son, do you know who the hell you're talkin to?" he barks while planting his huge hands on the desk to lean closer to John, another tactic to induce domination, which of course didn't work.

From his side of the desk John leans over to meet the man halfway, he comes within inches of the old man's face, "I don't give a rat's ass who you are and I'm sure as hell not your son!" he barks back.

The tension continued to grow thicker and thicker within the small space, and the walls seemed like they were closing in, making the space feel even smaller. Matt couldn't stay still any longer, he could smell the fight, see it playing out in front of him from start to finish. He wasn't good at head games like the Boss, so he stepped a few feet closer, ready to react in a split second.

"I know she's here," Dempsey spits into the room while looking at his phone, "my app shows it."

It was all John could do to restrain himself from flying over the desk at Dempsey, ignoring what little restraint he had left. "She who?" he demands, hoping Marco is close to shutting down the signal.

"My damn wife, that's who!" Dempsey screams.

Any time now, Marco!

As the volume in the office heightens with rage, Reggie and Abby find themselves watching Amee and Bud intensely. Abby moves in close and takes Bud's hand in hers whispering, "John's got this," followed up by a reassuring nod of her head.

342

Reggie does the same with Amee, moving close to her side but letting Suzie take the lead. Comfort is Suzie's thing, with her baby in her mouth she leans against Amee, where she sits in a chair next to Bud. Reggie notices someone has given her a cup of tea, she clutches the porcelain with her palm absorbing the heat as it flows into her shaky hands. Amee feels Suzie's comforting weight as it softly leans into her and is grateful for the closeness. Then, acknowledging Suzie's concern, she runs her fingers across her damaged head, the evidence proving once again how cruel man can be.

At this point, all Suzie wants to do is consume the pain and absorb all the heavy fear that Amee carries as she sits trapped in the chair. Suzie proceeds to do her thing by pushing her muzzle into Amee's lap, placing her baby there for comfort, and without knowing it, Amee reaches down and touches the pink fur. Suzie watches intently, giving off a satisfying whimper when she witnesses Amee momentarily forget her burden of pain. Suzie's eyes take in the transformation, and she vows that she will hold Amee's burden for as long as she can, because this woman needs her attention.

Back in the office Darwin continues, "my son's technical do-dad shows this is the place," the man roars.

Any time Marco!

"Well, your phone app must be wrong!" Matt begins...

"Shut up little man!" Darwin spits in Matt's direction.

343

John glances to his left where Matt stands. He's poised and ready, waiting for a nod that would allow him to show just what kind of damage this 6'1" *little man*, could do.

"Wait, what the hell just happened?" Dempsey yells as he looks intently at his phone, "My signal just went dead." Looking up and locking eyes with John he screams again, "I know my wife is here, you did something to my signal."

Thank you, Marco!

Roaring with defeat Darwin grabs his son's phone and sees a blank screen where there was once a blinking icon. How could he not have control of this situation? He didn't know what to do, so he fell back on the bully he had always been while growing up. He looked at the two men in the room then barked like a rabid dog, "hand her over now!" he demands.

"I'm sorry you feel a wife is a piece of property to be controlled and mistreated," John says calmly, "so if you lost yours, it's probably because she didn't like it and took off, couldn't blame her much if she did. Now you have about five seconds to get the hell off my property," John says to both men as he once again points at the door.

Darwin DuPree could hardly contain himself as a red rage bubbled within, he was a man who was always in control, always. He looks at his dip shit son, then at John and Matt before turning to the door to escape the humiliation he found so foreign to him. He was down but he wouldn't be for long he thought to himself already plotting his revenge for this humiliation. "This isn't over by a long shot," he declares over his shoulder.

"Wait, Dad," Dempsey says before Darwin's hand hits the door, "just wait."

Dempsey looked around the small space, taking a few deep breaths, trying to make himself as tall as possible. He finally had something to say and enjoyed the drama the wait was causing. It felt good to be in control for once.

"Amee, Darlin," he yells sarcastically over Matt's shoulder at the entrance into the Club House, "I know you're back there, so you better listen up Sweetheart. If you don't get your little ass out here right now, you will never see your son!"

Chapter 62

Dempsey's parting words and the satanic laugh that accompanied them sent a ripple of paternal pain through Amee. The shattering of porcelain as it hit the cement floor of the Club House picked up where the declaration of sorrow and cruelty left off. It was like an old, black, and white silent movie playing in slow motion; it took forever for the cup to fall from Amee's hand and shatter to the floor. However, no one immediately noticed the liquid spooling up among the shards of glass at Amee's feet because they were trying to make sense of the threat that traveled the hallway from the small office. The mess on the floor surrounding her boots seemed to dance with extreme cruelty in front of Amee's eyes, causing an unbelievable blackness to course through her veins. Dempsey's shocking words seemed to call to her, brutally taunting her; all she was capable of at that moment was to mutter one word over and over, *"no... no... no,"* as the cement floor came rushing towards her, she was falling from her chair!

Large, gentle hands scooped her up before her face met the floor. Mountain lifted Amee into his arms like she was a small rag doll, his boots scraping through the glass and tea. He sat down in the chair next to Bud, placing Amee in his lap where he cradled her protectively. She sobbed quietly into the big man's shoulder with disbelief; she couldn't bring herself to believe what she had just heard. It was just another level of torment and cruelty her husband enjoyed inflicting. There was no way this could be true, or could it? He certainly was an evil Bastard.

Suzie began to panic about what was happening to Amee, and she needed to get closer to be by her side. But she would have to go through the broken glass to do it, leaving Reggie barely enough time to pull her back to safety. "It's okay, Suz; Mountain has her," Reggie whispers reassuringly.

"Amellia, girl, I'm so sorry for his cruelty," Bud says, taking her hand from where it grasped the front of Mountain's shirt.

"Oh, Daddy, it hurts all over again."

"I know girl, I know," he whispers sadly.

As John and Matt enter the Club House, they are confronted with the carnage Dempsey's cruel parting words managed to inflict. Amee was being held tightly in Mountain's arms, sobbing into his chest. John had no trouble recognizing the big man's rage, for it mirrored his own.

"Son, the dentist is here when you're ready," Michael speaks up.

"Marco, you still jamming Amee's signal?"

"Yes, Sir, and the tracker on the cruiser is transmitting their direction is North."

John makes eye contact with Mountain and Reggie; both acknowledge and begin to speak in calming whispers to Amee.

The little pinch at the back of John's neck was pulsing with a determined purpose, he was coming up with a plan, and they needed to move on it now.

347

"Amee," Reggie says, "I can only imagine the pain you are feeling, but right now, the only thing I can do to help is to walk you through the next few steps so we can figure out what he meant by that. But first, we need to remove that tracker from your tooth. Are you ready?"

Still in shock and visibly shaken, Amee whispers she's ready and begins to climb off Mountain's lap while wiping multiple tears from her cheeks.

"Just hold on, Amee, I've got you," Mountain says, standing, keeping her cradled to his chest.

"Suzie and I will go with Amee," Reggie says to John as they pass the crowd heading to the Med Bay.

"Bud, I know Dempsey's declaration must have shocked you too. Do you think there's any truth to what he said?" John asks.

"I have no idea, but knowing him and Big Daddy, I wouldn't put it past them. So, what do we do to find out if it's true? I'm worried about Amellia; I don't know how much more she can take."

"Agreed, so I'm going to have Dominic and Matt start their investigation into this by asking you some questions, okay?"

"Anything I can do to help, but I was in the facility in Leavenworth during the whole pregnancy."

"You may know something that doesn't seem like it would help, but you never know."

"Okay," John looks up at Marco, "keep jamming Amee's tracker and keep me updated on the other; I need to know where they are at all times."

"Copy that, Boss."

John enters the Med Bay and hears his father say to a familiar face, "thanks for coming Simon; this is an unusual emergency."

Amee is in the same make-shift dental chair as before, and Mountain is at her side. "Open wide, Miss," the dentist says. He examines Amee's tooth and then looks at the X-ray provided.

"Very interesting."

From the doorway, John asks, "can you remove that tracking device without damaging it?" The plan he wanted to set in motion depended on the tracker still sending out a signal.

"Probably not; I need to drill into the porcelain that caps it. I could try, but there are no guarantees I could remove it intact."

"Just pull out the tooth, I don't care, and I don't care what I look like after you do. So JUST PULL THE DAMN THING, PLEASE! And if it helps end this nightmare, I won't even ask for Novocain," Amee declares from the chair.

"Well, it isn't a matter of just pulling the tooth; if the idea is not to damage the thing-ma-jig embedded in the tooth, sorry, I know that isn't very technical, I will have to remove it surgically. Which will mean you'll have to go under anesthesia. Is that going to be a problem?"

"Not to sound bitchy or ungrateful for your concern," she says to the dentist, "but that's the least of my problems. Go for it!"

349

"John," she looks at the man, "when this is over," she says, pointing to her mouth, "will you help me find out if my son is still alive?"

"That's the first order of business; I promise you'll know the truth. As you can imagine, we'll have many questions about that time, the delivery and such. Will you be able to hold it together and relive that day?"

She begins to cry as the possibility of her son being alive wraps itself around her heart and begins to squeeze it with hope. Then, without warning, Mountain hands her a tissue from the counter behind them. It's just a few tears filled with hope and a couple holding fear, but she wipes them away, anxious to get on with the process. "Oh yes, I'll tell you what I can remember, but I was pretty out of it during the delivery."

"How long do you need, Simon?" John asks, looking at the Dentist.

"Give me about an hour, I'll have to put her under. I'll need to have a second set of hands; can I recruit Michael for help?"

"Absolutely, I just need to speak to him for a second then he's all yours, and thank you Simon, your help is much appreciated."

"Mountain, you good here?" John asks the big man.

"I'm good here, Boss."

As John heads to the door, he indicates for Xander and his father to follow him out. Once outside the door, he stops and begins. "I know you said the Kid is good to go medically, but I want to hear it again. Can I send him out on a mission?"

Both Doctors immediately give him an affirmative nod.

"Good, because once we have that tracker in hand, I'm sending him out to lead Dempsey and Big Daddy on a wild goose chase; he will keep them scrambling in multiple directions and out of our hair while we deal with this new development. Thank you."

All Xander and Michael can do at this point is watch John as he walks away; they know he will elaborate on his plan when he's ready.

Clearing his throat, Michael looks at the other man, "I never thanked you for what you did in DuPree Xander; I'm very grateful; Abby and I are very grateful."

"You're welcome.

I'm just glad we got there when we did; it would have been too late for all concerned otherwise."

"That bad?"

"You have no idea."

Chapter 63

The window of one hour stretched into two, but the dentist and Michael worked together flawlessly. Once Amee was put under Michael began monitoring Amee's vitals while the dentist performed the extraction of the tooth. Even before Amee began to wake up John found himself holding the tooth, with the transmitter completely intact, in the palm of his hand. Doing his best to keep his rage at bay, he realized he was running out of time and energy to continue to internalize this madness.

"Kid!" John bellows across the core of the Club House.

"Yo, Boss!"

"You up for a road trip?"

"Does my Momma dye her hair?" Oscar-D responds with his dopy grin.

"Jesus Kid, I don't know, and I don't care. Just get your ass over here!" John barks: as his patience continues to fray.

"Oscar-D, this is what I want," John says as soon as the young man stands at his side, exuding pure, youthful adrenaline.

"Boss, let me just say thank you, I was going crazy standing on the sidelines."

John acknowledges the kid's enthusiasm with a quick nod.

"This is the hardware Simon just dug out of that poor woman's mouth," John says, holding up a small baggie containing the bloody molar and transmitter. "I don't want what she endured to give us this," John holds the baggy up to eye level between the two of them, "to be for nothing. Feel me, Kid?" John asks with determination, wanting to make sure what he was saying was getting across.

"Whatever I can do, Boss," Oscar-D says, using the adult part of his brain.

"Right now, Marco is still jamming the signal, so this is what I'm thinking. Head East for now, your final destination will be DuPree, but not until I give you the go-ahead. So, for now," John says, handing over the baggy and its contents, "take those two bastards on a chase, stop at towns along the way, play hide-n-seek, if you know what I mean."

"Can I engage and interact, make conversation and such?" Oscar-D asks, looking extremely hopeful.

"Yes, you be you Kid, but comms on the entire time per usual protocol.

Have some fun out there, use that weirdness some of us love; anything goes as long as you're careful. You feel me, Kid?"

"Like a winning jackpot in Vegas, Boss," the young man says, beaming with anticipation.

"Just get to the Motor pool," John says, pointing in its direction, "Pete has your ride ready."

"Jeez, what have I done?" John sighs to the room as he watches the Kid practically skipping through the Club House.

"Marco," John says, turning to the man, "give the Kid about fifteen minutes, then un-jam the signal to Amee's tracker."

353

"Copy that, Boss; I'll send him a text when it's back online. It looks like you made him a happy guy."

"Listen up, team," John says, raising his voice, looking around the Club House, "I need everyone in the conference room in five. Mom, I need you to bring your laptop; we need to look at the names on the black files again."

"Reggie, will you wheel Bud in while I get Mountain and Amee, please?"

"Of course," she replies and steps behind Bud's chair.

In less than a second, John heard a demanding bark from you know who. Translation: *What about me, John?*

"You," he says, pointing to Suzie, "come with me; Amee is going to need you." As usual, he finds himself in a holding pattern while waiting for Suzie to look up at Reggie to receive the go-ahead nod. Once Suzie is at his side, cradling her baby in her maw, they head to the Med Bay. On the way, he looks down at Suzie and asks, "when will you realize I'm the Boss around here?" She responds with a: *"We've had this conversation before, John,"* snort.

"How are you doing, Amee?" Reggie asks as the woman enters the conference room behind John, with Suzie at her side and Mountain bringing up the rear.

"Still a bit loopy and numb, but fine for now," she says as she takes the empty chair next to Bud, who instantly takes her hand in his to lend support, and no one is surprised when Mountain takes the empty chair next to her.

After everyone is settled in, the room becomes charged with anticipation, waiting for John to begin.

"Simon extracted the molar embedded with a tracker from Amee's mouth successfully, and Marco will un-jam the signal shortly. So, I have set the Kid free to have some fun at the DuPree's expense, a road trip to drive them crazy and keep them occupied while we work from here and try to dig up information concerning Dempsey's claim."

Everyone in the room knew the claim; they had all heard it and were ready to move forward. The team has seen a lot of cruelty since they started Mickey, but this emotional beating was beyond comprehension. Whenever they think they can't see anything they haven't witnessed or confronted already, the Devil sends them an updated message.

"Okay, moving on," John says. "Even though Amee and Bud are safe right now, we still need to act against the Duprees, but first, let's find out if there will be another extraction he says."

"Dig hard team we need to find the truth, and we will, that's a promise." If there's a baby out there, it needs to be with his mother, bottom line!" The sadness in the room was palpable, the urgency of the situation swarming the occupants seated at the table. Their thoughts: *could this be possible?* It didn't matter; everyone was ready to do whatever it took to find the truth for Amee and Bud. The gray area that usually surrounded and motivated their actions had changed instantly to black and white; this was an innocent child, and the vast consequences they could incur would never put a dent in their resolve. And even if the consequences were presented by a giant, flashing neon light showing the outcome not to be in their favor, these people would still forge ahead because that's what they do; that's who they are, and they have to try.

"So, it's possible," John continues, "we may have another extraction before delivering our message to Dempsey and Big Daddy. We leave no stone unturned, are we all on the same page here?"

All heads nodded in silence, a show of agreement all around.

"Dom, can you quickly search the Seattle branch of the FBI for us?"

"What ya thinking, Boss?"

"I want to know who runs the show."

Dom immediately opens his laptop and begins the search. "Okay," he says, "The Special Agent in charge of the Seattle branch is Royce Delgado, appointed in 2015."

"Does anyone recognize that name?" John asks the room. No one spoke; the name wasn't familiar. Hopefully, that was a good sign. "What about negative press, anything out there?"

"Only that he's a Rams fan," Dominic says with disgust.

"Okay, Mom, will you put up the names from Darwin's black files, please?"

Abby's fingers flew across the keys, and the result instantly appeared on the room's large monitor. "Did you find any other files when digging, maybe something you didn't think was relevant?"

"John, seriously," his mother says indignantly, "you know better!"

Smiling, he looks at his mother, "forgive me, Mom."

"In time, if you're lucky," she laughs, and the team follows suit.

Matt, who was studying the blacklist of names, or the list of corruption as he referred to it, said it first. "I don't see the Special Agent's name on the list!"

"What is this list of names?" Bud asks, studying the monitor information intently.

"It's a God damn payoff list, Bud," Matt growls, "All those names are getting payoffs from Big Daddy."

"I knew he had to be doing something like that all along; he was getting away with so much. Remember Reggie? I told you that!"

"I do, Bud," Reggie responds.

"Oh, my God!" Amee hisses from her chair, "the Doctor that came to DuPree to monitor my pregnancy and deliver my baby is on that list, and the Dentist that wired my jaw shut is there too!"

"Hurtful Bastards," Bud says, squeezing his daughter's hand, while Mountain silently takes the other.

"I recognized the Doctor's name when we first saw this list," Michael interjects.

"Dom!"

"On it, Boss."

357

A quick google search of both names provided their private practice information. The team was supplied with addresses, phone numbers, a short bio, and a picture, giving them all the information they needed to proceed.

"Ok, this is what I'm thinking," John says to the room. "We need to talk to each of those men, but we can't take a chance that after we do, they will warn Darwin, so this will be our play. We're going to pay each Doctor a surprise visit," he says to his team. "We'll extend an invitation, which will most likely end up being by force because they won't come willingly to sit down with us." And before anyone could question the idea of bringing them back to the Club House, which was against all protocols, he clarified. John couldn't help but notice every eye in the room displayed a bit of shock, but not enough to interrupt him. "I'm going to have Pete clear a space in the adjacent hangar, the one we use mainly for storage. Then, we can bring them back here to get the information we need while at the same time keeping them from reaching out to DuPree."

"Isn't that a bit dangerous?" Matt questions, "I mean, we've always gone to great pains to keep the Club House location secure."

"I agree, Matt," John says, "but if we keep their hands shackled behind them and blindfolded through the entire transport, I'm not too worried. I think the manhandling and discomfort will instill enough fear into them that they'll talk."

"Only if you make them more afraid of you than they are of Big Daddy," Bud interjects.

"We know how to do that," Matt smiles at the man wickedly.

"Okay, getting back to the plan," Pix says, "do you mean we're going to kidnap them?"

"Yes, we're going to kidnap them," John says matter-of-factly. "Well, that's a new one for me, sweet!"

"Matt, Dom, you two are to extend our non-negotiable, uncomfortable invitation to the Dentist. Don't forget the zip ties and blindfold for his traveling pleasure, and I always want usual protocol with comms on."

"Roger that," both men say in unison as they look at each other and grin; boys will be boys.

"I can't wait until the Kid finds out he missed a real kidnapping," Dom laughs.

"Mountain, Pix, you two do the same with the Doctor. But, Mountain, I need you to restrain yourself during transport? He's no good to us if he can't speak."

Mountain stands from his chair to his full height, casting a towering shadow over Amee, "I think I can manage," he says, looking down at her.

"I'm going with you," Amee declares, "no discussion. It's my son we're talking about!"

"Amee," Reggie begins but is shut down so forcefully it feels like the words Amee spits at her have physically picked her up and moved her backward a few feet. But Reggie isn't surprised by the outburst; she can relate to the extent of Amee's pain; she has lived through the torture of losing a child herself and the inability to have another. A mother's pain for the loss of a child settles deep into the marrow of her bones; it becomes part of the body's makeup, as real as appendages like hands and feet. The pain may lay dormant for long periods but awakens quickly by the chance giggles and smile of a child. At this point, the longing and desperation flood the marrow with sorrow, and all the body can do is pick up one of those appendages and then the other to move forward. But one can't walk away from reality; it always catches up.

"No discussion," Amee says again forcefully in Reggie's direction, "you can come with us if you want! But you can't expect me to sit back and wait; I'M GOING!" she declares, looking around the room as if daring someone, especially her father, to object.

Chapter 64

Before leaving the Club House, Oscar-D had grabbed an armful of mission essentials, like hats, coats, and some fake glasses. He was heading East like the Boss said, waiting for the text from Marco informing him that his operation was going live. Could his smile be any bigger?

As instructed, Marco had given the Kid some time before un-jamming the signal to Amee's tracker. He then monitored the tracker Mountain had planted on the Police Cruiser and watched as it started following Oscar-D. It didn't take very long for the games to begin. "Have some fun Kid," he whispers to no one.

His phone pinged with the text for him to start having some fun, and he had every intention of doing so. It felt so good to be back in action and out in the field again; God, at this moment, Oscar-D loved his job. There's no college degree needed, no job description, and no 9 to 5 behind a desk. Right now, his assignment is to lure, make soft contact if the opportunity doesn't put him in danger, then the fun part, evade the target to set the chase in motion again. Lure, soft contact, evade, damn, this is better than Disneyland.

Oscar-D: Marco how far behind?

Marco: You've got about a 20-minute window.

Oscar-D: Roger that.

"I'm feeling like a beer," Oscar-D says to himself and heads to a small Bar & Grill he knows that doesn't sit too far off the main road, about fifteen minutes away. Was it mentioned that you could drink on this gig? Is life not grand?

He picks up the plastic bag with the tracker and shakes his head; the unbelievable cruelty of men can still hit him with surprise, even after all this time.

"Come on, you piece of crap," he says, looking at the tracker as if Dempsey can hear him, "let's get to know each other over a beer."

The parking lot of the Bar & Grill was located behind the establishment itself, and as Oscar-D made his way around the corner of the building he noticed only a few cars parked there. He assumed at least a couple of the vehicles would belong to employees, so the clientele was going to be minimal, but it was still early.

Once parked, Oscar-D gets out of his vehicle and heads to the front of the building, as the sign in the back instructed, but before he enters, he grabs his phone and triggers his comms app. He opens the door and steps into the muted lighting, moving slowly as his eyes take their time to adjust. Two men sat on stools, bellied up to the bar conversing amongst themselves, his entrance not interrupting one of the men from exaggerating the point he was trying to make with his meaty hands.

The music funneled low through the speakers, but Oscar-D could hear Miranda Lambert singing, *If I Were a Cowboy,* making him smile. He loved that little woman.

He still held his phone in his hand and looked at the time; he figured he had about twelve to fifteen minutes before the games began, so he made his way to the bar. After nodding to the two men seated there, the Bar Tender asked what he could get him, and Oscar-D replied, "Bud Light."

With beer in hand, Oscar-D heads to a table in one of the back corners and sits facing the only entrance and waits.

At twelve minutes on the dot, the entrance door opens with a bang as it hits the wall it's affixed to, allowing the daylight to dance through the dust bunnies as the violent swing of the door displaced them.

"Dempsey and his Daddy just slammed through the door," Oscar-D whispers for the tuned-in ears at the Club House, "this is going to be fun."

Looking around the primarily deserted bar and not seeing Amee, Dempsey growls at the man behind the counter, "ladies' room?"

With his mouth hanging open, all the Bar Tender can manage is to point to the restroom sign on the wall, which indicated with an arrow where he could find it.

"Amee," the few patrons of the establishment hear the crazy man scream, "what the hell do you think you're doing?" And obviously, since Amee was nowhere abouts, there was no answer.

"Can you hear him?" Oscar-D laughs quietly, hoping they can.

"You got any good Scotch back there?" Big Daddy growls at the still stunned bar tender as he leans on the bar, waiting for his son to retrieve his property.

"Yessss, Sir," the man manages to say, "I got some 18-year-old Jameson."

"Well, if that's all ya got," Big Daddy says disgusted, "two fingers, neat, I'm goin to need it."

Big Daddy takes his first sip of the Whiskey, saying, "you got young'uns Bar Keep?

"No, Sir."

"Well, if you ever decide to take that plunge, make sure the lady you choose to house them for nine months has a brain in her head; otherwise, you could end up with what I did," he says, pointing toward the restrooms.

"Yes, Sir, thank you, Sir."

After finding the ladies room empty, Dempsey made his way back to the bar area, stomped up to the counter and began screaming at the poor Bar Tender. "Where's Amee?" he demands.

Barley able to stammer his reply, the man informs Dempsey that there hasn't been a woman in this place all day. Not satisfied with the information, Dempsey pulls up a photo of his wife on his phone and shoves it into the faces of the two men seated at the bar, and then shows it to the Bar Tender.

"Have you seen her?" Dempsey hisses at each man individually.

One by one, the men shook their heads in the negative while screaming internally, *I need to get the hell outa here!* Which was fine and possible for the two patrons sitting at the bar, but the poor Bar Tender didn't have the luxury.

"Son-of-a-bitch!" Dempsey declares, then looks around the area and spies a young man slouched at a table in the back. "You," he calls out, heading toward him.

"First contact," Oscar-D whispers.

"What's all the unhappiness about Sheriff," Oscar-D asks, in his best slurring manner, "did she escape your custody or something?" doing his best to perform like a man who'd been drinking all afternoon.

"Look at the picture, you idiot," Dempsey says, shoving his phone under Oscar-D's nose.

"Oh God," Oscar-D gasps in horror and starts to cry, "she looks just like my Darlene. Do you know my Darlene? She's beautiful like that," he says, doing his best to push another tear down his cheek. "Not ugly like her sister Sharlene, now that's one U-G-L-Y woman. My Darlene is beautiful; I miss her so much," he says and continues with the fake waterworks, "you sure you ain't seen her?"

Hearing enough about beautiful Darlene and ugly Sharlene, Dempsey grabs the sobbing lump by his shirt and lifts him off his chair. "You are a worthless air breather; do you know that?" Dempsey screams inches from Oscar-D's face. "It's pathetic how you are sitting here crying like a baby over a piece of ass. At least I'm looking for mine, and God help her when I find her."

365

Dempsey roughly pushes the blubbering lump back into the chair he was grabbed from and gives him another disgusted look before turning and heading to the door. "What the hell is going on with this app?" Oscar-D hears Dempsey say before stepping out of earshot and making his way to the bar.

"Marco, Oscar-D whispers, jam Amee's tracker again so I can get on the road, this guy is pissing me off."

Chapter 65

An hour and a half later, Mountain, Pix, and Amee enter a new medical complex on the East side of Seattle. A bank of elevators and a directory of the offices of the building present themselves to the right. Finding their destination, they call an elevator and head to the 6th floor.

Once the elevator stops on the sixth floor and the doors slide open for them to exit, they do so and quickly find the office they are looking for to the right.

Upon entering, they walk through an imposing reception area and stop at the front counter. The blonde receptionist looks at each individually and becomes visibly alarmed when her eyes land on Mountain's immense presence.

The woman behind the counter looks like she has spent most of her wages on Botox and cosmetic surgery. Her overly plump lips are set in a permanent pre-pucker like a grandma chasing after a visiting grandchild, making it almost impossible to understand her due to the fact her lips don't move when she speaks. And because she's had so many nips, tucks, and lifts the only parts capable of movement on her face are her eyes, moving side to side under stationary eyelids. Her face is stuck in a constant state of surprise, her eyebrows look like they were painted onto a cream-colored canvas, the canvas being her forehead, which has been pulled, tucked, and stretched to the max.

Her eyes begin a terrified dance, and it looks like she's going to try and say something, but Mountain feels the need to launch forward. Even though he'd promised the Boss to follow restraint, his patience seemed to have disappeared at the door. His need to find the Doctor began to cloud over any restraint he may have had left, he was losing it, big time. "Now!" he demands.

The two Botox lips fight to open, she looks like a goldfish kissing the glass of its bowl. The visitors standing in front of her watched as she continued to try and speak, it was an excruciating display of ridiculousness to suffer through when the only words they could understand were; *zoom appointment.*

"Which room is he in?" Pix demands.

The eyes held prisoner within the hardened face shift, look down the hall to the left. Mountain leads the way into the hall and as the receptionist begins to stand in protest, Mountain gives her a Medusa look causing the rest of her body to freeze in place like her face. "Stay!" he declares.

Mountain and Pix begin to open closed doors as they move down the hall, a couple had patients waiting and were given an apology before the door was closed again. Finally, of course it's the last door, they find who they're looking for and enter.

The Doctor is sitting behind his desk with his laptop open, and when he sees three strangers standing in his office, he begins to pump up his tiny chest for the benefit of the patient on the screen and say, "who are you and what do you think you're doing?" But suddenly, all the traces of indignancy he was portraying drain from his demeanor, causing him to turn eight shades of pale. Once the fake demeanor had drained and an abundance of hidden guilt surfaced, an apparent bout of panic set in when he recognizes Amee as one of the intruders. He suddenly realizes he has no control over his body and visibly sags back into the desk chair as he closes his laptop without speaking to the patient. Sweat begins to break out on his forehead in larger than regular beads, and he can't seem to catch his breath. *Is there a doctor in the house?* And what is up with the uncontrollable shaking of his hands?

"You're coming with us, Doc," Mountain announces with his deep angry voice, leaving no room for debate. A debate is the last thing coming because the Doctor can't speak from the surprise and knowledge of the consequences that will come his way because Amee is standing in front of his desk. Still staring at Amee in disbelief, there is no resistance when Pix spins his desk chair around to face Mountain.

Leaning in with his most dominating presence, Mountain speaks directly at the Doctor so there won't be any misunderstanding. "I said, your presence is requested elsewhere!"

"What? Who are you?" he asks as the initial shock of seeing Amee begins to wear off, "he will kill me if I talk," he says looking at Amee for understanding.

Mountain finds himself disgusted and enraged by the little worm's statement, "right now, that's the least of your problems," he says, grabbing the Doctor by his shirt and tie, dangling him a foot off the floor, "which way to the private entrance of this office?"

The Doctor says, "down the hall and through the employee kitchen."

"Good, You, have an appointment to keep!"

"Pix, Mountain says, still holding the Doctor above the floor, lead the way. Once in the hall, we'll take the stairs down to the ground floor and exit into the parking lot."

"Copy that!"

"You, doing, okay?" Mountain asks Amee as they begin to exit the office.

"Best I've felt in a long time; my heart is beating with optimism after his reaction to seeing me in his office. It makes me think that Dempsey's declaration has merit. Oh, and I think he still may wet himself, so watch for that when you're sharing the back seat," she says, smiling.

Pix sends a text to the Boss.

Pix: Our guest has been retrieved, on the way back.

John: Copy that!

Chapter 66

Marco gives Oscar-D the time he wants before un-jamming Amee's tracker again, and knowing the kid as he does, Dempsey is going to go bat shit crazy by the time this is over.

Meanwhile, Dominic and Matt were extending the invitation to the Dentist and feeling seriously let down. They encountered no heart-pumping adrenaline surging through their bodies, no anticipation as to kicking down a few doors; in fact, there was no excitement to be noteworthy. The actual snatch-and-grab was so easy they could have accomplished this OP while in grade school.

The Dentist's office was located right in the middle of downtown Tacoma; the building stood eight levels high with four levels of underground parking.

Once they found a parking place, the two men exited their vehicle and headed to the elevator; always diligent, their eyes never stopped surveying the dark surroundings. It was quiet for the most part, just a few cars coming and going.

As they approached the elevator, the down arrow on the wall next to the elevator doors was blinking the car's descent; once it arrived, the doors opened, and to the would-be kidnappers' surprise, there stood the Dentist, *the mark*.

Through their shock, the duo watched the Dentist nod hello in their direction before exiting the elevator. Then, reflex overriding surprise, they return the Dentist's nod and watch him pass. Dom and Matt instantly eye their surroundings and see no one, so they do an about-face and catch up to the Dentist. With Matt on one side and Dom on the other, they extend the non-negotiable invite from their Boss, and with their luck still holding; they make it to their vehicle unobserved. Standing next to the car, Dom opens the back of the SUV and reaches inside, then throws a roll of duct tape to Matt to dress the Dentist up like a Thanksgiving turkey.

Once the Dentist is secure and sitting in the back seat, Dom leans in and places a wool beanie on the man's head, pulling the front down over his eyes, surprising Matt, and Dom that they still hadn't received any resistance.

It was as if the guy woke up this morning resigned to the fact that today was the day he would be atoning for his sins, which was a relief, for the guilt was becoming so powerful he didn't know how much longer he could carry it. That would explain why the Dentist just turned into a pliable lump when Matt and Dom first grabbed his arms and lifted him off the ground, no fight as they extended the invitation. It's possible an unused portion of conscience was done lying dormant within the Dentist. Fearful at first, the newly awakened part of his conscience opened an eye, looked around its questionable existence, and decided it was time to show itself. It popped its head out tiredly, portraying the fact it knew the jig was up, and continued to acknowledge within the awakening that he had, indeed, sold his soul to the Devil.

It didn't take the Dentist long to realize his guilt was more than ready to comply with anything. But it still wasn't clear what was going on; he could only imagine it had something to do with the off-the-books favors, *favors my ass,* he had been doing for Big Daddy. So, if that were the case, he would need to start weighing

372

his options between the Boss these two men mentioned or the wrath of Big Daddy.

But he didn't need to speculate for long as he sat in the dark with his hands tied behind his back and a blindfold pulled down over his eyes. It quickly became clear what was going on when one of the men in the front of the car turned around and said, "by the way, Amee DuPree says hi!" Now he knew and quickly decided he had a better chance with the "Boss" than Big Daddy. And, to move things along, he would have started spilling his guts right then and there if he didn't have a piece of duct tape covering his mouth.

"I'll send a text to the Boss, Matt says.

Matt: Invitation delivered and accepted.

John: Any problems?

Matt: I wish, BORING!

John: Copy that, hurry back.

Chapter 67

Reggie has finally received the go-ahead to begin working out her shoulder, and a lot sooner than she was told originally. So, she thought she would start while waiting for their guests to arrive. In her mind, the best way to work out her shoulder was the batting cage. To begin, she dials back the pitching machine, which will force her to make slower, smoother swings to get warmed up because she could be her own worst enemy at times by jumping in full throttle. "So far, so good," she says after the first couple of swings to her sidekick sitting outside the netting where she will be safe from foul balls.

Suzie has always been her biggest fan and staunchest supporter of these workouts, she may be a dog, but she knows this is not just physical exercise for Reggie but an emotional recharge as well.

After a dozen or so more swings on this setting, Reggie increases the speed of the pitching machine. Her body is working out all the kinks from her bed rest; she's beginning to sweat and feel her muscles respond to the movement, and she feels invigorated with each swing. But the workout isn't complete; with each swing of the bat, Reggie has begun her mental ass kicking of Domestic Violence, the one that keeps her going. The one that helps her stay emotionally fit and mentally strong. The formula for each excursion varies depending on current circumstances, but the result is always the same. Because no matter how productive the physical and emotional workout is, Reggie has accepted that she will always live her life on the practice field, dreaming of a day she will send her past over the center field fence. Just once she would like to send the ball, AKA the head of the devil himself, screaming through the air, over the center fielder's head and fence, to land in the domestic darkness where he is confronted by all the victims that arrived there first by his hand.

No matter how many times she swings the bat, how many times the bat connects with the ball, and how many abusers the team takes out of play, she will always have her demons. Hence, the life of a survivor. But Reggie has never wallowed within the confines of a pity party, asking herself, *'why me'* because she knows there's no answer to that question. And most importantly, she's very aware she's not the only one to walk through hell and come out the other side; sadly, the number is astronomical.

All victims of any violence, not just domestic violence, will be scarred emotionally, if not physically, when they are finally set free of the darkness they were trapped in for so long. A freed victim learns over time that they may have escaped physically, but their mind will always be held prisoner within a purgatory that keeps them wondering when the next trigger from their past will descend like a dark locust. It can be an emotional shackle that hinders their quest and ability to move on, exposing the blatant reality that some will make it, and some won't.

Every team member has witnessed Reggie's constant struggle to remain a Survivor, and their admiration for her strength is solidified every time they watch her fight her past. It's heartbreaking to witness the acts of courage she performs to sidestep the darkness as it rushes in on her, each step placed strategically within its muck as it surrounds her with fear and memories. It's a grueling consequence of once being a victim, but over time she has found the strength to fight and maintain her footing, which at times is still so fragile.

Because of their work and insight, each member can acknowledge that the physical escape for a victim is always dangerous, but with their help, it's doable. However, the never-ending emotional journey a victim will have to face once the escape is complete saddens them deeply because they continuously witness the fight and see it every day with one of their own.

It's an emotional highway that continues to lay more miles of asphalt and construct more steel bridges for them to traverse mentally. There are times when they will see what looks like a life of peace, devoid of fear and pain, coming into view, giving them the illusion that their journey is coming to an end and all they must do is take the next exit to arrive. Then, WHAM, he's back in their head, pushing them toward his dead-end detour of horror and fear, disrupting their progress, striking them down with a sharp reminder of the consequences. He causes an emotional U-turn, wiping out the miles of progress they had worked so hard to claim. But the ones that will make it will set out again, by passing his detour to find one of their own.

Trying to become a Survivor leads one on an endless journey due to the emotional exits, and the mental OUT-OF-ORDER rest stops along the way. It seems like a cruelty of colossal proportions played by the GPS gods, their favorite joke continually telling you to follow a different route. They hold court as they ride the closest satellite laughing at the turmoil they cause below and screaming into space, NOPE, NOT YOU, MUST RECALCULATE, MUST RECALCULATE!

Reggie takes one more swing, relishing the sweat drenching her T-shirt, feeling physically spent, but mentally and emotionally recharged. She reaches up, removes her helmet, and pushes the stray hair that has become dislodged from the band at the nap of her neck away from her face. Then she wipes the salty sweat from her forehead and face by lifting the bottom of her shirt in a not-so-classy move. Dropping her shirt, she reaches for the remote control connected to the pitching machine, but before she turns it off, she notices the digital number flashing from the wall behind it. She watches the display continue to blink, showing the mile per hour the machine sent the pitches hurdling across the plate. A satisfying smile begins to form across her face as she happily acknowledges that physically, she's almost back, "now that's what I'm talkin about!"

Chapter 68

While the two teams that were dispatched to extend the warm invitations to a not so warm, mandatory sit down, *wink, wink*, checked in and gave their returning ETA'S, Oscar-D was more than happy to continue his cat and mouse game.

He pulled into the parking lot of a small diner off US-2 E, found a parking spot as far from the front entrance as possible, and cut the engine. He immediately texted Marco and gave him the go-ahead to, once again, un-jam the tracker.

Before getting out of his vehicle, he reaches over the console and grabs a duffle bag from the passenger seat and begins pulling out his stash of clothing items. The items consisted of the usual hoodies, T-shirts, and hats, a young man's wardrobe of choice.

Oscar-D, the self-proclaimed biggest fan of Coach Mark Few of Gonzaga University, pulls out a Bull Dogs Hoody and a baseball-style cap with the Coach's autograph emblazoned in black sharpie across the bill. "Now that guy can coach," he constantly tells anyone who will listen. He quickly slips both items on, looks into the review mirror, and decides if he didn't get too close to his pursuers, he wouldn't be recognized or even noticed, for that matter. But before exiting the vehicle, the young man can't help but take one last look in the mirror, he's satisfied with his choice of clothing and says to the face staring back at him, "Go Zags!"

The first thing Oscar-D did upon entering the diner was look for the sign indicating where the restrooms were located. He made his way to the men's room, mostly because he really needed to use the facilities. He begins to laugh, just loud enough for Marco, who is listening over the coms, to hear the steady stream of urine flow into the urinal and then the loud flush that follows.

This happens every time he's sent out, Oscar-D enjoys his time in the field and takes his instructions seriously when the Boss says, "coms on at all times." But Marco hates that he's forced to sit and listen to Oscar-D's bodily functions, and he really gets irritated when the sound of the flush travels through the coms, it's so unprofessional. Oscar-D can imagine the string of expletives flying around the Club House when Marco hears him take a leak and he can't help himself by saying in a wicked whisper, "you'll be okay Marco, see ya soon Brother."

When his current torment aimed at Marco is complete, he opens the men's room door and takes a quick look in both directions of the hallway, first left, then right, all clear. Oscar-D slips out and takes a few steps to the left, then using a knuckle, he taps on the door to the lady's facilities.

"Hello," he says quietly while opening the door just enough for his face to breach the gap, "anyone in here?" When there's no reply, he slips in and fumbles with the lock attached to the inside of the door, sliding it into place. He takes a moment to look around the space, realizing things haven't changed since his high school antics, but that's a story best left in the past.

There's only one toilet, so it's easy to find what he's looking for. Remembering Miss Reggie's suggestion to Amee about the Tampax box, he makes his way to the toilet and lifts the lid on the silver metal receptacle attached to the wall for used feminine articles. He's relieved the garbage bag inside is empty and lifts it out, placing the tracker at the bottom of the receptacle, then replaces the paper garbage bag on top to cover it.

Satisfied with his plan, he quickly moves to the door, slips the lock back, and silently steps out into the hall. Suddenly a thought slams into him when he realizes the possibility that the empty bag in the receptacle may not be empty when he retrieves the tracker. *Could Marco really rain down that kind of Karma on him?*

Yes, it would gross him out, but he has three sisters and was exposed to weigh more than any teenage boy should have been growing up. Oh, the education he had acquired and the things he had endured at the hands of his sisters. But still, what was gross then is going to be gross now!

Oscar-D was enjoying the view from a booth at a dirty window facing the parking lot. He had ordered a half-pound Mega burger, apparently their specialty, and an obscene amount of fries to go along with it. He intended to take his time eating, and enjoy every second of the show, that at this moment had begun in the parking lot just a few parking spaces from his window. He was confident, at least for now, that between the dirty window and his disguise, Dempsey or his Daddy wouldn't be able to recognize him from their earlier encounter at the Bar & Grill.

His food arrived at the same time both driver and passenger doors opened on the cruiser marked with the DuPree Police Department logo, causing Oscar-D to chuckle to himself because the DuPree Police Department was a total farce.

The two men were screaming at each other over the top of the cruiser. Dempsey stood at the open driver's side door with his phone in his hand, while Big Daddy stood on the passenger side with his door still open as well. Both men were trying to outshout the other to make their point and get the last word in.

This display continued for another two or three minutes before Dempsey waived his phone in the air, stepped back from the cruiser, and like a belligerent child, slammed his door shut before heading toward the diner entrance. Seconds later, Big Daddy did the same with his door and began stamping frustratedly after his son.

Dempsey never took his eyes off his phone as he reached the door, so he didn't see the young man on the other side who was one step away from opening the door so he could exit. Before the young man's hand grabbed the door handle to pull it open, Dempsey pushed the door from the outside with frustrated anger, slamming it into the young man so hard it knocked him off balance and he landed on his ass.

"Hey, what the hell, man?" the young man screams as he scrambles to his feet, intending to confront the bully at the door. But one look from Dempsey stopped him in his tracks, causing his hands to rise in defeat as he took the necessary steps to retreat.

"WHAT?" Dempsey barks at the young man before stepping into the dining area.

"Asshole," the young man says, making a hasty retreat around the bully to the exit. It was as if the diner and its customers were placed on pause, all activity ceased after the confrontation at the door. The suffocating silence engulfed the diners as their eyes became trained on the two men, including Oscar-D's.

Looking around the diner, Big Daddy shouts into the room, "Listen up, all you Lib-tards; we're looking for this woman. Show them the picture, you idiot," Big Daddy bellows at his son, the biggest disappointment in his life.

Dempsey begins at the closest table, and with Amee's picture on his phone, he stops at each patron while screaming her name at the top of his lungs. All the customers could manage in response to the situation was a negative shake of their head, causing Dempsey to become even more riled up.

"I know you're lying," he screams at the patrons because we tracked her here," he says, looking at the app on his phone again.

"Boy, check the shitter!" Big Daddy bellows.

"He's heading to the restrooms," Oscar-D says into his pile of fries so the Club House can visualize what's happening.

The diner still sat in absolute silence except for what sounded like the restroom's door being dismantled followed by a beastly rage one associates with a Pitbull who's been trained to kill in a warehouse ring.

Popping the last fry into his mouth Oscar-D says to the empty basket sitting on the table in front of him, "jam it again Marco."

"Done," Marco says into the coms.

Now he will have to wait for Dempsey's reaction to losing the signal before he can retrieve the tracker. And once he realizes he's lost it again, everyone in the diner will witness a rage, one Oscar-D hopes will not bring harm to the innocent people sitting around him.

During the wait, he begins thinking of the poor woman this animal is hunting, imagining the dark world she has lived in and the pain that went along with that existence. The thoughts fill his brain with sadness, as they do every time the team is on a mission, so he tries to draw strength from the many positives of their work and the successes they have achieved. Unfortunately, it's all he can do while shackled to the booth at the dirty window, listening to the Pitbull's pitiful and desperate screams of rage because he's lost control of his victim.

Chapter 69

As hard as Bud tries, he can't give John and his team any information concerning the day of Amee's delivery, except the date. He knew nothing about the medical aspect of his grandson's birth and still feels the profound loss he had felt that day when told the baby didn't make it. Sadly, Bud still fights his feelings of inadequacy because of his inability to protect his family. He trembles with self-hate as he keeps reminding them, while slapping the armrests of his wheelchair for emphasis, that he was stuck in Leavenworth at the time, well out of the way of everything.

He *was* able to tell them that on one of the rare visits he was allowed with Amee, she had told him she was pregnant. And then, on her next visit six months later, she told him she had lost the baby, stillborn, she'd said, between sobs of emotional pain.

Even though the only information they had was the date Amee said she had lost the baby, Marco had confidence in his skilled techs and set them in motion. There wasn't a computerized secret they couldn't ferret out, no thread of information they couldn't pull, or any lie they couldn't decipher. Each workstation was running a different program, many of which Marco had developed himself, to search through the parameters given, but so far, they had gleamed nothing. But that only made the techs more diligent in their efforts, ramping up their resolve. They were dedicated and emotionally invested; they wouldn't stop until they found the information that would help solve the question of the baby. Is he alive, or isn't he?

There searches came up blank for a birth or death certificate; the net gave them nothing for a baby boy with no name who was stillborn on April 2nd, 2020.

As frustrating as the process was becoming after hours of searching and finding nothing, the Club House chose to take it as a good sign, maybe Amee's son was alive.

"How's it going Marco?" John asks as he walks up to the man's workstation.

"Still nothing Boss, I'm hoping no news is good news."

"You?"

"I'm afraid to speculate, there are a million scenarios of how this could have played out and I won't get my hopes up, not yet! But we'll get more info soon enough, both my teams of kidnappers should be here shortly, and we'll get the answers we need," John says with a wicked smile.

"How's the kid doing?"

"He flushed again, Boss, and he didn't wash his hands!" Marco says in horror.

"Well, that's a given, Marco; you should be used to that by now, but I didn't need to know about the hand washing thing; some things are better left unsaid," John says.

"Now you know how Dominic and I feel, Boss; the kid slithers into our heads and plays with our patience neurons," Marco says, tapping his temple to show he's as serious as a heart attack. But getting back to the hand washing thing, you might want to remember that the next time you shake his hand Boss, and just remember you heard it from a reliable source, and that source is me." Marco smirks.

Not liking the idea of giving any semblance of an attaboy or admitting to anything that could be construed as positive, Marco says reluctantly, "he's doing good for the most part but needs to learn you don't talk over the coms with your mouth full. I don't think he'll ever grow up!"

"That seems to be the consensus, but what can we do? He *is* family," John says, shrugging his shoulders in defeat.

"Back gate to the Club House," the voice says coming through the strategically placed speakers affixed to the walls within the interior, "both teams just got home, and we have guests."

Looking up, John sees Reggie and Suzie coming his way. He greets them with a sinister smile and says while taking her outstretched hand, "time to have some fun!"

"You are way too excited about this," Reggie says, trying to curb her own excitement.

"Damn right, I'm done letting everyone else have all the fun!"

"Oh, the burden of leadership, you poor baby."

As John, Reggie and Suzie exit the motor pool; they watch as their guests are escorted into the storage space with their wrists bound and eyes still covered.

Suzie hears the shuffling of feet and turns her head to greet Michael and Xander as they fall into step.

"This ought to be fun, "Xander says with a dark drawl.

"Just what I was telling Reggie," John comments.

Upon entering the storage unit, John sees it's cleared of all the junk, and for effect, Pete has extended one bare bulb at the end of a dangling wire above a table with two chairs sitting on one side. Their own version of interrogation 101. Their two guests of honor were seated at the table, eyes uncovered now and wrists free. Their eyes were large as saucers as they took in their surroundings and tried to judge the meaning of their predicament. And strangely enough, neither had found their voice.

In one corner stood the menacing Mountain, with Pix and Amee at his side, and in another, trying their best to seem cool and calm, and failing miserably, were Dominic and Matt. These two men still felt robbed of any excitement and were hoping that might change now. That left John and his gang to plant themselves in front of the table. They didn't speak to the men, but Reggie performed spectacularly, bending down and whispering into Suzie's good ear. Suzie becomes visibly rigid, the team knows this is also a performance, but their guests do not. Finally, after the nod from Reggie, Suzie turns and begins to circle the table, teeth bared and a guttural growl emanating into the room. John almost laughs but manages to hold it in.

"Hey, what the hell is this?" the dentist screams with panic as Suzie makes her rounds.

Suzie plants herself between the two honored guests and continues playing the tough canine.

She sniffs them individually, growls, and shows her teeth, which causes the dentist to lose control and pee himself.

"Suz," Reggie says, calling her back to her side, where she leans down and whispers, "Good job." Suzie, still playing her part, continues to quiver. She plants her backside within inches of the concrete floor, just waiting for the game to be over so she can launch herself over the table.

The room is silent except for the heavy breathing of the two men, and the urine drip from the dentist's chair as it hits the cement floor.

The silence is broken by John, "Amee," he says not turning from the men, "will you step up here please?"

Amee immediately takes a few steps forward but is stopped by Mountain's large hand as he places it on her shoulder. She turns slightly to look into his tender eyes; she feels him squeeze her shoulder and hears him whisper, "you got this, girl."

"Thank you," she responds before joining the others at the table. Her stomach begins to churn with anticipation, whether it's good churning or bad, she doesn't care, she needs answers one way or another.

As she takes her place at the table between Reggie and John, she realizes she doesn't have one iota of sympathy to waste on the men sitting in front of her.

An image of them set on fire while tethered to a stake, fuels her mood, and she begins to let her rage toward these two men take root. All the sorrow and pain of loss spread through her veins again; it pumped with embers of heated hate she had never felt before, not even toward Dempsey.

Neither of the men could look at her; their eyes lowered to the table they sat behind and acknowledged with their silence that they were cowards who sold their souls to Darwin DuPree; there was nothing to be said, and they offered no excuse. Their cowardice was of the worst order, and they knew they deserved every bit of reprisal.

"Does he know we're here?" the doctor asks as he finds the balls to lift his head and plead with the room.

"Who?"

"Darwin DuPree!"

"At this particular moment," John says calmly, leaning over and planting his fists on the table directly in front of the man, "he's the last person you should be worried about!"

"Easy for you to say," the doctor cries in John's face, then quickly looks to Amee, "please tell him what Darwin is capable of!"

Amee maintains her strength and doesn't say a word, letting herself ride the merry-go-round of satisfaction when she sees the fear emanating from the man sitting at the table. *Welcome to my world, she thinks, you sorry excuse for a human being.* Like John, she leans close, her face about a foot from the doctor, and delivers a shrill scream of disbelief. "Are you serious right now? You want me to have pity on you, to help you the way you *DIDN'T* help me? Again," she screams and slams her palm onto the table, making him whine with surprise and guilt, "you pathetic piece of crap!"

"Well," he says hesitantly, "I was hoping."

"IS MY SON ALIVE?" she screams with rage into his face, drowning out his incredible pleas for help.

"YES!" he screams back.

Chapter 70

Amee wants to pray, but first, her belief in prayer needs rescuing from the darkness, where it's floundered dormant for years. So, with every deep breath, she silently recites every prayer suddenly remembered because she needs the declaration Dempsey made in John's security office to be fact, to be a truth she so desperately deserves. Amee's legs threaten to buckle, but somehow, their quivering muscles hold her upright. The truth of her son's existence ignited her strength, and she screamed for every mother's vindication concerning their child.

Sensing the pain emanating from Amee, Suzie lets out a genuine growl that begins deep in her chest; she goes to Amee's side with her eyes locked on the doctor. Games over, Suzie isn't acting this time.

Reggie knows she should call Suz back but thinks, what the hell?

The doctor deserves much worse than anything Suzie can do to him. She steps up to the table and tries to comfort Amee with a slight touch to her shoulder. The woman's mind and soul were coming together in a blind rage, and even though Amee deserved the act of delivering some justice, it wouldn't get them anywhere now. Reggie is familiar with the term 'blind fury'. She's experienced it herself many times, and now she knows what the team sees when she hits that point of no return. The point where she delivers that fury in an explosion of justice.

So, before Amee could launch herself over the table and rip the doctor's head off, Reggie screams in his direction, *"WHERE THE HELL IS HER SON?* And don't waste our time by lying; there's no reason for you to bide your time here because there's no way out of this for you!"

"Answer the question you piece of crap," Matt hisses from his time out corner.

"Darwin took him!" the weasel screams into the room, not having the guts to look at Amee.

"What do you mean, he took him?"

Physically squirming in his seat, the doctor elaborates. "But don't worry, he's a happy healthy little man," the doctor screams hoping to placate his captors, as if that will make things okay.

"How do you know that?" Amee demands.

"Because I'm his private pediatrician," the man declares to everyone in the dimly lit room, as if there's nothing to worry about and all is fine. But what he saw on the faces of his captors was nothing but rage, and all his declaration did was fuel it.

"Oh my God," Amee cries and begins to fall, but just like before, Mountain is there to catch her.

"Start from the beginning Doctor, and don't leave anything out," John says sharply.

Remembering what Michael had said earlier, Matt speaks. "Especially the reason you would ever betray your oath about doing no harm," he demands from the dark corner he has been occupying since the visitors were brought in.

392

"Please understand," the Doctor pleads to the room, "Darwin will kill me if he finds out I talked about his grandson." The statement concerning his own safety felt like nails on a chalk board making everyone cringe with loathing for the worm squirming in front of them. And the reference of the baby being Darwin's grandson sent Amee into a spiral of nausea that began churning like sour milk with no escape, because unfortunately it was a true statement.

"Doctor," Amee screams over the table, "when this is over, you will welcome your death by Darwin's hands because what I promise you is a pain so dark and twisted it will eat you alive for the rest of your days. I swear to you that you will suffer, emotionally and physically, to the point you end up in a blubbering pile of skin and bones, living in the corner of a cement cell. Now, do you understand you will get no mercy from me?'

The doctor doesn't know what to do as he looks around the room. On the one hand, he knows Darwin will kill him after all this is over, but on the other, he has no delusions that Amee was just being emotional at the moment; no, he knows her threat is real. Until now, he had no idea how far a mother would go!

"I want to know where my son is, please, you owe me something, you owe me that at least," she declares through choked sobs.

"Suz!" Reggie says through clenched teeth, her dark command registered not only to Suzie, but everyone standing with her.

Immediately Suzie moves around the table and bares her teeth, emitting a dangerous growl as she creeps closer to the doctor. She places herself between his knees while continuing to growl and takes a good long look at his manhood, while saliva dripped ever closer to what by now would be a shriveled stump. Suzie, taking her orders seriously continued the intimidation by jutting her tongue out and licking her lips, leaving the doctor to be the only one who didn't know it was just an act. "Start talking," John demands, "looks like she's ready for lunch."

Resigned to the fact he had only two choices, bad and worse, the doctor let out a heavy sigh while throwing glances at Suzie. "Okay, Okay," he stammers, "but call the mutt off!"

Reggie snapped her fingers, and Suzie immediately stopped growling and showing her teeth, but she wouldn't move. She sniffed loudly, staying where she was between his legs, and plunked her butt onto the cement, glaring at the doctor and continuing to lick her lips. Her reason for such diligence is that she may still get lunch after all.

Surrendering to his fate, the doctor began to try and explain. "I'm married, you see," he says pleadingly to the audience, who are glaring down at him.

John picked up on the eruption building from the back of the room; Mountain was ready to explode. He needed to put a cap on it before all hell broke loose, and Mountain ended up killing the man before he told his story.

"Mountain!" John said, raising his hand in a declaring manner to defuse the thoughts going through the big man's brain.

"So, you're married," Reggie says to the man, "our condolences to your wife."

"And I have two lady friends I frequent and support." He's jabbering, the explanation sending him deeper into the recesses of his desperate attempt to vindicate his actions. "My wife doesn't know, but Darwin found out somehow, that Bastard," he hissed. "Anyway, getting back to my situation, do you know how expensive it is to support three women?" He waited, looking around the room as if seriously expecting an answer. "You have three mortgages, three cars, the usual monthly expenses times three. I was almost to the point of having to cut one loose before Darwin walked into my office one day. He sat down at my desk and said, very bluntly, you're a stupid son-of-a-bitch, three heifers, really?"

"He told me he'd been having me tailed for months, then offered me a solution, a financial solution, a way I could keep all my ladies and keep them happy. I asked if he was going to tell my wife, and he said not as long as our little arrangement didn't hit any sudden potholes caused by ethics or a conscience on my part, he wouldn't tell her."

Looking over at Amee, he said, "I had no idea at the time what the arrangement would entail. All I saw was the financial solution to my problem. But once I realized how demented that man was and what he expected me to do medically, not just for you but the poor bastards his son decided to play with, it was too late. I'm so sorry I was such a coward and chose my ladies over you and what's right.

Matt couldn't stand it any longer, he had to move, "you're telling us you stole this woman's baby? You told her it was born dead, just so you didn't have to cut one of your Bitches lose?"

395

"Well, I guess when you say it like that it does sound pretty awful, but yes, that's what I'm saying."

"You guess !!!!" Matt screamed and moved so quickly that he was a blur in jeans and a T-shirt as he catapulted over the table. He hit the man so hard that his chair collapsed beneath him, causing a fearful scream to enter the room from the Dentist, who up until now had been silent. If he hadn't already emptied his bladder, he would have then.

The single light bulb swaying from the ceiling after Matt hit it while flying over the table caused the whole scene to resemble a bad movie. Watching from the sidelines, the rest of the room's occupants could only stand in stunned shock. Suzie began a frenzied dance while John tried to pull Matt off the doctor. Feet were kicking, and bloodied fists were flying with determined accuracy as the pummeling continued.

"Sergeant!" John commands using the rank Matt held while in the service, and just like it did then, it resonated now, as it will for infinity. The command silenced the room and stopped the fist that was held in the air bloodied and extended, ready to add another pummeling blow to the already damaged doctor.

"You contemptable piece of SHIT!" Matt screams at the lump cowering on the floor, blood dripping from a broken nose.

Once Matt was under control, having stepped back to his corner, the table was lifted and put in place with the two attendees sitting in their chairs beneath the still swinging light bulb above the table. One guest a bloody mess and the other needing a change of clothes.

"You broke my nose," the doctor cries into the room while wiping the blood that had spread down his chin and across his cheeks with the back of his hand. How am I going to explain this?"

"Don't much care!" Matt declares from the corner where he stands struggling with a rage that is so raw he wants to climb out of his skin.

"Where's my baby now?" Amee demands.

"With his nanny in Leavenworth. Darwin bought a house there, even before you delivered, he had this all planned."

"OH, MY GOD, OH, MY GOD," Amee keeps repeating from the background. The jacket of torment she has worn since the day she believed she had lost her son has become more restrictive. It begins to devour her with a new rage and heavy contempt for this man and the other men involved. She slumps to her knees connecting with the cold cement floor, she has no control over her own body. She wraps her arms around herself and begins rocking back and forth, digesting the pain and sorrow all over again. It feels just as raw and jagged as it did the first time, the internal eruption awakens the dormant pain and restricts her ability to comprehend what shouldn't need to be comprehended. "I will Kill you for this," she hisses, "if it's the last thing I do, I swear I will see you dead!"

Fighting her contempt for the man, Reggie demands the address in Leavenworth. "You act like you have a choice here; believe me, you don't. NOW WHAT'S THE ADDRESS!" she screams across the table. When the doctor continues to sit silently wiping his nose, Reggie snaps her fingers, and we all know what that means. Growling again at the man, Suzie moves in and stands on her back legs, placing her large fore paws on his knees and piercing him with black orbs of hate in her eyes. She scrapes her large nails across his legs, enhancing the threat as it's delivered from her maw to slither over and through her teeth.

"I can't," the doctor says trying to exact Suzie's paws from his legs. "PLEASE CALL THIS MONSTER OFF!" he screams.

"Suz!"

Once Suzie has stepped back from the man he says, "I can't tell you, he'll kill me."

"You still think your life is going to be worth living after this?" Reggie asks with heated sarcasm. "Either way you're royally screwed doctor, NOW GIVE US THE ADDRESS!" And he did.

Suddenly the focus in the room shifts to the dentist and he starts to stammer without being asked, he'd seen and heard enough, and didn't want to pee himself again. There was no prodding necessary to make the man start singing.

"Gambling, lots and lots of gambling. I owed so much money at Washington State Casino's and Darwin found out about it, he'd had someone following me too. He told me all my debts would be paid in full saving me from the broken limbs the casino thugs would deliver if I didn't pay. He settled with all my creditors. You don't understand, I had been banned from every casino in the area and down the coast, that included all the underground card games I knew of. I knew I was in trouble, there was no way I could win enough cash to save my ass from those guys. Darwin said all I had to do was come when called, do what he asked and keep my mouth shut. After he paid off my debts, money started coming into an overseas account he set up for me, after that it was too late to back out. Money was deposited after every off the books task I performed."

"I have one of those accounts overseas too," the doctor chimed in.

"Jesus, you're pathetic," Matt snaps.

"Just like the doctor," he says pointing to his brother in crime, "I'm sent to treat the damage inflicted by that son of his. He loves prowling the bars far and near just to find a victim and start wailing on him, or her, for no good reason."

As the dentist continued to spill his guts he seemed to become smaller with every word he spoke, if he had many more confessions he may end up swimming in his puddle of urine below his chair. Looking to his right he gives the doctor a sick look of camaraderie, "I figured out a while ago I'm not the only shit head he has control of. Every time I was summoned to fix the dental damage of one of the poor schmucks Dempsey set his sights on, law enforcement from that town or county would show up and convince the victim that proceeding with filing charges wouldn't be in their best interest."

John stands tall and imposing on the other side of the table, so disgusted he doesn't think he can form words, his anger is so intense. But heaving heavily he states, "so you just turn a blind eye to all of it?"

"Yes, and I'm sorry to say that I still gamble and am still bad at it, but now I can afford to lose."

After the team had asked all their questions, the rage in the small space was as pungent as the puddle of piss under the Dentist's chair, but they had no choice but to endure it and continued to evaluate the information.

"What do you want us to do with these two pieces of crap, Boss?" Dominic asks, the question full of contempt. His European accent sounded thicker than usual. John commanded this man into battle more times than should ever have been needed, and because of that, could read him well. Dom's voice always became thicker when his blood began to boil, and one thing that always turned up the heat was atrocities against women and children. But as much as it pained John to hold Dom back, the boiling pot needed to simmer with the lid affixed tightly. But he promised himself that it would only be temporary.

"Hold them for now Brother, I have a feeling we just had a taste of the shit we'll be walking through before this comes to an end. Besides, they may come in handy down the road."

"Roger that, Boss," Dom says, letting his disappoint show; he was hoping for a green light to do, you know, WHATEVER.

As the team swiftly exited the supply shed, leaving their guests to tend to their wounds, one nursing his injuries and the other desperately wishing he could change his soiled pants, John managed to catch up to Xander.

"We need to talk," John says. I think it might be time to call in that favor we've been sitting on."

"Yep," Xander replies, "I was just thinking the same thing."

Chapter 71

Back inside the Club House, Reggie and Suzie accompany Amee as she goes in search of Bud to tell him that his grandson is alive.

"When can we go get him?" Amee asks impatiently.

"As soon as we check out the doctor's story and come up with a solid plan."

"I want to go with the team when it's time, Reggie, I have to."

"I know, Amee," Reggie says, reaching out and touching her shoulder. "Goes without saying."

"Thank you. I just can't believe he's alive. I should have known; I should have felt something! I'm his mother, for God's sake!"

Standing outside the conference room, John stops and sends Oscar-D a text:

John: "We need a bit more time before you head to DuPree. Can you manage?"

Oscar-D: "No prob, Boss."

John: "Be safe, kid."

Oscar-D: "Copy that."

After the communication with Oscar-D is complete, John makes his way to the inner sanctum and heads to Marco's workstation. "I just reached out to the kid and let him know we need a bit more time and for him to keep the game alive, so he'll be in touch."

"That's some heavy intel you just got out of our two guests, Boss. I wish I could have seen Suzie do her thing," Marco laughs. "It's just not the same listening to the words and not witnessing the actual acts that go along with them."

"Agreed. Now we just need to figure out the best way to utilize that info and form a plan to get that boy to his mother."

"Understood and agreed, Boss."

John looks around the room and finds his two ladies. There they are, Reggie and Suz. The sight begins to lighten his fatigue and brighten his world, as it always does. The last two hours of disgust and rage he'd acquired with their guests seem to melt into a simmer. Reggie must have sensed his eyes, because she slowly turns in his direction and shyly places her hand on her heart while meeting his penetrating eyes with a pair of her own.

Suzie, on the other hand, senses she has work to do. She is consumed by the act of comforting Amee and Bud. Her baby lies snuggly in Bud's lap, and Suzie waits for it to do its magic. Always the gentle nurturer, our Suzie is.

Sadly, the emotional connection he and Reggie just shared is suddenly replaced with the weight of the daunting tasks taking up residence on his broad shoulders. He knows working through what is needed won't be easy, but he's managed before more times than he can count.

He wonders what time it is, then realizes he isn't as curious as he thought, because the act of looking at his watch feels too disheartening and is forgotten in an instant. His exhaustion is smothering, emotionally and physically, but he doesn't have time to slow down or shut down—there's a baby out there who belongs with his mother and grandfather. His head spins with the fact that two extractions just turned into three.

He closes his eyes, takes in a deep breath, and begins to pull from his training. There were times when he and his platoon stayed awake for days at a time, with only ten to fifteen minutes of shut eye at various intervals, if lucky. They would lean against anything they could find—a wall, a tree, a bombed-out vehicle. Sometimes, they would stand back-to-back, leaning on a brother. He remembers with astonishment how Marco could be standing alone and begin to snore in seconds.

Chapter 72

John and Xander sat behind the small desk in John's security office, having a FaceTime conversation with Robert Statsmore from the Department of Justice.

"Well, this must be important if you two are reaching out," the man says through the laptop screen.

"It is, Sir. We need your help, if you can," John says.

"Of course, Lieutenant, I owe you both an enormous debt. What do you need?"

Xander clears his throat. "Sir, do you by chance know of Royce Delgado, the head of the FBI's satellite office in Seattle?"

"Is this some kind of joke?" the man laughs incredulously.

John and Xander turn to each other with questioning eyes, suddenly feeling like they're seated in front of a high school principal's desk, waiting for punishment. Turning back to the screen, John replies, "No, Sir, not at all!"

"He's my son-in-law, married to my oldest daughter Judith." Adjusting his position in his chair, he leans a little closer to the screen. "What's this about?"

"Well, we're going to need his help, Sir, and want to know if he can be trusted, to put it bluntly."

"Well, to throw the bluntness back at ya, he's as straight as they come. He's had an amazing career and worked damn hard to achieve it. Men, Royce can be trusted; you have my word."

If luck and fate were something you believed in, this was the proof of their existence. All John and Xander could do was sit in shock, looking at the man. Finally, something was going their way.

"Why don't you explain, Gentlemen," he says, settling comfortably back into his chair.

Thinking quickly, John decided it couldn't hurt to have a high-ranking official in their corner, so he and Xander, taking turns, started from the beginning, the very beginning. John relayed how his family lost his aunt to abuse and then sadly explained how that loss led to the formation of Mickey. Xander interjected here and there but left most of the intel to be delivered by John. He shared their current situation concerning Amee, Bud, and the baby, leaving off with the battle they were up against, fighting local and state-wide corruption with Darwin DuPree being the puppet master of all of it.

The man suddenly sat military-rigid and alert, with looks of sadness, shock, and rage—the whole gamut of emotions—tramping across his face like boots across a battlefield. What he was hearing brought back scenes of his time in Afghanistan and the atrocities he witnessed concerning that despicable culture and the treatment of their women and children. But, like so many, he was naive about the subject here at home. He had no idea there was a need for a group like this in the civilized world. It made him question his awareness and pained him to realize how out of touch he was. He had a sudden need to do something.

"What can I do, John? What do you need?"

"If you could reach out to your son-in-law and let him know we will be in touch, and that he should take our call, that would be great. But, Sir, you can't say anything about what my team does—for our safety and every victim we help. We need to stay off the radar; you can understand, I'm sure. We will inform Royce ourselves on what we need and why; again, I'm sure you understand."

"Of course, understood!"

"Thank you, Sir. We appreciate your help and discretion. By the way, Sir, how is Charles doing?"

Years ago, toward the end of John's last tour, he was escorted into a dust-covered officer's tent. Once his eyes had adjusted from the piercing, insufferable sunlight outside to the heavy darkness inside, a voice that sounded like it was being filtered through the hot sand surrounding them told him to stand at ease. A high-ranking military man sat behind a makeshift desk, and John realized, once he could see, that it was a colonel. *At ease, my ass!* The man's eyes, heavy-lidded, were filled with the same shame and sadness that John had witnessed just minutes ago. The years hadn't taken away the sorrow within his eyes when thinking of his son.

"Lieutenant," the Colonel says, acknowledging John's presence.

"Sir," John responds.

"I need your help, Lieutenant," the Colonel says, while throwing a few papers into his out basket. "But first, I need you to know this is not an order; it's a personal request, one that can be refused if you choose. Do you understand, Son?"

"Sir, yes, Sir!"

"At ease, man, this is not a formal meeting."

All John felt he could do at that point was nod his head in acknowledgment and do his best to calm down.

"I am going to ask you to take on a very risky extraction in Fallujah. I've heard nothing but good things about your special abilities, and because of them, I'm asking for this personal favor."

"Sir?"

"My son Charles was captured two days ago, along with two other journalists assigned to follow leads concerning drug trafficking from this country into ours. At least that's what everyone thought they were doing," he says, fidgeting in the rickety chair he was seated in. "I'm sorry, Lieutenant, this is very hard to admit, but my son wasn't covering a story; he *is* the story. Yes, he's a journalist, but he wasn't there in that capacity; he was there moving drugs."

Now that the information the Colonel relayed hung in the suffocating heat of the tent, he slowly began to deflate while sitting behind his desk. If one bothered to look, all the man's strength could be seen surrounding his chair in a shameful puddle of disappointment. Anger, embarrassment, and fear plagued his every thought. He felt as defeated as their efforts in Afghanistan had been.

"Here's the intel I have as of now," he says, handing John a very thin file. "Which, I admit, isn't much, but you needed to see what you would be up against so you could decide if you would help. Again, this is not an order!"

"If you decide to go, there is someone I insist goes with you."

"Who's that, Sir?"

"Me," John hears a strong voice travel from a dark corner of the tent. He was there the whole time, and John hadn't a clue. The man steps from the dark corner, tall, muscular, and obviously fit — a sand eater like him.

"The Lieutenant and I are acquainted, Sir, but he was a lowly sergeant then," the man says, taking a few steps toward John with his outstretched hand in greeting.

John recognizes the man from his time in basic training and his first deployment. He steps toward the man and grabs his hand in return. "Long time, Xander," John says. "How's the medic business?"

"Unfortunately, very busy. Never hurting for patients. I went on to the Rangers and plied my skills there."

"Rangers!" John exclaims. "I guess it's true they take anybody with a pulse."

As one would imagine, it was a very tricky extraction. John and Xander had to constantly push themselves mentally and physically. Both men used their individual strengths and covered the other's weaknesses to finally accomplish the extraction of the Colonel's son and the other two journalists. Twenty-four hours of constant encounters with the Taliban pushed their physical endurance to the limit, even for these two men. Exhaustion affected their mental fitness, and lack of sleep didn't help.

During their travels to the extraction point, one journalist, a young woman, was captured and beheaded so quickly that the act was complete before it registered to the group. The other journalist, a man, was wounded in the leg by gunfire approximately 100 yards from the pickup point. Charles was unhurt physically but mentally shut down.

"Men, I'm sorry to say Charles is dead, killed by inmates while serving his time for the acts you risked your lives to save him from. He was a disappointment to his mother and me; he never felt remorse or hated himself for his actions. It won't make a difference now, but I still try to figure out where we went wrong with him."

"I'm sorry to hear that, Sir," John says.

"Xander," the man says, "did you finish medical school after your stint in the sand waylaid it for a bit?"

"Yes, Sir, I did."

"He's one of the best, Sir. He and my father run the medical end of our endeavor. But rest assured, he's still a Ranger through and through," John says, recalling Doc's actions in DuPree.

"I'm glad to hear it. Okay, men, I'll get on the horn after we disconnect and let Royce know you'll be reaching out."

"Good to see you again, Sir," the men say into the laptop monitor. "Thank you."

"You as well. I'm humbled by your endeavor. Don't hesitate to contact me in the future if there is anything I can do on my end. Take care, gentlemen, and Godspeed."

The two men sat in silence after the monitor went black, each one remembering that mission and all the close calls that could have changed their futures. They didn't know Charles, but they knew his father and respected him deeply. They had seen that same look of sorrow on many faces from their past and found themselves clearing space upon their shoulders to help carry a portion of it. Their shoulders were broad and made of chiseled muscles, ready to bear the enormous and heavily dispiriting weight.

Chapter 73

After John and Xander informed the team, they had it on good authority that Royce Delgado, the head of the FBI office in Seattle, would soon become their best friend concerning the town of DuPree and the monsters running it. They knew they would have to wait and see how it all played out, but with Abby's intel, the hope was that it would go something like this: every ounce of corruption connected to that town, the surrounding counties, and the state government would be ferreted out and dealt with permanently. Every weasel on all levels would soon be adjusting to a cement cell after prosecution. The courthouses, both county and state, would need to install revolving doors to accommodate all the scum they envisioned passing through them.

Of course, the team had questions concerning "the good authority," but they were quickly shut down. John said the important thing was that Royce Delgado was not included on his mother's list of corrupt individuals, and from what they found out from their source, he never would be.

"Now," John says, as he stands at the head of the conference room table, "it's only 1700 hours, and I want to shut this operation down and retrieve Amee's son." He couldn't help but feel for the woman, her eyes brimming with hope as she met his gaze. Hopefully, all the years of her painful, empty existence would only be a dark memory that, over time, would eventually fade to gray. Looking at her engulfs him with sorrow because he knows that's as good as it will get—a damaged soul can only be healed so far.

All members agreed enthusiastically. They were so close to getting another win that they could taste it. They could feel all their hard work and emotional investments were coming to a favorable end. And for some of the members, Dom and Matt especially, the next step would be fun. The monsters of DuPree could never imagine the hell that was coming their way.

Going around the table, each member threw out ideas for the baby's extraction and the takedown of the two men who ran that town. After an hour or so, the team pulled together the best ideas from each suggestion. The final plan meant two teams: one to go and retrieve the baby in Leavenworth, and the other to head to DuPree and take down the evil. Logistics and timing were paramount for their success, but they had Marco coordinating every step as usual.

"Before everyone disperses to get ready," John says, looking around the room and settling on Amee, "we need to know how far you're willing to go to end the nightmare concerning the town of DuPree, Dempsey, Big Daddy, and the two deputies."

Amee sat rigidly in her chair, her face and demeanor heightening her thought process. With the turmoil churning through every pore, she looked each team member in the eye. These people had supported Bud and herself from the minute they received the call for help, with no qualms or hesitation as to what that help would entail. She looks over at Bud seated next to her and meets Mountain's eyes again before heaving a determined sigh that fills all four corners of the room.

"This is so hard for me," she says to the people in the room. "I can't remember the last time I was allowed to decide anything on my own, and this is a big-ass decision right out of the gate." She begins slowly, hesitant at first because all she feels now is rage for herself, for Bud, and for the torment that consumed her life for the last eighteen months because she thought her son was dead.

"I've been thinking about the nanny," she says. "It could be possible she doesn't know anything about the circumstances surrounding my son. I mean, Darwin probably came up with one whopper of a story. So, I want to wait on deciding how to deal with her until I hold my son in my arms and look her in the eye."

Finding the courage to continue, she stands, taking shallow breaths while closing her eyes and shaking her head. "As for the town's innocent residents, I don't want them hurt or held accountable for the filth that ran that town, because they were prisoners just like I was. They lived with threats of foreclosures on their homes, which would force them to leave town with nothing because Darwin held their mortgages, and worse, in some cases, physical abuse to them and threats to family members." She pauses, then continues, "But there are plenty of not-so-innocent persons, and I'll give you their names—those who enjoyed being on Dempsey's good side."

Like Piggy Face and Praying Mantis Guy, Reggie says to herself, remembering the two tow truck drivers whose real names are Carl and Stew.

"Now," she continues with the rage of a caged animal, "you can judge me harshly if you want, but remember you asked. I want Darwin and Dempsey DuPree to be buried somewhere in the deepest recesses of the Okanogan Forest; it can be dead or alive—I really don't care. And if that's not something within your means, or there's a code of some kind, I'll do it myself. Sorry, Bud," she says quietly to her father.

"No need to be sorry, Amelia, I agree!"

"There's no judgment here, Amee, from any of us," Matt says from the end of the table.

"As for the two deputies, I will defer their fate to the FBI. I have no qualms about testifying against them as many times as it will take to put them behind bars."

She sits again, fighting the fatigue, and releases a labored sigh that indicates how drained she has become. The exhaustion envelopes her body like a second skin, and she can't seem to shed its constricting bond. A large hand touches her arm for support and assurance. She looks over at Mountain and manages a sad smile. She can't believe her life's drastic turn in such a short time. The day Suzie stuck her head around the corner of a bookshelf in the back of her store, holding her baby in her mouth, was the catalyst to a new beginning, and she wasn't going to waste one minute of that new beginning. Her son was alive, and because of that, she and Bud would find a way to move forward.

Silence emanated from the people sitting around the table. As so many times in the past, they have compartmentalized their emotions. No one will judge Amee or themselves for their actions moving forward. As always, the goal of the team is to protect the people counting on them and themselves as they walk the too-familiar slippery slope of, "I don't give a shit what I need to do." The time has come to finish the mission and live up to the promises given.

"Alright, Amee," John says, "we'll handle the DuPree's per your wishes, and I don't mind saying it will be a pleasure."

"Amee, what do you want to do about the doctor and dentist? I want to volunteer to escort our two guests sitting in the shed to the authorities unless you want to make good on your threat?" Matt asks, sounding way too hopeful about the last option.

She lowers her head to the table in front of her. The cool surface feels good on her forehead as she rocks her head side to side, the question spinning around in her brain. She's not used to being judge and jury, but then whispers, "FBI as well."

"I want in on that delivery," Dominic adds.

"Roger that, but it can wait until we're done in DuPree."

"Thank you all," Bud whispers his gratitude to the room. Suzie hasn't left his side since he found out about his grandson. She keeps a vigil by his chair and continues to move her baby around in his lap, her soulful eyes registering to him that he deserves this happiness, and she's sorry he and Amee had to live with this pain for so long.

"Okay," John says to the room, "let's go get us a baby!"

"Marco, where are the Duprees at this moment?"

"The auto tracker has them immobile right now, but Oscar-D has them in his sights. He said they're at *The Gentlemen's Steak House.*"

John takes a moment to remember what he can about the geography surrounding the Leavenworth area while considering what should come next. "Tell the kid you're activating Amee's tracker and for him to head back west and drive for about fifty minutes, find a secluded spot, park, and wait about twenty more minutes, then head to DuPree. Hopefully, he'll have a tail. The first team will leave now and head to Leavenworth to retrieve the baby. Once they have taken care of business there, they will meet us in DuPree. I'll take the second team now and head directly to DuPree, where we will arrive in enough time to formulate a plan for the ambush of Darwin and Dempsey."

Chapter 74

"That's it," Amee points through the darkness to a nice house set back from the main street. "That's the address! Oh my God, I can't believe my son is in there!" She's been sitting on pins and needles the entire ride from the Club House to this address, nervous energy dancing around her in the back seat. As hard as she tries not to, she continues to tell herself that this could be one of Darwin and Dempsey's demented acts orchestrated just to keep her in pain. But they couldn't be that cruel, could they? OH YES THEY COULD!

From the driver's seat, Mountain slows to a stop at the foot of the driveway and places the car in park, leaving it running for the time being but killing the headlights.

"The front porch light is on, and it looks like a lamp is glowing through the front window," Pix says. "The nanny is probably still up; it's early."

"Hopefully, the baby is asleep, so he won't see a confrontation if it comes to that," Xander comments. "So, what's the plan, Mountain?"

"What do you mean, what's the plan?" Amee bites out a response, on the verge of hysteria. "We go get my son!"

"Yes, that's what we're going to do, Amee," Mountain says, turning to look at her in the back seat. "But we can't just rush the house and barge through the door. We have no idea what to expect.

417

It's possible the nanny isn't alone; we need to take this slow. But I promise you, we will not leave without your son, no matter what."

"I'm sorry, I know you're right. It's just so hard," she acknowledges.

"I'm going to move up a bit and park under the trees covering that small gravel turnout," Mountain says, putting the car in drive and moving slowly. "I think the best way to do this is if Pix and I follow the tree line up to the house, staying in the shadows and working our way to the back. Hopefully, we can find the baby's bedroom window and get eyes on him. That will give us some idea of the layout once we're inside. Doc, you and Amee stay put for now."

Mountain holds up a hand to stop the outrage he can see coming from Amee. "Once we know what we're up against, I'll text you with a plan. I'll leave the keys under the floor mat, so remember not to lock the doors when you get out. Everyone understands?"

Xander nods in agreement from the darkness of the back seat, silently hoping it will be that easy. But the fact that he was sent along tells him it probably won't be.

"Then what?" Amee asks.

"I told you; we're not leaving here without your son."

After Mountain and Pix exit the car, Xander and Amee take their places in the front seats.

"What is taking so freaking long?" Amee asks Xander, staring intently at the lights from the house filtering through the trees. She's wound so tight she could put a toy top to shame.

In the dimly lit space of the car, Xander reaches out and touches her hand. She turns her head to meet his gaze, his eyes piercing her with a silent acknowledgment of the turmoil churning within her.

"I understand," he begins, his voice a steady anchor amidst the storm of her fears. "The past has a way of casting long shadows, making it hard to see the light of future joys. But remember, we're not bound by the chains of yesterday. Our team, our unity, is stronger than any dark history with the DuPree's." He pauses, allowing his words to sink in. "And as for your son, let's hold onto hope together. The doctor's allegiance may be questionable, but our resolve isn't. We'll find the truth and we'll do it side by side. Your heart's plea for happiness isn't unheard, and it's not a joke. It's the very thing that'll carry us through to that happy ending."

His assurance is strong and steady, a perfect promise she so needed to hear.

Xander's phone lights up, pinging with a text:

> **Mountain: Now, but when the nanny opens the door just do something to stall, keep her occupied.**
>
> **Xander: Roger that, good luck.**

"Time to go," Xander tells Amee. "Done any acting?"

"What?" Surprised by the question, she asks, "A little in grade school, why?"

"Good. When the nanny opens the door, just follow my lead. Got it?"

"I've never been any good at improvisation, but I'm with you," she says as she opens the car door.

The sound of their boots displacing the driveway's gravel seems to echo through the darkness. It's so loud. As they enter the front porch's light, Xander notices a silhouette crossing by the front window, heading for the door. Amee follows Xander as they make it up the two steps to the front door, but the door opens before his knuckles can connect with the thick wood.

The woman leans closer to her visitors and pushes her heavy glasses up her nose, the lenses as thick as the bottom of Coke bottles. She reminds Xander of Mr. Magoo, the cartoon character, and he smiles. She is probably in her 60s and has a slight build. Her blue eyes are noticeably huge as they blink through the thick lenses encased within large blue frames.

"Yes," the woman says, "can I help you?"

Before Xander can speak, he and Amee catch a glimpse of Pix standing in the shadow of the hallway behind the nanny. She's holding Amee's sleeping son in her arms, putting her finger on her lips to keep them silent. Then she mouths "window" and points behind her, giving them a thumbs-up.

Amee can't help her reaction as she sees her son cradled in Pix's arms and lets out an involuntary sob of relief as her legs threaten to buckle under her.

"Now hold on, Cupcake," Xander says as he reaches out to steady her. "It'll be fine. I'll just call that dumb-ass brother of yours for help," he says, holding Amee close, making sure she can remain standing.

Amee gathers her wits about her and tries to calm her beating heart. She knows she can do this because her son is alive and safe. "Okay, Teddy," she sniffs, "but what if he's hit the shine too hard again?" Amee manages a couple of fake sobs and adds some realistic despair as she chokes up. *Not bad, girl.*

At this point, the woman is looking at her surprise guests, waiting for an explanation.

"Is there something I can help you two young people with?"

"Well yes, ma'am," Xander responds. "We were on our way to meet my wife's dear mother for dinner," he says, pulling Amee to his side, "and began having car trouble."

"Car trouble, Teddy, seriously?" Amee says, delivering disgusted laughter. "That's what you call being an idiot and not putting gas in the tank!"

"Now, Cupcake, you..."

She doesn't let him finish before launching into the role of a pissed-off wife. "Don't 'Cupcake' me, you probably did this on purpose. I know you've never liked my mother," she declares for effect, before scrunching up her face and hiding behind her hands.

"Now, Cupcake, you know that's just not true," Xander says, doing his best to sound chastised while looking shyly at the woman.

"Oh, you poor dear," the woman says with sympathy to Amee. "What is it you need, young man?" The woman asks, her huge eyes blinking through the Coke-bottle lenses.

"If possible, can I use your phone? My cellphone is dead, and my wife forgot hers." Xander almost laughs out loud when he notices Amee looking at him through her fingers, still covering her face.

Dropping her hands from her face, she turns to challenge him with a wife's disapproval. "Oh my God, Teddy," she screeches at him, "you probably did that on purpose, too!"

"Now, now," the woman says, "come right on in here and use mine," she says, pointing to the old-fashioned phone hanging on the wall behind her. "Would you like a glass of water, dear?" she asks Amee as she closes the door behind them. "Or maybe something stronger? I find it calms my nerves when I'm upset."

"No, thank you, but I do appreciate the offer," Amee says, still standing at the door, hoping to keep the woman's attention on her. She watches Xander pick up the old receiver and make a show of punching in numbers, then waits a few seconds.

"Hello, hello, George, yeah, it's me. I know she'll have my hide for not getting there on time, but we had car trouble," Xander explains to the dial tone.

"Call it what you want, Teddy," Amee says in the best pissed-off tone she can muster. "What is it with men?" she asks the nanny to keep her attention engaged.

"I know, dear. My late husband Gerald was the worst," the woman says to Amee, giving her a large wink to show sisterhood.

"Just hurry up, dumb ass!" Xander tells the receiver. "We'll be waiting by the car." As he hangs up the phone, he gives Amee an affirmative nod, indicating it's time to go.

"Thank you so much for your help, ma'am. We really appreciate it," Amee says to the woman as she wipes non-existent tears from her cheeks.

"You're very welcome, young lady," the woman responds, looking over at Xander. "Young man," she says, "I suggest you pull your head out of your ass and get on with making this girl and her momma happy."

"Yes, ma'am, I'll work on it."

"Do better than that!" she snaps.

Chapter 75

Amee's heart raced with a cocktail of anticipation and motherly love, each step propelling her forward as she began to shed months of tortured sorrow and despair with every stride she took. The driveway, a ribbon of gray amidst the encroaching twilight, seemed to stretch and bend with her eagerness. Xander's voice, a distant echo of caution, was drowned out by the drumming of her own pulse and the anticipated reunion. The darkness hovering over the driveway was not a threat but a curtain, behind which waited the light of her life—her son. With open arms and a spirit unburdened by fear, she ran. She pushed on, then ran faster, ready to embrace the moment when dreams would solidify into a joyous reality.

Amee got to the car and saw her son wrapped in a warm blanket with two strong arms holding him securely.

"Oh, my God!" she says, closing the distance in a millisecond. Tears of joy fall down her face as bright blue eyes look at her with wonder.

"Hey, little man," Mountain says, "that's your momma."

Then Amee receives an unexpected gift—the bundle in Mountain's arms sticks out his chubby little arms to her, and giggles escape from his mouth as he waits for his mother to take him. Hesitantly, she steps forward, mouthing a thank you to the big man.

Pix takes a picture of the mother and son, then sends it via text to the Club House with a caption that reads, **PACKAGE SECURE**.

She then follows up by letting them know they're on their way to meet up with the second team in DuPree. Once she has relayed their status, she looks over at Mountain and says, "We need to get out of here," and they all climb into the car.

As they pull away, Xander grabs his go bag from the floor and asks Amee to hold the boy on her lap so he can do a quick check.

"He seems healthy from what I can tell under these circumstances, but I'll do a thorough check when we get back to the Club House."

"You're sure he's alright?" Amee asks, holding him tightly.

"Yes, I'm sure, Cup Cake."

"Thank you, Teddy," she says, laughing at him while she kisses the two chubby cheeks in front of her.

In the front seats, Mountain and Pix glance at each other with "what the hell" looks on their faces.

"No matter what it takes, you two, I will find out what that means," Pix says over her shoulder.

Her declaration only causes more laughter from the back seat.

"What's the status with the second team and Oscar-D?" Xander asks.

"We spoke with Marco when we got back to the car; everything is going according to plan. All the trackers are online and showing movement heading to DuPree. The second team is about twenty minutes ahead of the kid, and the DuPree's are following at about that same time frame. Marco informed us we should be arriving

about the same time as Oscar-D. It sounds like the kid had some
fun," Mountain says with a laugh.

Chapter 76

Entering the town of DuPree is an eerie experience for Reggie and Suzie. Sadness, intertwined with their emotional and physical pain, is overwhelming. It engulfs them from every angle, restricting their breathing as they fight the onslaught of dark memories. Neither can shake the time of terror they were trapped in.

Sadly, Reggie knows this experience will be another side note to her personal story, but she is confident that when this operation is over, it won't be the side note she remembers. She looks out the window into the darkness and speaks to the inside of the car, "There is so much evil in this town." She begins to massage her shoulder; she can still feel the hot lead piercing her body and winces at the memory.

Sitting in the back seat next to her, Suzie becomes tense and agitated when movement catches her eye out the window. Her canine instincts overwhelm her, and a primal whine of fear kicks in.

"Stop!" Reggie tells John abruptly after she sees the golden glow of eyes running along the tree line, keeping pace with the SUV.

"What the hell?" Matt exclaims as he watches the animal materialize in the glow of the car's headlights. A giant gray wolf bounds out of the trees and plants its huge paws in the middle of the road. Its eyes peer through the windshield just seconds before throwing its head back and letting out a primal howl of canine despair into the darkness.

"Well, that's surreal," John says in shock from behind the wheel.

"Yes, that's the same one," Reggie replies. Suzie's intense reaction beside her leaves no doubt. Her body begins to shake with intensity, and her moans of sadness are heartbreaking. Reggie instantly throws her arms around her protector, trying to calm the animal's rage, screaming for release, as everyone watches the wolf take off into the shadows of the forest on the other side of the road.

The car's occupants sit immobile, unsure how to take in the scene as it slowly begins to register with disbelief. Suzie's sorrow is overwhelming. It penetrates the inside of the car, eventually entwining with the shallow breaths of the humans surrounding her.

"Boss, up ahead, on the right, is the entrance to the sawmill. I think that's a good place to end this, you know, away from the town itself."

Everyone in the vehicle agrees as John lifts his foot from the brake to move forward. After turning onto the gravel entrance to the sawmill, they immediately see that the chain-link gate is closed and padlocked.

"Well, shit!" Matt says. "I don't think we have bolt cutters."

"No need," John says with anger. "Hold on." He hits the gas pedal with his heavy boot and pushes it down to meet the floorboard. The front of the SUV connects with the gate and snaps the lock, allowing the giant vehicle to crash right through.

"Well, that works, too! Boss."

"Bolt cutters are overrated," John says, looking at Matt. "Assess and adapt, Brother."

"I'm glad you were the one to 'assess and adapt' on this one, Boss, because Pete is going to blow a gasket when he sees the front end of this rig!"

"Probably, but I bet he supplies all the rigs with bolt cutters from now on."

John pulls up to the closest building, where a security light burns brightly, illuminating the parking lot. Without a word, everyone and Suzie step out of the car and gather at the front of the battered SUV.

"Now we wait!" John says, letting the built-up anger he's felt brewing since the day Reggie and Suzie were retrieved from this hellhole—battered, bruised, and maimed. "You doing okay?" he asks, looking over at Reggie intently.

"Yep! Well, no, I'm not, but let's go with 'Yep' for now."

Chapter 77

A few minutes later, the screen on John's phone lights up with Marco's caller ID.

"Talk to me, Marco," he says, putting the phone on speaker.

"Team One and the Kid are about ten minutes out from your location. Mountain is right on the Kid's tail because the DuPree's pulled off into a Quick Stop on the outskirts of Leavenworth. Mountain said as they passed by, it looked like they were having another screaming match back and forth over the top of the squad car. Because of Amee's tracker, they have to have figured out by now that she's heading back to DuPree, so they're not in too much of a hurry."

"Probably right; that gives the others time to get here ahead of them. Please let them all know we are waiting at the sawmill. Mountain and Xander know where it is already. Tell the Kid once he takes the road to the right heading to DuPree, he will be taking another right into the sawmill entrance after he's traveled about three miles."

"Will do, Boss."

"Thanks, Brother," John says before disconnecting. He looks at his team, making eye contact with each one as they stand beside him under the glow of the light, looking for their acknowledgment of the information. Every head responds with an affirmative nod as they begin to prepare mentally.

Suzie is extremely agitated as her head turns from side to side, and her eyes, ever diligent, scan the tree line. Her body leans into Reggie's leg, her protector role surging off her quaking shoulders as her attention stays glued to their surroundings. Minute by minute, the spring inside her coils tighter with the desperate need to act.

Talking amongst themselves, each team member acknowledges the vehicle headlights coming their way. Two sets of lights make the turn slowly, continuing through the gate and heading to the parking lot.

"Hey, Dominator!" Oscar-D yells through his boyish grin. "Did ya miss me?" he asks before shutting the car door.

"NO! But you did good, Kid!"

"Agreed," John says, pulling Oscar-D into his chest like a father would do to a son after a long separation. Looking the young man in the eyes, John says, "Yes, you did damn good, Kid!"

When all the greetings for Oscar-D are complete, Team 2 exits their SUV with a yawning little man snuggled up in his mother's arms. Amee walks forward, still wearing the smile of happiness plastered to her face from first taking her son into her arms. Suzie sees the little addition to the group, and happiness engulfs her. She begins to whine a bit and wants nothing more than to give the boy some love, but she knows she needs to stay with Reggie with all that's going on around them.

"It's okay, Suz, John's here," Reggie whispers in her ear. "Go!"

Suzie takes off, sprinting toward Amee and the bundle in her arms, stopping inches from Amee's feet. Happiness engulfs her entire being; she begins wagging her tail so hard that her entire back end has no choice but to follow. Amee bends down on one knee so Suzie can smell her son and give kisses of joy to those little chubby cheeks. The baby is suddenly awake; sleep and sweet dreams are forgotten as he pats Suzie on the nose.

"Doggy," he says through a toddler's giggle of happiness.

Chapter 78

Headlights began to float through the tree line. Their prey was getting close. This was going to end tonight. The DuPree Sheriff's Department vehicle came to a screeching halt at the entrance to the sawmill but didn't enter.

"Mountain," John says, looking over his shoulder, "take Amee and the boy into the shadows until I call you out."

"Roger that," Mountain replies, putting his arm around Amee and leading her into the shadow of the closest building.

"Doggy, doggy," a tiny voice cries over his mother's shoulder as they walk into the shadows.

"Matt, Pix," John commands, not taking his eyes off the threat sitting at the entrance to the sawmill, "on my right. Dom and Xander, on Reggie's left!" The orders are acknowledged silently and carried out instantly, each team member taking up their assigned posts.

"Why are they just sitting there?" Matt manages to ask, letting all his pent-up rage ooze like a heavy discharge through an infected fistula.

For the next ten minutes, the team remains silent but diligently aware of the danger at the sawmill's entrance. The vehicles' headlights seem to bore right through each member as if trying to ferret out their level of anger and test their resolve.

Finally, Oscar-D suggests, his voice carrying a hint of concern, "Maybe they're looking for Amee since the tracker is still active."

"You may be right, Kid. Mountain, bring Amee back out here and stand in the light so they can see her," John says over his shoulder.

"Well, that worked. Good call, Oscar-D," Reggie says as the team stands and watches the cruiser's lights begin their intrusive strobing, followed by the wail of the siren just before the driver slams down on the accelerator, heading right for them.

Darwin opens the passenger door as soon as the car stops. Upon its approach, gravel had been displaced in all directions, and dust can be seen settling around the group through the vehicle's headlights.

"What the hell do you think you're doing with my grandson, woman!" Darwin screams at Amee, advancing on her with his barrel chest puffed up and out in his usual dominating manner.

"I wouldn't come any closer, you piece of crap," Mountain warns Darwin, stepping in front of Amee.

"Who the hell are you?"

"I'm your worst nightmare," Mountain says, stepping closer to the man, "and I hate bullies."

"Big Daddy, that's one of the guys who caused the trouble at the office!" Dempsey shouts at his father while climbing out of the cruiser, shutting the door, and racing to the front. "And the others," he says, pointing at Pix, Reggie, Xander, and Dom. "That one,"

Dempsey says, pointing at Xander, "is the one who destroyed Deputy Tack's knee!"

"Seriously," Pix laughs, "are you tattling to your daddy right now?"

"You better mind your lip!" Dempsey warns, pointing his finger in Pix's face, "or I'll finish what Deputy Tack started."

"Matt, no!" John barks out the order, stopping him from bulldozing into Dempsey. "You'll get your turn."

"You dumb canker sore!" Darwin screams at his poor excuse for an offspring. "I don't give a rat's ass about that, or you, for that matter. That woman has kidnapped my grandson, and that is NOT going to fly; he's mine!"

Mountain steps even closer, cutting Darwin off as he advances on Amee. "Not one step closer," Mountain growls at the pompous piece of shit. "She will not be abused anymore. Not by you, or by that weak son of yours."

"She kidnapped my grandson, and that's a federal offense," Darwin proclaims to Mountain and the others. "She will hand him over, or I'll call the authorities!"

Dempsey has seen and heard enough. "Amee, you get your ass over here right now, or you will have a lot more healing to do when this night is over!" When Amee doesn't move or acknowledge the threat, Dempsey moves to his right, thinking he can grab her arm and pull her out from behind Mountain. Of course, that is a colossal mistake because now Suzie is the one who has seen and heard enough!

In a flash of fur rippling with muscle and her maw open, showing all her canines and tongue dripping with saliva, Suzie launches herself at Dempsey, hitting him with all her weight and knocking him to the ground onto his back. Not giving him a chance to catch his breath, she jumps onto his chest on all fours, her body rigid with hate. Suzie hears the call from the forest, pushing the anger inside her even hotter. She is determined to end this, not only for Bud and Amee but also for the canine cousin calling out to her. Suzie absorbs all the sorrow and loneliness the animal portrayed within its howls as they sift through the trees, begging for vengeance.

Reggie watches her protector balance her seventy-five pounds of rage on Dempsey's chest, thinking she deserves to have some fun, but the fun will soon be over. John notices it first: Dempsey's right-hand fumbling at his side, intending to pull his pistol from the gun holster at his waist.

"Not going to happen, Dumb Ass," John says, stepping closer and placing his boot onto Dempsey's arm to stop him from pulling his weapon.

"Get this mangy animal off me!" Dempsey screams at Reggie. "I should have put a bullet in her when she was locked up!"

"Suzie, hold tight!" Reggie says calmly.

While Suzie continues to hold Dempsey to the ground, Big Daddy speaks up again. "Girl, you give me my grandson, and I mean right this damn minute. You have no right to take him from his home!"

"Your way of thinking is so demented I am getting physically sick to my stomach," Matt says, stepping up to the man and placing his hand behind his back to grip the pistol he carries there.

"Who the hell are you assholes?" Darwin yells at the people surrounding Amee. "This is a private family matter!"

"Big Daddy, do something! Help me, please," Dempsey pleads to his father.

"Shut the hell up, you worthless piece of shit!" Darwin warns his son.

As Darwin finishes his demand, the tree line surrounding the parking lot becomes full of activity, wild paws of all sizes and colors step into the light. Growls of all octaves are thrown at Dempsey and Darwin, but the wild canines don't seem to be bothered by the rest of the humans standing close. It's as if they are invisible, or the animals know they don't pose a threat. But the same can't be said for the humans themselves—booted feet begin to shuffle, and hands can be seen caressing their weapons, a natural reaction for them.

With their heads lowered and ears laid back, the wolves begin to inch closer to Darwin and Dempsey. Their large shadows follow the animals closely into the light. Their eyes register nothing but revenge for being hunted so cruelly, and their sharp canines continue to show with each growl delivered. The lone female that Suzie has developed a connection with holds her head low and steps through the bodies; her interest seems to be only with Dempsey. Blood will be spilled tonight for revenge, is all she has left.

437

"Suz! Enough! Come!" Reggie commands, sensing there's going to be trouble and wanting her girl out of the way. "Good girl, Suz, good job!" Reggie praises as Suzie reluctantly retreats to stand at her side, but the dog's demeanor remains on high alert, her eyes never leaving her prey.

The only sound pushing through the light and into the night, besides the growling coming from their unexpected guests, is the whimpering coming from Dempsey as he tries to sit up now that Suzie has left his chest.

Chapter 79

But before Dempsey can get to his feet, the female wolf—whose mate had apparently been killed by him—flies at the man, knocking him down again onto his back. She stands, just like Suzie had, on his chest with all her bulky muscle and rage. It happens so fast. The canine's teeth sink into Dempsey's neck, followed by a blood-curdling scream and a thick spray of blood in all directions.

"Oh my God!" Amee screams, covering her son's eyes. "Oh my God, oh my God," she keeps chanting as the scene in front of her and the others continues in a grotesque display of vengeance. Dempsey is screaming for his daddy and keeps trying to launch the animal off him with his arms. But as the blood keeps pumping into the gravel around him, his attempts begin to dwindle, his strength depleting onto the ground along with his blood. As far as the team is concerned, it ends too soon, for they feel he deserves more pain before he checks out.

Darwin moves to Dempsey's side as the last bit of life ekes from his son's body. He can't take his eyes off the scene or the animal whose muzzle is dripping with blood as she lifts her head and just stares into the tree line. Vengeance really does taste sweet.

"You goddamn bitch!" he declares, turning in Amee's direction, placing his hand on the pistol at his side and advancing right at her. "This is all your fault; why couldn't you accept your place and be a good wife?"

And were those real tears streaming down the old man's face? No, that can't be; that would mean he had to care about someone other than himself. With the angered outburst directed at Amee, Darwin lifts his pistol and charges toward her, but the she-wolf launches off Dempsey's dead body and attacks him, chomping onto the wrist of the hand holding the weapon. But Darwin doesn't falter. He lifts a heavily booted foot and kicks her in the chest, sending her onto her haunches with a whimper escaping her maw.

"Now, give me my grandson, you stupid bitch!" Darwin demands as he advances on Amee, intending to rip the boy out of her arms. The man never looks back at his son once.

"NO!" Amee screams into his face, causing him to stop in surprise. She allows all the hate and years of emotional and physical pain to push her voice higher with rage. She turns before continuing her rant and hands her son to Mountain, where she knows he will be protected and safe. The years of fear and pain begin to take on a life of their own as she spits them at Darwin.

"You and that piece of crap," Amee says, pointing at Dempsey where he lays, "thought you broke me, but all you did was scar me inside and out, and even with all the scars, I promise you I'll find me again, you bastard! That is my son," she says, pointing at the little boy for emphasis, "and the only grandfather he will ever know is waiting for us to start a new life." She seems calm to the bystanders in the circle, but they know there is more coming. They've seen it before: once a victim believes they have a way out, they find some bravery. "There is no way you will ever come near him, Bud, or me again!"

After Amee finishes her promise to Darwin, she turns to Mountain, and with shaky arms, she lifts her son from his. There is a movement of unbelief crawling across Darwin's red face. He is at his boiling point; he can't believe Amee has the nerve to speak to him as she did. That is not acceptable. In the past, she had been dealt with by his son, but since that wasn't an option anymore, he would have to handle the punishment himself.

"You will learn your place, WOMAN," he screams through the light and into the night as he advances toward Amee. It only takes one step before Suzie begins barking a warning at the man, but Darwin doesn't seem to hear her, so he doesn't slow his advance. But the dozen other angry growls, he can't dismiss. The animals start closing in, surrounding him with a primal need to destroy as they have witnessed him, and others kill members of their pack. They want blood, and they are going to get it. Darwin can't move in any direction; he can't advance or retreat, and he is losing control of himself and the situation, which is foreign to him because Big Daddy DuPree is always in control.

Reggie is trying to keep Suzie from joining the advancing pack when the large black alpha charges in and latches his giant maw onto the thigh of Darwin's right leg, toppling him off balance as he does so. The man begins hitting the animal over the head with the butt of his gun but isn't having any luck dislodging himself. He turns the weapon, intending to shoot the animal in the face, but is stopped instantly by a bullet to his temple coming from the crowd.

The sight of the two men lying in the light, covered in their blood, is a scene of grotesque beauty. Even the animals seem to take the time to admire the picture before them. Then, one by one, they retreat into the darkness of the trees, leaving the humans to stare in wonder. But the female lingers for a time, catching Suzie's eye before she walks over and soaks up the closeness of her distant cousin. Suzie leans out and licks the animal's face in a gesture of saddened understanding before the wolf also retreats into the darkness.

"I'll get the shovels," Matt says to the crowd as he walks to the SUV.

Epilogue: Rising from the Ashes

The sun dipped low in the sky, casting warm hues of orange and pink over the trees. Reggie stood at the edge of the forest, feeling the cool breeze on her face. It was a different world for Amee now—one filled with hope instead of fear. She took a deep breath, soaking in the fresh air that smelled of pine and new beginnings.

In her heart, Reggie carried the stories of countless women who had walked the difficult path of domestic violence. Each face reminded her why she had chosen to fight: a reminder that no one should suffer in silence. Amee's courage, in particular, inspired her. Watching Amee reclaim her life filled Reggie with joy and pride. If Amee could rise from the ashes of her past, so could others.

In the last few weeks, Reggie, her team, and Amee organized workshops and support groups, turning places of pain into havens of healing. Women gathered, sharing their stories, laughter, and tears. In those circles, Reggie watched as fear turned into strength, and hope blossomed like wildflowers in spring. Together, they learned to lift each other, reminding one another that they were not alone.

As the seasons changed, so did the lives of those around her. Reggie saw women transforming—once timid voices becoming strong and confident. They began to share their experiences, spreading awareness like seeds in the wind. Reggie felt pride in their growth, knowing she had played a part in their journeys.

443

Reggie knew her journey was far from over. There were still battles to fight and lives to change. But with every step, she felt stronger, surrounded by women who believed in themselves and one another. They were a force, a family bound by shared experiences and unwavering support.

As the stars began to twinkle above, Reggie looked at the horizon. She was excited about the future and ready to continue her mission. With courage in her heart and a promise to never stop fighting, she knew they could create a brighter world for all.

Made in United States
Troutdale, OR
12/29/2024

27409012R00256